NO MEAN GLASGOW

Colin MacFarlane was born in the Gorbals in 1955. He has written for a number of newspapers, including *Scotland on Sunday*, the *Sunday Times*, *The Sun* and the *Daily Record*. He is also the author of *The Real Gorbals Story*.

NO MEAN GLASGOW

GLASGOW

Revelations of a Gorbals Guy

Colin MacFarlane

MAINSTREAM
PUBLISHING

EDINBURGH AND LONDON

First published in Great Britain in 2008 by
MAINSTREAM PUBLISHING COMPANY
(EDINBURGH) LTD
7 Albany Street
Edinburgh EH1 3UG

ISBN 9781845964238

This book is a work of non-fiction based on the life, experiences and
recollections of the author. In some instances, names of people, places, dates,
sequences or the detail of events have been changed for artistic purposes and
to protect the privacy of others. The author has stated to the publishers that,
except in such respects, the contents of this book are true

A catalogue record for this book is available
from the British Library

Typeset in Optima and Sabon

Printed in Great Britain by
CPI Mackays of Chatham Ltd, Chatham, ME5 8TD

CONTENTS

FOREWORD

I DIDN'T REALISE UNTIL I READ *NO MEAN GLASGOW* what curiously parallel lives Colin MacFarlane and I have led. Like him, I was brought up as a kid in the Gorbals (a single end in Moffat Street, if you're interested) and like him I found my road out into the wider world through a combination of chance and determination: in his case, via a lowly position in the catering trade and in mine a lowly position as stage sweeper and general dogsbody during the 1965 Lex McLean season at the Pavilion Theatre. Reading his book, I recognised that the same ambition that drove him to try to better his life drove me too. I also realised that we share a love of great jokes.

Now, I believe the thing that makes great jokes great is that the really memorable ones offer an insight into the human condition, as perceptive as anything by Dickens or Tolstoy. *No Mean Glasgow* is full of jokes, real laugh-out-loud jokes, and every one of them a window into the singular mindset of the Glaswegian. As an example, here's one of my own favourites. It was told to me many years ago by one of my acting heroes – the late, great Roddy Macmillan, who was a great connoisseur of all things Glaswegian – and I think this joke says everything that needs to be said about anyone who's ever tried to escape their Gorbals origins.

There's a wee guy from the Gorbals gets a job as a bus driver. Proud as punch he is, driving folk all over Glasgow in his smart Corporation uniform. But after a few years, there's a wee niggling voice in the back of his mind that's saying, 'Naw, there's got tae be mair tae life than this.' So he saves up and buys a taxi. He's happy as Larry, picking up passengers and dropping them off with a cheery word and a wave. But, again, after a while, there's this wee niggling voice in the back of his mind saying, 'There's still got tae be mair tae life than this. Ye're cut oot fur somethin' better, pal.'

One day, he's sitting in the rank reading the *Evening Citizen* when he notices an advert in the situations vacant column. It says: 'Wanted: chauffeur for the Queen Mother.' He thinks to himself, 'This is it! This is whit ma life's been leadin' up tae.' So he writes in and, would you credit it, gets the job. He's given an immaculate livery and a vintage Rolls-Royce, and all he has to do is drive the Queen Mother around whenever she's in Scotland. Anyway, one day he's driving her along a single-track road near the Castle of Mey when another Rolls-Royce approaches from the other direction. There's no room to pass, so the two cars slowly pull up and stop, bumper to bumper. After a minute or two of this stalemate, the driver of the other Rolls-Royce steps out into the road. He's immaculate in his burgundy livery, with a peaked hat and shiny boots. So the wee Gorbals guy steps out too and the pair of them stand there, sizing each other up. Eventually, the big guy says in a posh English voice, 'Excuse me, would you mind moving your motor? I have the Duchess of Kent in here.'

'Is that right?' the wee Gorbals guy replies. 'C'mere ower here a minute.' And he opens the passenger door of the Rolls-Royce to reveal the Queen Mother sitting there, resplendent in her ermine and pearls. 'And whit, pray, dae ye think this is?' he says, gesturing in her direction. 'An heap of shite?'

Aye, ye can take the boy oot the Gorbals . . .

Enjoy the jokes, enjoy the adventures: this is the real deal.

Alex Norton

PREFACE

WRITING THIS BOOK HAS BEEN A LOT OF FUN, AS IT brought back so many memories of my days spent hanging about with larger-than-life characters in Glasgow and beyond as a young man. Everything seemed so simple then and every day had its dramatic, funny and even sad moments. At times working on the book, half of me was laughing and the other half greeting about people and places that have long since gone. I miss the folk and the patter of the old Gorbals and the rest of Glasgow and, although I was a naughty boy at times, I don't regret one minute of it all.

Sadly, while I was writing *No Mean Glasgow*, my best pal, Chris Purcell, passed away at the comparatively young age of 52. The son of Irish immigrants, Chris was a great Glaswegian, who could bring tears of laughter to your eyes with his sparkling patter. He will be sadly missed by everyone who knew him and I hope that those who never met him will get a glimpse through this book of how funny and brilliant he was.

When I began this book, I was really fed up with books about Glasgow that were so grim and dreary that they made depressing reading. Anyone from the city will tell you that it's the banter that keeps everyone on their toes and makes life worth living, so really you can't write a book about Glasgow without giving it a full blast of the funny patter. I was determined to pack in as many stories, jokes and anecdotes as possible and, to this end, I have based some of the characters in the book on more than one person, while others are representative of types I met during my time working in kitchens and drinking in pubs in Glasgow, Oban and beyond, and I've used some artistic licence in recreating scenes and dialogue from all those years ago. Having said that, everything in the book is true to my experiences and I hope that I have created an accurate portrait of the times and places described. What I have tried to do is make the book serious and funny at the same time.

I must thank the team at Mainstream, including Bill Campbell, Claire Rose, Graeme Blaikie, Emily Bland and Kate McLelland, for their tremendous help in bringing it all together. Also, I would like to thank *Taggart* star Alex Norton – a real Glasgow gentleman – for kindly agreeing to write the foreword. I am grateful also to Jean Doig for providing exclusive photographs of Glasgow taken by her father, the late Michael Martin, who was born in the Gorbals in 1917. Mention must also go to John Evans, French teacher and adviser, and to the staff at Glasgow's Mitchell Library for their fantastic help.

Colin MacFarlane
August 2008

1

RAIN TOWN

A MILLION ASTOUNDING AND BIZARRE STORIES HAVE begun on the streets of Glasgow and this is one of them. It starts at the beginning of a new year, 1971. I had just left work on a dark, gloomy evening and the rain was pouring down as if God himself had begun to cry tears of sorrow onto the city; what he was crying for, I couldn't say, but he must have been very upset. Barely aged 16, I had a job as a lowly commis chef at the prestigious Royal Scottish Automobile Club (RSAC) in Blythswood Square. The wages were pretty meagre, around seven pounds a week, but it was the only employment I had been able to find after I'd left school in the Gorbals a few months before. 'Serves me right,' I often thought to myself. 'I should have looked at the blackboard more and learned something instead of trying to be a fly man.'

Blythswood Square was lined with fine Victorian buildings, including the club with its high-class restaurant, but the area was better known as a haunt of prostitutes, dozens of whom lingered there each night. The rain was so bad that I stopped in a doorway to keep dry for a few moments. I was joined by a buxom, soaking wet prostitute, who said, 'Bloody terrible weather, doll. Have ye got a light?'

'Naw,' I replied with a smile, following up with a familiar Glaswegian line: 'Ah don't smoke. If God wanted ye tae smoke he'd have put a chimney oan yir heid!'

She laughed and rummaged through her handbag until she found a lighter to try to ignite her damp cigarette. The downpour was getting worse and an avalanche of hailstones began to rattle down. Both of us were freezing. My teeth began to chatter and she started to shiver with the cold. It couldn't have helped that she was wearing a bright-red miniskirt, the shortest I had ever seen on a woman.

'Whit's a young boy like you daein' hingin' aboot here?' she asked. 'Ye're too young tae want business, ur ye no?'

'Naw,' I said with a laugh, 'Ah'm workin' as an apprentice chef jist roon the corner.'

She took a puff of her cigarette, her mascara running down her face. 'Oh aye? That's a posh bloody job. Ur ye busy at the moment, son?'

'Aye, we're always busy. The toffs o' Glesga have always got money tae eat oot and get pished oan the finest o' wines.' She gave out a loud laugh. 'Whit aboot you? Ur ye busy?' I asked rather timidly.

'If it wisnae fur this bloody rain, Ah'd be rushed aff ma feet,' she replied with a nonchalant shrug. 'In fact, business is sae good, if Ah had another pair o' legs, Ah'd open up in Edinburgh.' We both hee-hawed out loud and, as the rain showed no signs of stopping, I said, 'Ah'm offski. Look after yirsel.'

'Aye and you look after yirsel too, ma wee pal,' she replied, blowing me a kiss.

I meandered through the town and in Renfield Street I saw an image that has stayed with me all my life. A drunk man was lying face up in the pouring rain, a small black Scots terrier dog licking his face. With the rain coming down in torrents, there was something almost biblical about the scene. The inebriated man looked as if he had been crucified, taken from the cross and then thrown into the gutter.

I had had enough of this bloody rain. It always seemed to be pishing down in Glasgow. 'Rain, rain go tae Spain and don't come back here again,' I grumbled to myself as I trudged home. My shoes were leaking and it was a horrible feeling walking through the streets with soaking wet socks and feet. I went past the Horse Shoe Bar, not far from Central Station, and peeked through the door. My God, it looked so warm and friendly, and customers were laughing loudly. Everyone looked as if they didn't have a care in the world.

Earlier I had put on a flat cap to stop my head getting soaked, so I entered the joint with the bunnet pulled low on my forehead and hoped the barman didn't rumble me as an underage drinker. The place was so busy, rowdy and smoky that he didn't bat an eyelid when I said in my roughest accent and most grown-up voice, 'A pint o' heavy, pal.' He poured me a McEwan's Export and I looked around. A fat guy with a moustache was holding court with his band of inebriated cronies. He talked in a half-respectable Glaswegian accent and I surmised he was probably one of the many journalists who hung around such city-centre pubs telling outlandish stories. At the time, Glasgow was not short of local daily newspapers. There was the *Evening Times*, *The Citizen*, the *Glasgow Herald* and the *Daily Record*, all vying for the best stories.

As I picked up my pint, the journalist bellowed, 'Hey, did you hear this one?' Knocking back a large Bell's whisky, he said, 'There was two Celtic supporters walking through the bloody freezing cold and rain towards Parkhead when all of a sudden one of them pulls out an open razor and cuts his pal's nose off. "Whit did ye dae that fur?" screams his blood-soaked pal, and he replies, "Ah had tae dae it, Jimmy . . . yir nose wis turnin' blue."'

On hearing this, one man laughed so much that he spat out a mouthful of beer, while another grabbed his chest as if he was going to have a heart attack. One of their jolly cronies chipped in: 'Hey, Bill, here's one for you. What's a journalist got in common with a pint of Guinness?'

'I haven't got a clue.'

'Hundreds are drunk every day!'

There was more laughter, more drinks were ordered and I'll tell you what: it was a million times better than being stuck in that bloody freezing rain outside.

I looked over to the front door, where two men had just come in. They were a striking sight – little and large. The big man I recognised as a well-known Gorbals gangster. I had read the day before that he had been cleared at the High Court of two attempted murders. It was something to do with a moneylending scam; he had run two men over with his car because they'd double-crossed him. The Gorbals hard case had a long scar running down his left cheek and he was wearing the classic gangster outfit: Crombie coat with a white hankie protruding from the breast pocket, suit, white shirt and flashy tie. He also had on an assortment of gold rings, which I imagined he wore as surrogate knuckledusters in case he got into an altercation. The smaller man was dressed rather soberly in a pinstriped suit, wearing glasses that made him look far more intelligent than he probably was. The hard case talked in tough, guttural Glaswegian tones, every second word an expletive. His associate had the accent of someone who had been brought up in Kelvinside and sent to a private school. I realised then that this guy must be the gangster's lawyer, the fellow who had got him off the attempted-murder charges.

'Whit ye fur?' asked the big guy.

'Oh, I think I'll have a large brandy, if you would be so kind,' said the lawyer.

'Nae bother,' replied the hard case. 'Jist a good job Ah've got a few bob 'cause drinkin' wi you isnae cheap. F***in' lawyers! At least ye keep guys like me oot the nick.' He laughed and his companion did too, if rather nervously.

I was only a few feet away and I had lifted my bunnet back to reveal more of my face. The gangster looked over and recognised me. 'Hey, Ah know yir face. Crown Street, Gorbals, wan o' the wild young mob? Am Ah f***in' right or am Ah f***in' wrang?'

'Ye're right,' I replied.

'Whit ye daein' in here?' he asked.

'Jist keepin' oot the rain,' I replied in the toughest voice I could muster.

I always made sure I showed guys like him respect. That was the secret: show them a wee bit of respect and everything was hunky-dory; if you didn't, you were in more trouble than you could imagine. I had heard that this one had almost garrotted someone at Gorbals Cross for not showing him the required amount of deference. Respect was what all these gangsters wanted, so, 'Play the game,' I thought.

'Whit ye fur, young fella?' he asked me. I was tempted to make an excuse and leave but the rain was battering violently against the windows.

'Ah'll have another pint o' heavy,' I replied, nodding my head in nervous appreciation.

'Come and join us and gie's yir patter,' said the hard man. I couldn't exactly refuse – that would be a big insult – so I went over and sat down.

The lawyer immediately said to me, 'Young man, you don't look old enough to be drinking in this establishment.'

I didn't let the posh little bastard intimidate me. 'Ah'm no auld enough but it's pishin' doon ootside and it's cheaper than buyin' an umbrella!' I answered. 'Ah think Glesga must be the rainiest toon in Britain.'

With an air of superiority, the lawyer said, 'No, young man, you are wrong. I often have cases in Manchester and it rains all the time there. In fact, every time I go to Manchester I seem to have to buy a new umbrella!'

The gangster reflected for a few moments then said, 'Nah, Ah think the boy here is right. Glesga should be called Rain City. It's usually f***in' tippin' doon, especially durin' the winter.'

But the lawyer wouldn't leave it there. He was a man experienced in defending cases in the top courts of the land; he wasn't going to let a young uneducated scruff like me get the better of him. 'I think you are both misguided,' he continued pompously. 'If you look carefully at the rainfall statistics for Glasgow and Manchester, you will find that Manchester is unquestionably the winner.'

The hard case looked annoyed, a wild, almost psychotic look appearing in his eyes. 'Those are the eyes of a murderer,' I thought. He said to the lawyer, 'F*** you, ya prick, and yir statistics. Ah've done a few jobs in Manchester and spent time in Strangeways nick. When it comes tae rain, Glesga takes the biscuit.'

The wee man looked frightened for a second. His profitable criminal client had just called him a prick. It was a danger sign, right enough. However, he was cunning enough to divert the conversation to me. 'Have you ever been in Manchester, young man?' he asked.

'Nah,' I replied, 'but Ah watch *Coronation Street* and it never seems tae rain there. In fact, Ah've never seen Elsie Tanner or Ena Sharples wi an umbrella, so Ah rest ma case.' I was taking the piss and he knew it. The gangster burst out laughing. In an absurd way, I had just got the better of one of Scotland's top criminal lawyers and I'd not even turned 16.

'F***in' Elsie Tanner! F***in' Ena Sharples! Brilliant! Ah couldnae have put it better maself,' he blurted out. The lawyer looked somewhat bemused and had an air of defeat about him. He shook his head slightly and said nothing.

I stood up, shaking both their hands and saying, 'Ah'm away back intae the storm. See youse later.' Then I headed off through the drenched streets, pleased that I had just made mincemeat out of an advocate. 'This little light of mine,' I sang, 'Ah'm gonnae let it shine!' I headed down Jamaica Street and crossed the bridge. For a few brief moments, the rain had a well-deserved rest and a ray of sunshine broke through the clouds. It was as if God had now resolved to shine a spotlight on the Gorbals. I had lived in this part of Glasgow all my life. For years now, though, the area as I knew it had been gradually disappearing as the old tenements were boarded up or knocked down and new high flats built to replace them.

The rain had given the grimy streets an extraordinary polished appearance and the swollen Clyde looked magnificent as it flowed with a Herculean current through the centre of the city. An old man passed me by shouting, 'Some bloody weather, eh?'

'Aye,' I replied, 'it's been pishin' doon fur hours noo. It's stopped fur a wee while but Ah bet it'll be back wi a vengeance.'

'Aye, ye're right. But Ah'll tell ye whit – the ducks willnae be complainin'!' he replied, chuckling and heading off towards the town. I've always noticed that about Glaswegians: they have a propensity to find the funny side even in the most unpromising circumstances.

I continued on my way only to be greeted with the noteworthy scene of three police cars outside two public houses in Bridge Street on the corner of Eglinton Street. There were about a dozen police officers and I could hear them all effing and blinding. Some were on their walkie-talkies while others were walking up and down the rain-sodden street looking carefully at the pavement as if they were searching for something.

'Nah,' a big policeman shouted to another, 'nae sign o' the f***in' thing. It must have got washed away in the downpour.'

The other said, 'Aye, it looks like it's been lost. Ah feel sorry fur that poor bastard. Ah'll tell ye whit: let's get back tae the station, deal wi aw they jokers, then we'll come back and see if we can find it.'

They jumped into a Black Maria and sped off. A local character called Danny was standing outside the Laurieston pub and inhaling deeply on a Woodbine. I had known him for years, ever since I was a kid. I'd gone to school with his son. 'Whit's the score, Danny?' I asked. 'Whit ur they big polis lookin' fur?'

Danny drew deeply on his Woodbine and then replied, 'A finger. A f***in' missin' finger.'

I was taken aback by this strange reply. 'Whit, a real finger? How the hell did that come aboot?'

'There wis a bunch o' bluenoses in the Stevenson Taylor pub tearin' intae the bevy and jist across the road at the same time there wis a gang o' Celtic fans havin' a right auld drink in the Laurieston. Oan wan side they're aw wearin' blue scarves and oan the other they're aw wearin' green. Anyway, the two sides decided tae leave their respective pubs at the same time. Well, as soon as they saw each other, it was war. Wan side wis shoutin' aboot Rangers, King Billy and 1690, and the other wis givin' it all the Celtic, IRA, Pope patter. The next minute, they started throwin' bricks at each other and then it was face-tae-face, haun-tae-haun fightin'.

'Man, ye should have seen it. Ah saw a bit o' fightin' when Ah wis in the army but Ah've never seen anythin' like this! A Celtic supporter gets hit over the heid wi a bottle, another has his face smashed in wi a brick and another gets slashed. Then this big mad Irish bastard appears fae naewhere wieldin' a meat cleaver. He runs intae the crowd o' bluenoses and starts whackin' them. Wan o' them puts his haun up tae protect his heid and the next thing two o' his fingers ur flyin' intae the air.

'The polis wur soon oan the case and they arrested them aw except fur the injured guy. They've taken him tae the Royal Infirmary tae get patched up. The polis've found wan o' his fingers but they cannae find the other wan. That's why they wur searchin' the road when you appeared oan the scene.'

'Whit ur they gonnae dae wi his fingers? Sew them back oan again?' I asked rather naively.

'Ur ye daft?' replied Danny. 'There's no way they could have sewn those fingers back oan again. The polis want them fur evidence when the case appears at the High Court. The guy who did it'll probably get 15 years or mair.'

A steady stream of water was still running along the gutter and, as Danny was talking, I saw a small white object bobbing against a drain. It looked like a little fish. I walked over to inspect it and realised, much to my astonishment, that it was the missing finger. What really took me aback was that it still had the man's wedding ring on it.

'Look, Danny! There it is!' I shouted.

'There's whit?' Danny replied.

'It's the missin' finger, complete wi weddin' ring!'

Danny walked over and looked at it. He said, 'Ah'll bet ye when that ring wis put oan that finger, it wis a happy day fur the fella. But look at it noo. Funny how life turns oot! Somebody'll end up nickin' that ring and takin' it tae the pawn if the polis don't get back soon. Ah'm no that desperate fur money, though! Let's get the f*** oot o' here before the polis come back. Life is jist a series o' moments and it's time tae clear aff and move oan tae the next wan!'

I said goodbye and sauntered off round the corner to experience my next moment. I walked past Gorbals Cross into Gorbals Street, then Cleland Street. There was rubble everywhere, very few people; the Corporation bureaucrats had got their wish: they had almost succeeded in wiping the old Gorbals off the face of the earth, although there were still a few crumbling tenements standing. As I walked along Crown Street, I noticed a woman crying into a hanky in the close of one such building. I recognised her face. I knew her to say hello, so I asked, 'Hey, how's it gaun? Whit ye greetin' fur?'

She replied, wiping her eyes with the hankie, 'Oh, they're movin' ma mammy tae an auld-folks' home. She's been bedridden fur mair than 20 years and she's no been well at aw. Ah'm jist waitin' fur the ambulance tae arrive. Ah'm frightened that the shock o' bein' moved after aw this time might be too much fur her. It could kill her.'

I realised I knew the woman she was talking about. It was Mrs McGrath, an old lady whom my pals and I used to run errands for when we were growing up. She would sit upright in her bed and bark orders at us: 'Get me a pint o' milk, hawf a dozen well-fired rolls and a copy o' the *Daily Record*.' This old bedridden woman was always very generous, giving us as much as a shilling for running such errands. I remembered she'd shown us photographs of herself in her youth. We'd all been taken aback, because in her teens she'd been extremely beautiful. 'Ah won a few beauty contests when Ah wis a lassie,' she explained, 'even Miss Glasgow. But that wis when Ah wis young and ma heart wis full o' fun! Look at me noo – disabled, auld and useless. Time catches up wi everybody.'

She told us that, having been the belle of the ball and the winner of several beauty competitions in the 1920s, she had taken the fancy of a wealthy Glasgow bookmaker. They had one child, the daughter who was crying in the close, and moved to Newlands, a more prosperous area of the city. But the bookie had all the worst traits a husband could have: he was a gambler himself, a drunkard, a womaniser, a thief and a liar. Not long after they married, he began losing lots of money and took to hitting his wife. 'He had money tae begin wi but he wis a nae-user,' Mrs McGrath said. 'He'd get drunk and beat me. He wisnae a real man. He wis too scared tae fight other men but he battered me.'

I heard various stories about her husband. His gambling debts got worse and he ended up owing a team of Glasgow heavies a huge amount of money. This put him under a great deal of pressure, leading to more heavy drinking and more beatings for his beautiful wife. One day, he attacked her so badly that she ended up in hospital for a couple of weeks and was never the same again. She eventually left him but by that time she had difficulty walking. She moved back to the Gorbals with her daughter and the bookie took the honourable route, throwing himself into the Clyde. Not long afterwards, Mrs McGrath took a bad turn and the doctors said she would be bedridden for life.

'Look, here comes the ambulance,' her daughter said to me. Thunder crashed and lightning lit up the sky above as the rain lashed down once again. Two ambulancemen got out carrying a stretcher.

'Ur ye here fur Mrs McGrath?' asked the daughter.

'Aye. It would've been a lot easier wi'oot this bloody weather. Where is the auld woman?' said one of the ambulancemen.

'Two up,' replied the daughter. 'The door's open fur ye. But please be careful wi ma maw. She's no been oot that hoose in mair than two decades.'

'Don't worry, darlin', yir maw will be awright, we'll take good care o' her. She's in good hands,' he replied confidently.

A few minutes later, the ambulancemen were coming down the close stairs carrying Mrs McGrath on the stretcher. The stairs on the bottom flight were wet with the rain and one of the men almost stumbled. I had visions of it all going drastically wrong, with Mrs McGrath being thrown onto the ground. 'Hey, haud oan,' said one of the ambulancemen to the other. 'The rain's made this mair dangerous than we thought. Take it easy, step by step. Slowly, slowly catch the monkey.'

I went up to help them balance the stretcher and I looked at Mrs McGrath's face. It was full of defiance. Her eyes were angry but then she smiled and said, 'Ah've been bedridden aw these years and Ah could end up gettin' killed by a couple o' medical bampots who should know better!' We all began to laugh.

When we reached the mouth of the close, one of the ambulance guys looked out into the street and said, 'It's true what they say. It never rains but it pours.' His cohort ran out into the rain and opened the ambulance door, then rushed back to shelter, soaking wet. 'Come oan then, let's get her intae the vehicle,' he said. I stood near the stretcher just in case they slipped.

We got a few yards along the street and Mrs McGrath suddenly shouted, 'Naw! Haud oan! Ah don't want tae go intae the ambulance jist yet. Let the rain pour over ma face.' We all stopped and the heavy rain fell on her cheeks. 'Oh, that's so lovely! Heaven! Ah've been waitin' years tae feel the rain against ma face.' She was drenched; we were all drenched. Finally, they put her into the ambulance and it sped off through the glistening Glasgow streets. The next day, Mrs McGrath died.

I have never complained about the rain since.

2

IN A STEW

M Y WORK AT THE ROYAL SCOTTISH AUTOMOBILE Club was a real eye-opener. I found out a lot about how a high-class restaurant should be run – and quite a bit about how it shouldn't be run, too. The head chef was a Londoner called Joe who had a cockney accent and an extremely foul mouth. He was a wiry man with grey hair, who must have been in his 60s. On my first day, he took me aside and said, 'Look here, sonny boy, what you learn in this kitchen will stand you in good stead. We have more than 20 top-class chefs here. These people are the elite of the catering game and they've worked all over the world – Switzerland, Germany, the South of France, even the USA. Work with them, learn from them, and after the training you get here you'll be able to go to any hotel or restaurant in the world and land a job with confidence. The first rule is always clean up after yourself and the second rule is don't f*** up, otherwise you'll be out the door. A good chef needs discipline and you, being from the notorious Gorbals, probably haven't experienced much of that in your life. That's what you'll get here: a training with discipline.'

It was the sort of speech you might expect an army officer to give to a new recruit and someone told me later that Joe had indeed begun his career in the army. From day one, I watched the techniques Joe used to instil discipline in his employees with a certain amount of fascination. Every day, he'd pick on one of the chefs and they were all terrified of him.

'Hey,' he shouted to one fellow on my first day, 'come over here.' He looked the young man straight in the face and then, rather bizarrely, stroked his chin.

'When did you last shave?'

'Eh, two days ago.'

'Two days ago?' Joe shouted angrily. 'You look like you've been sleeping rough in a f***in' bus shelter, you dirty little bastard. Do you think people who dine here want to be catered for by a squalid little chef?'

'Eh, no,' the young chef replied anxiously.

'Well, f*** off out of my kitchen and clean yourself up. You look like one of those tramps that sleeps under the Suspension Bridge at the Clyde. For f***'s sake! How much do a bar of soap and a razor cost? Now piss off and give yourself a good scrub, and don't come back until you do. You horrible little man.'

If this was Joe's idea of discipline, it was certainly enough to make most people quake in their boots. The young chef was in tears when he left the kitchen. When he went to get changed downstairs, he was so shocked that his hands were shaking with humiliation and anger.

'Whit did Joe say tae ye?' asked a fellow chef.

'He called me a dirty bastard and banned me fae the kitchen until Ah have a shave and wash.'

'Oh, that's nothin'. Ah've had worse,' said the other. 'Wan time, he almost threw me intae the big stockpot jist because Ah curdled a sauce. But don't worry aboot it. His bark's worse than his bite. It'll be somebody else's turn the morra.'

The incident made me slightly nervous of Joe and each day I stroked my chin, relieved to find only a bit of bum-fluff as, at 16, I hadn't started shaving yet.

The next day, another chef got it in the neck. He had overcooked the soup of the day, giving it a burned taste. 'You f***in' no-good imbecile. You are a useless nincompoop. When I was in the army, they would have put an ignoramus like you up against the wall and shot him! Throw the f***in' soup in the bin and then throw yourself in the bin.'

Joe's sous-chef, Jimmy, was a different kettle of fish. A stout middle-aged guy, he was a Glaswegian through and through; he walked around singing songs at the top of his voice and had a cheery disposition. In a way, he was the perfect foil to Joe. It was as if they were a double act and Joe was the straight man while

Jimmy was the joker. Instead of shouting at people and giving them a rollicking, Jimmy would stroll around the kitchen telling jokes to lighten the atmosphere, especially if Joe had delivered another one of his tirades.

Jimmy walked up to me after I had been in the job only a few days and, with a serious expression on his face, asked, 'Did ye hear aboot the two vegetarians who got married?'

I thought he was asking a serious question and replied, 'No, whit happened?'

'There wis a big turnip at the wedding!' said Jimmy, walking off laughing to tell the same joke to someone else.

The club had a reputation for being one of the best places in the country to eat traditional Scottish food. On the menu were braised oxtail, sweetbreads, tripe and onions, and Aberdeen Angus beef. There was also a wide variety of steak and chicken options as well as more exotic dishes like caviar, lobster thermidor and escalope of veal Holstein. Politicians, showbiz stars, judges, lawyers, accountants and businessmen all frequented the restaurant.

One afternoon, the restaurant manager, a slick-looking Italian who never had a hair out of place, made a speech to the assembled kitchen staff. He spoke very good English, much closer to received pronunciation than my Glasgow vernacular was.

'Tonight, we have some very, very important people coming for dinner. The head of the party is a multimillionaire businessman who owns a chain of hotels all over Europe. His friends include extremely powerful and influential people: namely, fellow successful businessmen, politicians and a few solicitors and High Court judges. It is imperative that we give them the highest standard of service. Everything must be first class. The reputation of the club relies on people like this to spread the word. So please will you all be alert and on your toes tonight?'

Joe and Jimmy both had nervous looks on their faces as they listened to this speech. After the manager left, Joe said, 'Oh no! I hate that little millionaire bastard. All he does is complain, complain, complain. The last time he was here, he ordered lots of dishes that weren't even on the menu. Even when we managed to cook them for him, he still moaned about everything. But he's an influential guy and my job and Jimmy's are on the line if we don't get it right.'

Jimmy nodded his head anxiously in agreement. You could almost smell the fear. He said, 'Joe's right. That wee rich pain in the neck has a reputation fur gettin' chefs the sack. He's a horrible little guy but we've got tae make sure he disnae catch us oot oan anythin'. Everythin' has got tae be top notch, otherwise we're aw in trouble. Whit the wee bastard wants, the wee bastard gets. Unfortunately fur us aw, that's the way it is.'

The party arrived just after eight. I had a peek through the door leading to the restaurant. The multimillionaire, a small bald man, had a brandy glass in one hand and a big cigar in the other. I heard him say condescendingly to one of his guests, 'The concept of business is simple, really. All you've got to do is ensure that you have more money coming in than you have going out.' I thought he had a face like a bull terrier, or, as another chef put it, like a burst settee.

The chefs waited nervously for the first orders to come in. The starters they chose included the best of the menu – smoked salmon, caviar, prawn cocktails, Scottish pickled herring and the finest French pâté. Everything went smoothly and there were no complaints. So far, so good. Then it was time for the main courses. When the checks came in, the blood drained from Joe's face and he shouted, 'That little bastard has just ordered cauliflower au gratin and we haven't got any! It isn't even on the menu tonight. I told you he was a pain in the neck.'

Sensing desperation in the air, I chipped in, 'Chef, aboot two days ago Ah threw an auld cauli in the bin.'

Joe's eyes lit up. 'Which bin?'

'In the back lane,' I replied.

We both dashed out of the kitchen and ran down the steps to the back lane. When I opened the bin there was a terrible smell of rotting food. The cauliflower was lying right at the bottom, covered with rubbish, cigarette ends and potato peelings. When I picked it up, I saw that several used condoms were stuck to it. They had most likely been discarded by the prostitutes who frequented the area. 'Right,' said Joe, 'run up to the kitchen, cut all the rotten bits off, give it a wash, then stick it in boiling water. Get ready for service!' I did as I was told and the cauliflower was soon placed onto a silver dish and thick cheese sauce lovingly poured over it before being sent out to the restaurant. 'Brilliant, young man, brilliant!' Joe said to me. Clearly, I had gained brownie points.

About 20 minutes later, the manager came into the kitchen. Joe looked extremely nervous. 'Joe, you know the cauliflower au gratin?'

'Yeah,' Joe replied. 'What's the matter with it?'

'Oh, nothing. Our friend said to me that it was the best cauliflower au gratin he's ever tasted!'

'If only he knew,' I thought.

But the drama didn't end there. When the dessert orders came in, Joe shouted, 'Oh f*** no! Now the little swine wants fresh peach Melba. Where the f*** am I going to get a fresh peach at this time of night?' Then he looked at me, 'Hey, Gorbals kid! Get me a f***in' fresh peach, now!'

'But, Joe, there's naewhere open at this time o' night,' I replied.

'Look, get me a peach or you're sacked!'

I shrugged my shoulders. Joe calmed down a bit. 'No, I'm sorry. I won't sack you. But run outside and try to get me a peach somewhere. Come on, you were good with the cauliflower, now let's see if you can conjure up a peach!'

I left the kitchen and ran through the streets of Glasgow. Near Charing Cross, I spotted a small fruit-and-veg shop. It had closed hours before but there was a single solitary peach in the window. We were fated to meet! I picked up a brick but when I threw it, it bounced off the glass. I tried again and this time it shattered the window and I grabbed the peach. A man who was passing by shouted, 'What's going on here?' He looked the retired policeman type. I ran off with the peach in my hand and he began to chase me. 'Come back! Come back, you thief, you bloody vandal!' he shouted. However, I soon lost him in the maze of lanes near Blythswood Square. Puffing and panting, I ran into the kitchen and placed the peach before Joe. He was overcome with joy, shouting, 'I knew you would do it! Fantastic!'

One of the perks of working at the RSAC was the fact that fresh sparkling-white chefs' gear was provided to us each day by the club. On the ground floor, by the back door, there was a laundry room and every morning we went there to fetch our clean working clothes. For a while, an old lady called Miss Archer was in charge and I gave her the nickname 'Miss Bow and Arrow', which she loved. She had a great sense of humour and although she was from posh Kelvinside, she would tell the dirtiest of jokes.

Every morning, I would shout, 'Morning, Miss Bow and Arrow! How's it gaun?' She always laughed at that greeting and would often launch into one of her cheeky tales: 'There were two Glasgow guys called Joe and Jimmy who went on their holidays to Ayr during the height of summer. When they got there, the sun was belting down, so they both decided to sit in it and try to get a good tan. After a few hours, Jimmy says, "Ah've had enough. Ur we goin'?"

'"No yet, Jimmy. Ah wonder if ye could dae me a favour?"

'"Whit's that, Joe?" Jimmy said.

'"Every part o' me is tanned apart fae ma penis. Can you cover me aw in sand and leave a bit fur ma penis tae stick oot so it'll get a tan?"

'Joe agreed and covered his pal over with sand, leaving only his penis sticking out. Two old women were passing by when one of them spotted it and said to her pal, "Maggie, would ye credit it? Ah married ma man fur that 40 years ago and noo they're growin' wild!"'

Although she had a naughty sense of humour, Miss Archer had never been married. When I asked her why not, she just shrugged her shoulders and replied, 'Nobody has found me yet – I'm an undiscovered treasure.' I had to agree with her.

'Mad Martin', a French waiter, was another character. He was the classic good-looking Frenchman, moustache and all. He boasted to me that in his lothario days he had 'made love' to around 1,000 women. He had worked in all the jet-set places in France but fell in love with a Glasgow girl who was on holiday in Cannes and decided to join her in Scotland. If a diner was giving Martin a hard time, he'd rush into the kitchen and shout, '*Merde! Merde! Merde!*' more often than not then launching into a further series of French expletives.

Watching Joe and Martin in action, one thing I learned was never, ever complain about the food or service in a restaurant. If someone complained to Martin about the service or was a regular customer who rarely left a tip, Martin would break wind over the food before taking it out to the unsuspecting diner. 'Ha!' he said to me one day. 'They think because I wait on them in the restaurant they are superior to me. I am a proud Parisian and they are arrogant pigs. I fart over their food to teach them a lesson. Bastards! They are all fools. In France, we have a saying: "When the wise man points to the moon, the fool looks at his finger!"'

He was full of legendary stories about his time on the Riviera. He said he had become great friends with Pablo Picasso after meeting him in a restaurant in St-Tropez. 'Monsieur Picasso is a great man, not like the ignorant pigs and fools we get here.' He told me one day, 'I was with him in Antibes when he was contacted by a big art dealer from Paris. We walked along the beach with this dealer and he said he would give Picasso a great deal of money for his next painting. Like me, Picasso is a proud man and he said no. The dealer doubled his offer but Monsieur Picasso still said no. Then he stopped on the beach and with his walking stick made a beautiful drawing in the sand and signed it. He said to the dealer, "Take that."'

Like Martin, Joe felt distaste for diners who complained. Mad Martin came into the kitchen one night shouting his usual stuff and said to Joe, 'Ignorant fool, son of a whore, bastard! Chef, he complains to me that the steak is underdone, the no-good swine.' Joe wasn't in a particularly good mood that night and earlier on I had witnessed him devouring several pints of lager, nicknamed 'sweat pints', which in those days the management provided free to the chefs to help them cope with the heat. 'What a f***in' c***,' Joe shouted. 'He asked for medium rare and that's what we gave him. Give me the f***in' steak.' He beckoned to me and several other chefs. 'OK, boys, we're going to have a game of football with this steak.' He threw the sirloin to the floor, where it was kicked about for several minutes. The steak was then given a quick wash, placed in a frying pan for a couple of minutes and sent back out to the diner.

Another time, a customer complained about the soup so Joe promptly took off one of his dirty old boots and threw it into the big pot of soup. 'I wonder if the bastards'll like it now that I've improved the taste!' he joked as his big army boot floated in the pot. He had a knack for recycling the soup of the day. If it didn't sell well he'd keep it until the next day, then he'd throw some curry powder into it and it would reappear on the menu as mulligatawny soup.

One of the kitchen porters, Robert, was a reserved sort of fellow who spoke in a posh accent. To me and the rest of the chefs, he seemed a bit too classy to have stooped to cleaning pots and pans. I asked Jimmy about him and he explained, 'Believe it or not, that fella used tae be the director o' a big firm. At wan point, he wis a self-made millionaire. He used tae come here as a customer. Ah remember he had a flashy car. But he had a bad break-up with his missus and she grassed him up fur tax avoidance. He lost everything; it cost him the whole lot, so he couldnae afford tae come here as a member. But he's no a daft man. He worked it out that if he got a job here as a kitchen porter he could have the best food, jist like when he wis loaded. Joe has a soft spot fur him and gave him the job. Maybe one day he'll get on his feet again and make his millions back.'

Robert was a hard grafter and had great enthusiasm for cleaning the numerous pots, pans and trays that were flying at him every few minutes. As I handed him a dirty copper pot, I said, 'Hey, Robert, Ah heard ye used tae be a millionaire and a member here.'

He began to scrub the pot furiously with wire wool and replied, 'Yeah, it's ancient history. I had it all; the bulging bank balance, the nice car, the big house – but it all went down the drain because of her and the taxman. She knew too much and gave all my accounts to the tax inspector. Buggered me up, it did. Mind you, I'm philosophical about it. That's how they got Al Capone, you know: the taxman kippered him up. More than a million pounds I had to pay them. I couldn't get out of it.'

I got the feeling that Robert was building up to some anecdote and I was right. 'I hired the best advice that money could buy,' he said. 'Before my interview with the tax inspector, I asked my accountant what I should wear. He suggested that I wear my shabbiest clothes to let them think I had hit hard times. But my lawyer gave me the opposite advice, saying I shouldn't be intimidated and should wear my most elegant suit and tie. I was confused, so I went to the local priest and asked his advice. He said, "Let me tell you a story. A young woman who was about to be married came to see me recently and asked me what she should wear on her wedding night. Her mother suggested she wear a long, heavy flannel nightgown that went right up to her neck. But when she asked her best pal, she suggested she put on a sexy negligee."

'The priest seemed to be rambling on, so I said, "Father, what has this all got to do with my problems with the taxman?"

'"Simple," he replied. "It doesn't matter what you wear; you're going to get screwed anyway."'

I began to really enjoy my job at the club and Joe had been right: I was picking up skills that would stand me in good stead in the future. I was taught to roast beef, lamb and chicken, to poach, boil, fry and scramble eggs, to cook lobsters and legs of ham, to make béchamel, hollandaise and demi-glace sauces, to gut wildfowl and fish, as well as a wide variety of other culinary skills. It made me feel that I could have the ability to make it as a top-class chef.

The kitchen's German and Swiss chefs, however, masters of their trade, looked down on me. They said that I was just a good cowboy – not a real chef but a chancer. In fact, they said that about most of the Glaswegian chefs at the RSAC. The wages were pretty rubbish and the hours were long, and some of these European chefs became disgruntled and left for better-paid employment elsewhere. This resulted in a staff shortage and Joe was forced to lower his usual high standards by employing chefs who had questionable training.

Enter Alex from Partick. In his early 30s, he had told the club's management that he had worked in all the best hotels, including the Savoy and the Park Lane Hilton in London. Alex was a sharp-witted guy and always on the move but I realised pretty quickly that he was a bit of a con man. Although Alex told me that he had been in charge of all the big functions at the Savoy, a German chef called Heinz sneered every time he saw Alex at work in the kitchen. He said to me behind Alex's back, 'That man is a real cowboy. He can't even dice an onion properly.'

Alex was much like Jimmy in temperament, full of the Glasgow patter, with great one-liners and jokes. 'Hey,' he said to me one day as we began gutting chickens, 'how dae ye know yir missus is deid?'

'Ah don't know,' I replied.

'Well, the sex is the same but the dishes keep mountin' up in the sink.'

He continued with his banter: 'A fella goes intae a shop and buys wan bar o' soap, wan toothbrush, wan can o' soup and wan can o' beer. The lovely lassie behind the counter gies him a big smile and says, "Ye're single, aren't ye?"

'The fella says, "Aye. How did ye know?"'

'"Because ye're an ugly bastard," she replies.'

Alex with his chat was certainly a contrast to the European chefs, who approached their jobs in a highly serious manner. He once related to me a story about a woman in a prison kitchen, a carrot and a stockpot that had even me blushing.

I was suspicious about his account of his previous life and said to him, 'Did ye really train at the Savoy in London?'

'Shush!' he said. 'Ah'll tell ye the real score when Ah go fur ma fag break.'

Alex regularly went for a smoke in the lane outside the club. He favoured Capstan Full Strength, which were incredibly strong, and generally inhaled the smoke with an air of quiet contemplation. The next time he went out, I joined him in the lane and put it to him directly: 'Ye didnae really train at the Savoy, did ye?'

He took another puff of his cigarette and thought deeply for a moment before replying, 'Nah, did Ah f***.'

'So where did ye train?' I asked.

'Barlinnie Prison,' he replied. 'But don't be tellin' anybody. That's between you and me, right?'

'Aye, right,' I replied. 'But how did ye end up in Barlinnie?'

He took another drag and replied, 'It's a long story but a few years back Ah found maself oan the dole. Ah wis really skint and Ah made the mistake o' goin' tae the local moneylenders and borrowin' as much as Ah could fae them. The debts mounted up and these guys ur heavy people. Ah couldnae afford tae pay them back and Ah pleaded fur mair time tae get back oan ma feet but they wur ruthless. Ah suppose ye have tae be in that game.

'Anyway, Ah went tae see the big moneylendin' boss and pleaded ma case and, tae be fair, he gave me a way oot o' it. He said if Ah picked up some parcels noo and again and delivered them tae a secret destination, Ah could clear ma debt. Ah didnae know whit wis inside the parcels and Ah never asked. Ma first pick-up was in Oban, the next wis Ayr and it wis Edinburgh after that. It wis easy-peasy and Ah thought it wis a great way tae wipe oot ma debt. Put it this way: it wis better than gettin' slashed and endin' up in hospital.

'The big boss said Ah had done well and Ah only had wan mair pick-up tae dae before ma debt wis cancelled. Ah went tae Fort

William tae pick up the parcel and then headed back by train tae Glesga. But when Ah got tae Queen Street Station, there wis a load o' polis waitin' fur me. They took me intae a little office and opened up the parcel and it was full o' marijuana. That wis it – game over! Ah got sent tae the High Court but Ah told the polis nothin'. The judge said that, as a drug courier, Ah wis a menace tae society and he gave me five years. Five bloody years fur pickin' up a parcel!'

He lit another Capstan Full Strength and continued his epic tale. 'When Ah wis in Barlinnie, Ah didnae fancy sewin' mailbags so Ah asked if Ah could work in the kitchen. Even as a wee boy, Ah had always been interested in cookin'. Ma mammy wis a great cook. She used tae make her ain bread and the most fantastic stews, so Ah thought it wis in ma blood. Anyway, the screw in charge o' the kitchen saw Ah wis enthusiastic and he took a shine tae me and made me his right-hand man. He'd been trained in the army, like Joe, and he taught me somethin' new every day, so that Ah got to the stage where Ah could cook wi confidence.

'Every night, Ah would lie in ma cell and dream aboot workin' in the Central Hotel at the station or in this club. When Ah got oot a few months ago, Ah made up a couple o' phoney references claimin' tae be fae the Savoy and the Hilton. Ah applied fur a chef's position at the Central Hotel but they found oot ma references wur false, so Ah chanced ma luck here and, much tae ma surprise, they didnae check the references and Ah got the job. Bingo!'

We headed back to the kitchen, agreeing that his little secret would remain between us. A few hours later, Heinz was watching Alex work and he said to me, 'Where did that man say he trained?'

'The Savoy and the Hilton.'

'I don't believe it,' Heinz said, shaking his head.

'Naw, Ah'm tellin' ye, he wis wan o' the top chefs in London but he came back tae Glasgow because he wis homesick,' I maintained. Heinz walked off, still shaking his head.

Every day, I looked forward to taking a break with Alex, who always turned on the patter. The other chefs regularly joined us just to hear what funny stories he had to tell. One day, standing in the lane, holding court and puffing away at his strong cigarettes as usual, he began, 'A snail is goin' up wan o' these back lanes and he's mugged by a pair o' slugs. A big polis arrives oan the scene and says tae the snail, "Who mugged ye?" and the snail replies, "Ah don't know – it happened so fast!"'

We all burst out laughing but Alex had a terrible coughing fit. 'Fur f***'s sake, these fags ur gonnae kill me,' he gasped.

'Gie them up, Alex,' I said. 'They're nae good fur ye.'

But he regained his breath and said, 'Nah, Ah like ma fags too much tae gie them up. A fag is the only thing that cheers me up nowadays.'

The next day, he wasn't at work. I asked Jimmy, 'Where's Alex?'

'Oh,' Jimmy replied, 'he's phoned in sick. He's probably been oan the bevy last night.' But Alex didn't appear all that week and was still absent the next. Then Jimmy walked up to me and told me, 'Yir pal Alex has packed it in. He phoned in sayin' he'll no be back. Pity, though. That guy wis a good laugh.'

I was shocked and downhearted. Why he had quit the job was a mystery to me, as I knew he really liked it. The place wasn't the same without him and Joe's erratic temper only made the atmosphere in the kitchen worse. One of the things Joe had taught me was to make Yorkshire pudding. 'A pound of flour, a pint of milk and nine eggs. Always make sure the oil in the tray is piping hot before you put the mixture in it and then into the oven. If you don't, the pudding won't rise,' he said. Then one night there was a big function on and all the guests were having roast beef and Yorkshire pudding. I was given the task of making the pudding. I mixed up the ingredients as I'd been shown, poured oil into the tray and then poured the batter in and put it in the oven. When Joe had all the roast beef ready to go on the hotplate, he shouted to me, 'Right, Yorkshire pudding away!' I pulled the large tray out of the oven and, to my horror, it was as flat as a pancake. I had forgotten to heat the oil.

Joe went ballistic. 'You f***in' stupid bastard! You've f***ed it up, you imbecile, you f***in' moron.' He was in a frenzy. He ran over and grabbed the tray and threw it right across the kitchen. I had had enough of this. I picked up a pot and threw it at him; it missed his head by only a few inches. I shouted, 'F*** you and yir Yorkshire pudding,' and walked out.

A few days later, I went back to the club to pick up my wages and the manageress called me into her office. 'The chef says he doesn't want you to leave. He knows you're a good worker and he wants you to stay. So will you reconsider your position?' I picked up my wages from the table, thought about the offer for a few seconds and then said, 'Nah, missus, Ah've had enough o' this place and Joe's tantrums.' Then I walked out into the freezing cold Glasgow day.

My first thought was to go and see Alex and buy him a pint out of my wages. I took the bus to Partick, found his street and looked up to his second-floor tenement flat. Alex was standing at the window looking out. He didn't see me. I noticed that he didn't look well; he had lost weight and had a worried expression on his face. I rang the bell and when he opened the door he seemed pleased to see me. He slapped me on the back and shouted to his wife, 'Ma best wee pal fae the club has come fur a visit!' I sat down at the kitchen table and Alex made some tea. When he brought the cup over, I noticed that his body was emaciated.

It was then that I realised he had cancer.

I never mentioned a thing but he knew that I knew. He became philosophical. 'Ye know whit? Time passes by so quickly. It jist flies. It's like smoke through a keyhole.' I nodded in sad agreement: 'Aye, like smoke through a keyhole.'

A little while later, he showed me to the door. He looked me directly in the eye and said simply, 'Ah've arranged fur ma ashes tae be scattered over George Square.'

'How long?' I asked.

'A few weeks, maybe a month,' he replied.

I shook his hand, clasping it tightly, then walked through the streets of Partick with tears streaming down my face.

3

HIGH LIVING

JUST AFTER I QUIT MY JOB, WE MOVED FROM OUR tenement in the Gorbals to a more middle-class area of the city, Shawlands. It was spring 1972. We'd held on for so long because my father had always maintained that he would never move to one of the new housing schemes like Castlemilk or to an overspill town on the outskirts of Glasgow. He held out for the right location, turning down several offers from the Corporation, and his gamble paid off. We secured a small two-bedroom flat in a quiet little street, Eastwood Avenue, not far from Shawlands Cross.

Ironically, the new flat seemed like a bit of a comedown after the (admittedly faded) grandeur of our Victorian tenement in the Gorbals. This was a different kettle of fish. When we moved in, I immediately got the impression that the place had been constructed by gluing some cardboard together. Compared to our old flat, it was like living in a little box, a filing cabinet for humans. However, it did have its advantages. It had a bath, which we had never had before, there were trees outside and it was near all the shops.

The neighbours were far more sedate than the wild people I had grown up with and some of them had a pretentious attitude not uncommon among Glasgow's lower middle classes. My father joked that they were the sort of people who took their ashes down to the midden in a briefcase. Any conversations I had with my new, well-spoken neighbours seemed a trifle flat. We had been used to the patter and banter of the Gorbals and, after a particularly dull conversation with one of our new neighbours, my mother told me that she'd 'seen mair life in a tramp's vest'. She summed it up when she said, 'Hawf o' they people ur deid fae the neck up.' The contrast with the vibrant community I was used to got me down a bit at first but I knew it would take time to adapt to this new, petit bourgeois environment.

Funnily enough, although we had moved, we still kept up our old ways. For example, we hardly ever used the bath, continuing to boil a kettle and have a wash in the sink instead. You can take the family out of the Gorbals but you can't take the Gorbals out of the family!

The block of flats had a caretaker who was a law unto himself. He liked to exercise what power he had with great gusto. Just after the move, my brother Ross and I decided to have a game of football in the back yard. The caretaker appeared out of nowhere, shouting, 'You can't play football here! This is a respectable area – you're not in the Gorbals any more, you know. If you don't stop playing, I will have to confiscate your ball.' We went back to the flat with our heads bowed. We'd had a lesson in lower-middle-class culture and we didn't like it one bit. Sure, in the Gorbals some of us boys played football night and day. It was our great pastime, our lifeblood, and this man had stopped us after a few minutes. Shame on him!

The next drama came when my mother did the weekly washing and hung it on the balcony outside our front door. Afterwards, there was a lot of curtain twitching and I could tell these new neighbours thought it was very common to hang your washing outside. 'Gorbals ruffians!' they must have thought. 'Let's teach them a lesson.' None of them complained directly to my mother; they went to the caretaker instead. 'I'm sorry,' he said to her, 'but it's against the rules to hang washing outside and some of the neighbours have complained. Please do not do it again, otherwise there will be repercussions.' My mother and father were extremely angry and they suspected the informers were a curtain-twitching couple who lived opposite us.

Uncle Mick, a wild bus driver from Clydebank, turned up at the flat with a housewarming present of a few bottles of strong El Dorado wine. We all sat round and the patter was fantastic; our boring new neighbours could never have come near it. Like my father, Mick was a tremendous raconteur and always had a funny story or a joke to tell. 'A fella is fed up wi Glesga,' he began, 'and he decides tae join a Tibetan monastery. He goes tae see the head monk, who agrees tae take him in oan the condition that he can speak only two words every five years.

'Fur the first five years, he eats rice, sleeps oan a wooden bed and has only wan blanket wi holes in it. He tends tae the fields and looks after the cattle every day. At the end o' the five years, the head monk says tae him he can use his two words and the wee Glesga fella says, "Mair blankets!"

'Another five years pass by and the head monk comes up tae him again and says he can use two mair words. He replies, "Mair food!"

'Five years later, the head monk come up tae him and says, "You may use another two words now."

'The wee Glesga fella says, "Ah'm leavin'."

'"Good!" says the head monk. 'All you've done since you got here is bloody complain."'

We all burst out laughing and it wasn't long before a good old-fashioned sing-song developed. But the next minute there was loud banging on the living-room wall. It was coming from next door, where an old lady lived, a retired schoolteacher who spoke with a plum in her mouth. She must have been annoyed that riff-raff like us had moved in. 'Ah, whit is this?' my father shouted. 'Can ye no have a laugh and a sing-song in yir ain hoose noo?' We all got on our feet and began shouting, swearing and banging wildly on the wall. The old dear must have been terrified by this Gorbals-style rebellion.

After more wine had been consumed, my father and Mick contemplated the situation with the curtain-twitching, complaining neighbours across the way. 'Whit we gonnae dae aboot them?' my father asked Mick. They came up with a bizarre plan to wreak vengeance. They found a spare pot of black paint and a brush, and Mick sneaked over to their flat well after midnight, when the couple were fast asleep, and painted all their windows black. We couldn't stop laughing about this crazy stunt.

The next morning, it was our turn to twitch the curtains. We peeked out as the shocked couple summoned the caretaker and showed him their blacked-out windows. The caretaker looked confused and began scratching his head in bewilderment. But, for a moment, I saw him glance over at our house. Perhaps he had his suspicions but there was nothing anyone could prove. Mick said, 'F***in' brilliant! That'll teach they hawf-boiled toffs no tae mess wi the real Glesga people!'

A few hours later, I bumped into the retired teacher from next door. Nothing was mentioned about all the banging on the wall, shouting and swearing the night before. 'Good morning,' she said to me. 'Lovely day!'

'Aye, lovely day,' I replied. I realised then that, unlike the folk I'd grown up with, the middle classes hated direct confrontation and avoided disagreements at all costs. In a way, it was a nice change from the Gorbals, where a riot could have developed in similar circumstances.

That year, the Gorbals was never out of the headlines for a variety of unusual reasons. It was as if, as the old Gorbals was disappearing, figures from its past were returning to haunt it. The newspapers reported that a life-size mural of Benny Lynch, the former world flyweight champion, born in the area's Norfolk Street, had been discovered underneath six layers of wallpaper in the Norfolk Arms. Old-timers had always maintained that it was there, so the pub's manager took action to find it and, much to his amazement, he succeeded. Benny had drunk in the pub when his fighting days were over. Sadly, around the same time, Lynch's son John was found dead in a stream in the grounds of Woodilee Hospital, where he was being treated for the same condition that had caused his father's death – chronic alcoholism.

Another Gorbals legend hit the headlines when safe-blower Johnny Ramensky, 67, was found lurking on a roof above a shop in Ayr. In a lifetime of criminal activity, Ramensky had been sentenced to more than 56 years in jail. His lawyer, Joseph Beltrami, told the papers that Ramensky had 'been on more roofs than the famous fiddler'. 'Gentle Johnny', as he was known, came to an inglorious end in November 1972, when he died as a result of a brain haemorrhage after being rushed from Perth Prison to hospital. His funeral was held at St Francis RC Church in Cumberland Street and hundreds of people turned out to give him a good Gorbals send-off. There are worse ways to go.

We might not have been entirely happy with our new existence in Shawlands, but my father's decision to refuse a flat in the new Hutchesontown Area E complex in the Gorbals turned out to be right. As the flats were completed, the Queen arrived to present the first inhabitants with their keys. Soon afterwards, however, the residents began to complain of damp and mould. The £7.2-million flats, supposed to be an improvement on the crumbling tenements they'd replaced, were affected by severe condensation and water penetration. They were soon nicknamed 'the Dampies' and the newspapers reported that the inhabitants' brand-new furniture, wallpaper and carpets were growing a dark, ugly fungus. Within a few years, the flats would be all but uninhabitable.

By the time we moved away, most of the people I'd grown up with had already been rehoused. My maternal grandfather, Dan, had been moved to a flat in Pollokshaws, not far from Shawlands. The place was 20 storeys up; I went to visit him and was amazed by the view. My first reaction was that it was like a penthouse from a Hollywood movie. From his balcony, you could see most of Glasgow and the surrounding countryside, and the people down on the street looked like ants. He also had a beautiful bird's-eye view of Pollok Park, with its trees and wildlife. The flat was like a luxury penthouse and a complete contrast to the living conditions we had all been used to.

But was he happy? 'Aye,' he said, 'it's awright up here above the clouds – ma best pal is an aeroplane pilot! But livin' up here is no like the auld days in Glesga when everybody lived in a tenement. Then there wis a great community atmosphere. Noo everybody seems tae be stuck in the sky wi naebody tae talk tae.'

Many Glaswegian people felt disorientated being moved to such places. It could take a lot for them to adjust to the new high living. There was a story going round at the time about a wee woman who had lived in a tenement all of her life and was moved to a new flat 20 storeys up. She had just moved in when she suddenly went missing. Her family were worried and reported her absence to the police. They searched long and hard for her all over Glasgow, visiting all her old haunts. Eventually, they found her three days later on the ground floor of the flats clutching a scrubbing brush.

'Where have ye been?' asked the policeman. 'We've been searchin' fur ye aw over Glesga.'

'Oh,' the woman replied, 'somebody told me it wis ma turn tae dae the stairs.'

My childhood friend Wee Alex had been moved to one of the tower blocks in the new Gorbals. Like my grandfather's flat, Alex's new accommodation had brilliant views. From his window, there was a heavenly view of the Clyde and right across Glasgow Green. When I went to see the place, he joked, 'Ah'm gonnae get a parachute so Ah can jump right oot the windae and glide intae the bookies or the pub!'

Alex had been brought up in a cramped, damp single end in a crumbling tenement in Thistle Street. This was a complete turnaround; he even had an inside toilet, central heating and a bath now. He was delighted with his new environment. But I noticed it was extremely hot inside the flat. The central heating seemed to be on at full blast, even though it was a beautiful warm day outside. The sweat was pouring off me and I had to take my jacket off. I said, 'Alex, it's like Saudi Arabia in here. Have ye tried growin' bananas fur a livin'?'

Alex laughed. 'Look, Ah've lived aw ma life in the damp and cauld, so Ah'm takin' advantage o' this.'

'But whit aboot the heatin' bills?' I enquired.

He laughed again. 'Ah'm no worried aboot that. F*** the bills! Ah've got it aw sorted. Follow me and Ah'll show ye.' He took me into the hall and pointed to a device on the meter. 'That's whit ye call a meter beater. Ah met a guy in the pub who fixed it up fur me. It stops the meter clickin' up any units. It means Ah can have free central heatin' aw day and aw night!'

When I thought about it, we had all done pretty well out of the rehousing. I was in Shawlands, Alex and old Dan were in nice high-rise apartments and my pal Chris had moved to a comparatively comfortable council flat not far from the Gorbals in Govanhill. Others were not so fortunate, though: they had taken up the offer of a place on the Castlemilk housing estate, which would eventually accommodate around 40,000 people. The disconcerting thing about the sprawling scheme was that it was dry – it didn't have one pub. The story went that the farmer who had sold the land to the Corporation had been a strict teetotaller who had insisted that no licensed premises were to be built on it.

The locals had to catch a bus into the centre of Glasgow if they wanted a drink and, as a result, the last bus on a Friday or Saturday night heading back to Castlemilk became a bit of a folk legend, as it was always full of drunken characters and most weekends fights broke out on it. I got on it once and it was bedlam. People were vomiting all over the place, some were having a sing-song, others exchanging sweary banter and still others were fighting. I thought the conductor should have got a Victoria Cross for bravery.

One day, Alex, Chris and I decided to visit one of our friends who had moved out to Castlemilk. When we got there, we weren't sure where we were going, so we decided to ask for directions. Wee Alex and I went into a shop to speak to the woman serving behind the counter while Chris stayed outside, peering through the window at us. Alex said to me, 'Look at Big Chris. He looks like a cracked maniac, the way he's starin' through that windae.' I had to agree with him. Chris did look rather menacing as he scrutinised us through the glass. The woman was very helpful and gave us directions to our pal's house but Alex, who was a real master at winding people up, whispered to me, 'Watch this.'

'Hey, missus,' he said to the woman, 'see that heidcase ootside starin' through the windae?'

She looked over at Chris. 'Aye?' she replied.

'Well, he says he's gonnae come in and wreck yir shop.'

She looked horrified and was shaking with fear as we left the shop. Alex let Chris in on the joke and the three of us couldn't stop laughing as we headed through the streets to find our friend.

When we got to the new council house that our pal had flitted to, I was not impressed at all. There were a lot of dodgy-looking people hanging around, druggy and degenerate types, and the flat looked shabby and run-down compared to the ones we had moved to. We were invited to a party at another house in Castlemilk and my instinct told me that it would lead to trouble. However, against my better judgement, I was persuaded to go. The party was being held by someone else who had just been rehoused from the Gorbals. A group of guys whom I knew well from my schooldays were there and they gave me a warm welcome.

In the living room of the flat there was a group of out-of-control-looking, foul-mouthed women, all very drunk and guzzling from cans of strong lager. I was still comparatively sober when one inebriated woman staggered over to me and shouted, 'You f***in' told ma man tae beat me up, ya bastard ye.' I had never seen the woman before and I didn't know her man but she had it in for me. The next minute, she launched an attack and ripped all the buttons off my shirt. Then she began to scratch at my face and was punching and kicking like a woman possessed. I had no alternative: I gave her an uppercut to the chin. She went flying across the room and she was out cold. 'Oh, no!' I thought. 'What if I've murdered her!' In a panic, I legged it and ran through the streets of Castlemilk until I saw a taxi, which took me back to Shawlands.

When I got home, my face was covered in scratches and my shirt was in shreds. The next morning, I woke up still aching from all the bruises and scratches the woman had inflicted on me. I began to rerun the Castlemilk horror movie in my mind. I put the radio on and was making a cup of tea when the newsreader said, 'A woman was murdered at a party in Castlemilk, Glasgow, last night.' He said there would be more details later and I went over the incident in my head once again. Sure, the mad woman looked dead when I left the scene. The taxi driver had dropped me outside my Shawlands flat and had commented on the scratches on my face. The police would have no difficulty finding me. Sweating with fear, I listened to the news every hour until more details came through.

Finally, I was able to breathe a sigh of relief, as the announcer gave the name of the street where the incident had happened and said that a man had been charged. Phew! A close shave! It reminded me of what my mother always said when I narrowly escaped trouble: 'Why put yourself in that position in the first place?'

I have never been back to Castlemilk since. Years later, the first public house appeared there and the day it opened its doors there was a queue half a mile long to get in. The name of the pub? The Oasis Bar, or, as some of the locals later nicknamed it, 'the Stab Inn'.

4

ON THE RUN IN LONDON

BY THE TIME WE MOVED TO SHAWLANDS, HALF OF THE guys I knew from the Gorbals were on the run in London. There was a trend to get bail and then flee to London, avoiding further court appearances and possible imprisonment. 'The Big Smoke' was regarded as a safe haven, the ideal place to hide from the Scottish police. There was plenty of work on the building sites and many paid cash in hand with no questions asked. Half of the notorious Gorbals Cumbie gang had fled there and they were joined by gangsters and other rogues from all over Glasgow.

The Gorbals gangs had been rudderless for a while because many of the top leaders had been given lengthy terms of imprisonment. For example, one of the major gangsters in the city, Jimmy Boyle, had got life imprisonment for murder in 1967. But Boyle was back in the news again in '72, when he had six years added to his sentence for his role in a riot at the high-security Porterfield Prison, Inverness, during which a prison guard lost an eye. Boyle and fellow inmate Larry Winters, who had also taken part in the Porterfield riot, were transferred the following year to the new Special Unit at Barlinnie Prison, intended to focus on rehabilitation. It had been given the nickname 'the Nutcracker Suite', because it was set up to deal with long-term offenders who were prone to violence.

The guys on the run in London were all too aware that they could face prolonged prison sentences if they returned to Glasgow. The political situation at the time meant that unmerciful sentences were being handed down to gangsters and many decided it was time to lie low for a while until the Establishment in Scotland began to take a softer approach.

One day, there was a knock on the door of my flat and it was one of my Gorbals pals, a guy called Billy. He looked in a state, as if he had been crying, and the two of us headed off for a walk in Queen's Park to have a frank discussion about his problems. We sat on a bench, watching the pensioners feeding the ducks and swans, and everything seemed so tranquil and normal, a million miles away from the turbulence and violence of the gangs.

Billy told me, 'Ah've got terrible problems wi ma brother Johnny and ma poor auld maw. Ah jist thought ye might be able tae gie me some advice.'

'Aye, sure. So whit's the score?'

'Well,' Billy continued, 'ma brother's wanted by the polis fur a post-office robbery but he's jumped bail and ran aff tae London. Ah don't blame him. The courts ur really goin' over the top wi their sentences. Wan guy got 15 years fur somethin' similar last week at the High Court. So Johnny's decided tae go oan the run. It wis a daft thing he did but he only got away wi 30 quid and he disnae want tae dae 15 years in jail fur a measly couple o' bob. Until a few years ago, ye would've got a couple o' years but noo the judges have gone mental.'

He then unfolded a piece of paper and showed me it. 'This wis written by ma auld maw tae ma brother, askin' him tae come back hame and face the music. She's goin' oot her mind wi worry. It's killin' her slowly but surely. She's lost three stone in weight already. She wants him tae return tae Glesga straight away. But she jist hisnae got it intae her heid that he faces a long time in jail if he does gie himsel up.'

I read the letter:

> Dear Johnny,
> Ever since you were born I have loved you more than you will ever know. It breaks my heart to take in the terrible fact that you are on the run from the police. You've always been a good boy. I haven't seen you for more than six months and I feel as though I am cracking up with all the heartache you have caused. At the end of the day, I am your mother and you are my son, and I dearly want to see you back in Glasgow soon. Please return to your family and, no matter what, we will all stand behind you.

The police and all the judges in the world will never be able to take away my love for you.
    Love,
    Mammy

Billy's eyes welled up with tears and he said, 'Ah know Ah've got tae find Johnny in London and gie him this letter. Will ye come wi me tae lend a hand in findin' him?'

Well, I was unemployed and it sounded like an adventure, so I agreed. I was in. But London is a big place: it wouldn't be like looking for someone in the Gorbals or even in Glasgow. How were we going to locate Johnny? Later that day, I decided to ask one of the older guys who was in the know when I visited the Turf Bar in Hospital Street in the Gorbals. Sipping a pint, he said quietly to me, 'The polis would love this information: tell Billy tae go tae Highbury and try either the Gunners pub or the wan across the road, the Woodbine. Ye'll find some o' the guys in there.'

That night, Billy and I jumped on the overnight bus to London, Billy paying. It was a long journey in those days. The bus left at ten o'clock at night and arrived at seven the next morning. We'd had a few pints in a couple of city-centre pubs beforehand and we slept most of the way. When we arrived at Victoria, we caught the Tube to the West End. I felt shattered at first and the vastness of London and the apparent unfriendliness took me aback. In Glasgow, everyone happily talked to strangers; but here in the big metropolis, no one seemed to talk to anyone else at all. Trafalgar Square and Piccadilly Circus were quite impressive sights, though. I had only seen them in the movies and I felt as though I was on a film set. We meandered through the streets of Soho and soaked up the seedy atmosphere. There were notices and signs everywhere advertising the services of prostitutes. It was clear to us that there was more vice on one street there than in the whole of Glasgow and perhaps the whole of Scotland.

When we got some lunch, it dawned on us that everything was much more expensive than in Glasgow. To cheer both of us up, I told Billy a joke about a Scotsman in London that my grandfather had told me: 'A Glesga fella goes tae London and, after a week, he phones his son back hame.

'"Whit's it like, Da?" enquires the son.

'"Great, but very expensive."

'"How expensive, Da?"

'"Well, Ah've been here a week and Ah've spent a pound already."'

We ended up in Carnaby Street, where we tried on all the latest fashionable clothes. We had never seen gear like it. Both of us put on Afghan coats and Billy looked at himself in the mirror and said, 'Ah'm havin' this.' He then bolted out the door, still wearing the coat. I wasn't far behind, although I'd discarded my coat. We were hotly pursued by the foreign owner of the shop, who was shouting at Billy, 'Stop, you thief. Stop or I kill you. Give me back my coat!' I looked back and saw he was waving a large machete. We ran even faster, rushing into Oxford Circus Tube station, jumping over the barriers and racing down the stairs to the platform.

Just as the train appeared, the owner arrived; we jumped on as the doors were closing. He was banging on the windows, shouting at Billy, 'Bastard! You thief! Bloody thief!' As the train pulled out of the station, both of us were sweating profusely and out of breath.

I looked at Billy with his new Afghan coat on and said, 'Ye wur hawf mad daein' that. Ye're jist like yir brother!'

'Ah know,' he replied, still gasping for breath. 'Ma family ur aw known fur actin' oan impulse. Ah think we're aw crazy. Ah don't know whit came over me.'

We got off at Waterloo Station. By this time, it was late afternoon. We passed by the Young Vic theatre and I noticed a sign outside proclaiming that *The Great Northern Welly Boot Show* was there. It was a musical set in a welly-boot factory and inspired by the Upper Clyde Shipbuilders' work-in. It had been written, songs and all, by the poet Tom Buchan and a new Scottish comedian called Billy Connolly. Connolly played shop steward Big Jimmy Littlejohn. I had read about Connolly in the Glasgow newspapers and I was intrigued. We went inside. The foyer was deserted so we pulled open the door to the theatre.

A Scottish actress, Lesley Mackie, was on stage singing one of Connolly's songs called 'Good Love'. Then Connolly, with his long hair and beard, took to the stage and, as we sat in the darkness, we laughed as the director gave him instructions about how to throw away a fish-supper wrapper. We thought we could have done that directing job without any problems.

Connolly noticed us watching the rehearsal and afterwards he came right up in the stalls and asked who we were. I don't know what came over me but I said, 'We're a couple o' reporters fae the *Melody Maker*.' His eyes lit up and he joined us for a coffee in the theatre's café. It was a bizarre and very funny conversation. Understandably, he was acting as if we were interviewing him. He used loads of funny lines like, 'I've just written a new song called, "How Can I Love You When You're Sitting on my Face".' In reporter mode, I asked him how he dealt with hecklers back home. He said he had a number of well-prepared lines such as, 'There's ten thousand manholes in Glasgow and that guy has to come in here.'

Connolly then sat with us for about 20 minutes explaining in great detail how to make a lampshade out of plastic cups. 'You get one and then you cut it down the middle, glue it to another one and then make a circle with them, building it up until you've got the size you want,' he advised. I was impressed with his patter and I could tell he was going to be a gigantic star in the future. We bade him farewell, saying that we would be in contact again to give him a write-up in the *Melody Maker*! Suddenly, I was beginning to enjoy my London adventure.

By the time we got to Highbury, it was about 8 p.m. When we walked into the Gunners pub, I couldn't believe my eyes: a load of the Gorbals mob were there, all knocking back the beer. These guys were wanted men in Glasgow and I thought, 'If the Devil were to cast his net here and now, he would have a very good catch.' Johnny was there, as predicted, and he looked shocked when he saw his brother. He jumped up from the table, ran over and gave Billy a hug. Then we sat down with some of the most wanted men in Scotland.

As well as the guys from the Gorbals, there were others from Glasgow and the rest of Scotland, all in the same predicament. Some of them were working hard on the building sites, others were into crime: shoplifting, breaking into shops and stealing cars. Some had even been working as muscle for gangland figures in the city. But, apart from their nightly meetings with one another, most of them found London a lonely place. 'When Ah first arrived here,' Johnny said, 'it wisnae like Glesga. Ah didnae know anybody. Ah ended up goin' intae a telephone box and phonin' directory enquiries jist fur someone tae talk tae.' There was a lot of alcohol being consumed and when Johnny read his mother's letter he began to cry. But he just shook his head, saying to Billy, 'Tell her Ah cannae go back yet but Ah'll come hame when the time is right.'

After the pub, we were taken to the Paris Hotel, a cheap dosshouse where the guests all seemed to be lunatics or guys on the run. Johnny gave the owner money for a room for Billy and me. A lot of the residents had just been released from asylums and, as I lay in bed, their screams kept me awake. 'Aaaargh, aaaargh, aaaargh!' The screams sounded as if they were coming from the centre of hell. The place would have been an ideal setting for a Hammer horror movie.

A few days later, Johnny arranged for us to start as labourers on a building site. My work in the RSAC kitchen aside, I had never undertaken hard drudgery before. The other builders took the mickey out of me because of my age and my slight build – not exactly the typical physique of a labourer.

The three of us, Johnny, Billy and me, were the only non-Irishmen on the site. Back in the Gunners pub, Johnny told an anecdote that seemed to sum up the situation: 'A Glesga guy arrives in London and he's desperate fur work. He goes tae a buildin' site and asks the big Irish gaffer fur a job. The Irish fella says, "I'm sorry, pal, it's only Irish people we start here."

'The Glasgow guy is desperate and says, "But ma mother's fae Donegal."

'"Why didn't ye say that in the first place?" says the Irish gaffer. "I'll tell ye what then . . . tell her to start first thing Monday morning."'

Back in the Paris Hotel, I lay on the bed exhausted after a hard day's work with a shovel. Suddenly, there was a loud banging on the door. I jumped up and opened it. A guy who didn't look the full bob was standing there clutching a bottle of Domestos bleach. He had grey hair and a deranged look in his eyes. In a cockney accent, he blurted out, 'I just thought I'd tell you because you're my neighbour.'

'Tell me what?' I replied.

'I'm going to drink this. I'm going to end it all.'

'Don't be daft,' I said.

I spent the next hour trying to persuade him not to swallow the bleach. He eventually agreed but said, 'OK. But if I don't end it this way, I'll do it another way – the sooner the better!'

I lay on my bed, mentally and physically shattered. I had enough stress as it was. I was in a strange town, living in what was effectively a mental asylum, surrounded by wanted men. I didn't need some lunatic pestering me for life advice.

When Billy, Johnny and I got to the building site the next morning, I was no good to man nor beast but I struggled through the day. Afterwards, we were in the Woodbine with all the Glasgow guys. One of them, Harry from the Gallowgate, was throwing bundles of money around. The buzz was he had just carried out a 'profitable wee job'. A group of young English guys were standing near the bar and they seemed extremely jealous when they spotted Harry flashing his money about. 'A Jock spending money – now that's a miracle,' said one of them.

Harry ignored this insult but the fellow carried on. 'What's the difference between a Jock and a coconut?' he shouted. No one replied but he continued, in a sneering tone, 'You can get a f***in' drink out of a coconut.' His pals numbered about 15 and they all chuckled at his witticism. We stayed silent. There were 12 of us, some of the hardest cases in Scotland among us, and this guy was talking to us as if we were just a bunch of bampots. Wanted men being ridiculed – how dare he!

The cheeky Londoner kept on going: 'What's the difference between the Italian Mafia and the Scottish Mafia? The Italian Mafia makes you an offer you can't refuse and the Scottish Mafia makes you an offer you can't f***in' understand.' He and his pals all burst out laughing. Harry and the boys had had enough. 'F*** this,' Harry said, promptly picking up a chair and hitting the Londoner over the head with it.

It was like a Wild West brawl. Another one of the Glasgow guys pulled out a bicycle chain from his bag and began to lay into the English mob. 'Take that, ya cheeky c***,' he shouted. The rest of the Scottish contingent waded in and the place was wrecked.

Tables and chairs went flying and some of the Londoners ended up lying in a pool of blood. It was like watching a dozen Bravehearts in action.

Afterwards, we headed back to the Paris Hotel, some of us bloodied and bruised. 'We taught they English bastards a lesson, did we no?' shouted Johnny. 'That London diddy'll no be tellin' anti-Scottish jokes again. He wis messin' wi the wrang people . . . us!'

When we got to the hotel, Johnny said, 'Ah'm away fur a pish and tae tidy up some o' these cuts and bruises.' There was a dilapidated toilet with a wash-hand basin at the bottom of the corridor. He had walked only a few feet before he shouted, 'Oh no! That f***in' imbecile has done himsel in.' The door to the room next to us was ajar and we looked inside. I could feel the shock rise from my feet right through my testicles and up to the top of my head. Mr Domestos had hung himself. He was swinging from a rope attached to the rafters, which were making a strange creaking noise. Oddly, he was smiling; it was the first time I had seen a smile on his face. We alerted the manager, who called the authorities to deal with the situation.

The next morning, we all headed off to the building site absolutely shattered; the fight in the pub and the demise of our fellow guest had taken their toll. After work, we decided to head straight to our beds and have a decent night's sleep. Besides, it was better to avoid the local pubs just in case the police were looking for us. But when we got back to the Paris Hotel, the manager rushed towards us.

'The police have been here for you,' he said. 'They've come three times already today.'

Johnny feigned ignorance. 'The polis wur here? Whit did they want tae talk tae us aboot?'

The manager blurted out, 'They say you and your gang left three men almost dead in the Woodbine pub last night. It's a very serious matter. They told me they'll be back later to arrest you all.'

It was time to vamoose. We grabbed our stuff and headed for the nearest Tube station. We slept in Euston Station that night and it was freezing cold. I did not feel well at all. In the morning, Johnny had an idea, one of his many. 'Some o' the boys have digs at Blackstock Road in Finsbury Park,' he said. 'They'll put us up nae bother at aw until the heat fae the polis cools aff.'

I felt weak and my hands began to tremble. 'Nah,' I said, 'Ah think Ah'll head back tae Glesga.' Billy said he would stay on with his brother for another few weeks to make sure he was all right. That night, I climbed aboard the overnight bus to Glasgow at Victoria. Billy and Johnny waved goodbye. As the bus left the city centre, I began to cough and shake uncontrollably. It was then that I started to suspect that I might have pneumonia. My London adventure was over.

5

PNEUMONIA DAYS

'THERE'S NO DOUBT ABOUT IT,' SAID THE DOCTOR, 'it's definitely pneumonia.' He was a large, fat man with a posh Scottish accent. I was finding it difficult to breathe, lying on the couch in the living room gasping for air. My wild few weeks had caught up with me. The doctor gave a sigh as he clutched his stethoscope and added, 'Your parents tell me you have been having a rather tumultuous time in London. What exactly were you up to?'

'Oh,' I gasped, 'jist hingin' aboot wi people Ah shouldnae have been hingin' aboot wi.'

The doctor emitted another exasperated sigh. 'The folly of youth!' he must have thought. 'My young friend,' he began, 'let me tell you this: good health is all to do with avoiding situations that can lead to illness, mentally and physically. You have obviously been mixing with the wrong people in the wrong sort of environment and it has led you to this sorry state. You must be careful in the future. Otherwise, you won't make it to the age of 30.'

His words had me alarmed. Sure, I was only 16 and he was predicting that, the way I was going, I had only 14 years left to live. It put the wind up me. But he was right: my London adventure had been folly. Some of the things I'd witnessed during my time there, as well as the physical hardships, must have been a massive shock to my system and as a result my health had been affected.

'There is nothing for it. We must get you to hospital straight away,' the doctor said. Then he turned round, looked me straight in the eye and added, 'Remember, what goes around comes around.'

'Whit dae ye mean, doctor?' I replied, still gasping for breath.

In a gentle voice, he said, 'We are all responsible for our actions and what we do and say affects the lives of other people. You have been mixing with negative characters in destructive circumstances. In future, try to socialise with people who do good, and they will do you good.'

When he said that, I realised I knew this man. However, the memory was hidden in the back of my mind. The pneumonia, along with the penicillin he had given me, had blunted my mind and I was finding it hard to recall where I had seen him before. He wasn't my usual doctor but a locum who had been called in to deal with emergencies.

'Remember, what goes around comes around,' he repeated. 'Let me tell you a story. Many years ago, a schoolboy was playing on some farmland when suddenly he fell into a deep pond. He was drowning and shouting, "Help me! Help me!" Luckily, a farmer called Fleming was passing by on his tractor. He rushed over and pulled the drowning boy out of the pond. The next day, Farmer Fleming was feeding his pigs when a large chauffeur-driven Bentley pulled up. An aristocratic-looking gentleman got out and approached Fleming, who was a poor but proud man.

'"Good day to you, my man!" said the gent. "I believe you rescued my son from drowning yesterday."

'"I did indeed," said Fleming, "but it was the least I could do in such circumstances."

'"How can I reward you?" asked the gent.

'"Oh, it's all right," said Fleming, "I'm not looking for your money. I have a son of my own and I know how boisterous they get – boys will be boys!"

'The gent said, "Is your boy at a good school?"

'"No," Fleming replied, "I am too poor to have him educated to a high standard but he is a bright boy and if I had the money, I would make sure he went to university."

'The gent replied, "You saved my boy's life, so let me save your boy's life by paying for his education. There will be no argument about it. I insist!"

'They shook hands on the deal and the Fleming boy did indeed make it to university, where he proved to be a brilliant science student. Years later, the gent's son went down with what you have got – pneumonia – and was on his deathbed. By then, a new drug had been found: penicillin. It saved him. The man who discovered it was Alexander Fleming, the poor farmer's boy. And the child he saved was Winston Churchill, the son of the gent, Randolph Churchill. So you see, what goes around comes around.'

The tale sort of cheered me up, although even then I wasn't convinced that it was true. The doctor escorted me to the ambulance that was to take me to the Royal Infirmary. I still had the nagging feeling that I had met the doctor before. But where and when? As the ambulance sped off, his face played on my mind and it all came back to me in a flash. 'What a hypocrite!' I thought as an oxygen mask was placed over my face.

I did indeed know this medical man with his pan-loaf accent and psychobabble. A few years back, a gang of us street kids in the Gorbals had regularly made a bit of pocket money watching the motors that punters parked outside the Clelland bar in Hospital Street. One night, we agreed to look after a Volvo estate driven by a man with a posh accent. This was the same guy. Later on, he was thrown out of the pub shouting and bawling and obviously very drunk. 'F***ing Gorbals riff-raff!' he bellowed at a couple of passers-by. 'Most of the people in this area are the scum of the earth. They have no class, no education, no money, no nothing.' With that, he staggered towards his car.

A couple of local gang members had decided to beat him up. 'That big bampot wis in the pub slaggin' us aw aff, sayin' we wur low life, and he got chucked oot. Noo he's gonnae get it. Ah'm gonnae dae him in,' said one hard case. Then he pulled out an open razor and walked towards the drunken fellow. But I stood in his way and said, 'Nah, pal, let it go. He'll be away in a minute and he knows he's no welcome, so leave it there.' The guy reluctantly agreed and then went back into the pub.

We called him Dr Doolittle because, as far as we could gather, that was what he did – very little for a lot of money. We used to see him around the city centre, always drunk and often with women who looked like prostitutes. He never came back to the Clelland, though. He knew it was too dangerous for him. I had, in a way, saved his life, although, of course, he was unaware of it; now he had played a part in saving mine. Perhaps, then, he was right: what goes around comes around.

At the Royal Infirmary, I was carried on a stretcher to a ward where a variety of characters were lying in their beds, some gasping for air like me, others with quiet, resigned looks on their faces, as if they were expecting an inevitable fate. There were two nurses: one was an old Highland battleaxe who took no nonsense from the patients and the other was an extremely beautiful young thing with a great figure and blonde hair. Incongruously, this angel had an extremely thick Glaswegian accent and a foul mouth. While the old matron talked in sophisticated tones, the younger nurse swore under her breath most of the time, although always out of earshot of her colleague. 'F***in' bedpans, f***in' full o' pish, dirty bastards,' she would murmur as she worked. Despite this, she was a joy to watch as she went about her business, a work of art in motion.

In the bed next to me was a man who had both his hands bandaged and was on a saline drip. He was a fellow in his late 20s with an extremely pale complexion. When I first saw him I thought, 'My God, that guy is as white as sheet.' I presumed he had lost so much blood that it showed in his face. We exchanged greetings. The inevitable first question in a hospital ward is: 'What happened to you, then?' Everybody had a story to tell; sure, that was what landed them there in the first place.

Paleface Peter told me his tale. 'Ah'm fae the Gallowgate. In fact, ma close is a couple o' doors away fae the Sarrie Heid pub. Ma da wis a hard-workin' plumber until he got laid aff a wee while ago. He's in his early 60s and it wisnae easy fur him tae find a new job. So he had too much time oan his hands and the inevitable happened: he started tae hit the drink. At first, it wis jist a few pints. Then he started oan the wine and whisky. That's when it got worse. He began hittin' ma maw and she moved oot tae her sister's.

'She wanted me tae come wi her but Ah said Ah'd stay behind tae try and get him oan the straight and narrow and back tae work. But it wis a mistake. Because ma maw had left, he started drinkin' even heavier and he took it oot oan me. Ah don't drink maself and ma only hobby is goin' tae the country tae birdwatch. Ah even bought a big pair o' second-hand German binoculars. Magic, they ur. Anyway, yesterday Ah had jist come back after a crackin' day oot birdwatchin' when ma da staggered in. "F*** it!" he shouted, "Let's go tae the Sarrie Heid fur a drink." He had nae money and he wanted me tae pay fur him. Ah told him tae get tae f*** and the next thing Ah knew, he wis comin' at me wi a machete in his hand, wavin' it like a man possessed. Ah put ma hands up and he cut them, so Ah grabbed ma binoculars and started hittin' him over the heid wi them. He was lyin' oan the floor unconscious in a pool o' blood. Ah thought Ah'd killed the auld bastard.

'The polis and the ambulance arrived and took us both tae hospital – separate wards, mind you. They tell me he's still alive, the dirty nae-user. The polis have told me there'll be nae charges. Neither o' us wants tae get the other done fur a serious assault. So we'll leave it at that. But when Ah get oot o' here, Ah'm movin' in wi ma maw and ma auntie, and Ah'm takin' ma binoculars wi me. That auld bastard can go and lie in his pish fur aw Ah care.'

The battleaxe matron approached my bed, picked up my chart and said, 'Pneumonia, I see. Have you had it before?'

'Aye,' I replied, 'when Ah wis a wean in the Gorbals, years ago.'

'The Gorbals,' she sniffed. 'No wonder you contracted pneumonia with all those dirty slums there. You know my advice to you?'

'What's that, sister?' I enquired.

'Take up swimming and try to swim every day in the local baths. I tell that to everyone who has had bronchitis or pneumonia. Swimming will ensure you'll not have pneumonia again. It clears your chest and makes you less susceptible to infections. Those who have followed my advice have always come good.'

She talked sternly but she had very kind blue eyes and I thought her harsh-but-fair demeanour disguised the fact that she was an extremely caring person. She had grey hair and a stout build. She told me she had been in nursing for more than 30 years.

'Now, then,' she continued, 'it's time you had a bed-bath. I can do it later on or Angela can do it for you tomorrow morning.'

Angela was the name of the beautiful young nurse, who was now standing behind her. She sort of blushed and murmured something under her breath when I replied, 'Ah think Ah'll leave it tae Angela in the mornin'.'

'I thought you might!' said the matron, before walking off in a huff.

The man in the bed the other side of me began to laugh out loud. 'Nae contest, young man! Ye made the right decision there. Ye wurnae at the back o' the queue when God wis handin' oot brains, wur ye?' he said. Compared to Paleface Peter, this guy was a real ray of sunshine.

He was called Stuart and said he was from Glasgow Cross. He told me, 'Ah've got a story aboot two nurses like them, an ugly auld wan and a lovely young wan. The battleaxe gave a patient a bed-bath and afterwards she went over to the lovely girl and said, "I feel a bit shocked."

'"Why's that?"

'"Well, as I was giving him his bath I noticed he had the word Ludo tattooed on his penis."

'The young nurse said she'd go over and dae some medical check that involved pullin' the man's pyjama troosers doon. She came back and said, "Matron, you're wrong. It doesn't say Ludo – it says Llandudno."'

Stuart said he'd been brought up all over Glasgow, living in the Gorbals, Castlemilk, Townhead, Govanhill, Queen's Park and Easterhouse before, at the age of 18, he settled down with his young wife in a tenement at Glasgow Cross. He'd had a variety of jobs over the years including taxi driver, nightclub bouncer, barman, waiter and making plastic basins in a factory. Now, he said, he ducked and dived to make money and had a part-time job as a bingo caller in Parkhead.

'The problem wi me wis Ah got married far too young, at 16,' he explained. 'It aw started when Ah met this bird. She wis 16 as well and she wis an ugly-lookin' bitch. She wis so ugly she had a job in the local bakery stampin' her face oan the Hallowe'en cakes. We ended up shaggin' in a midden and the next thing Ah knew she wis pregnant. Ah thought Ah should dae the honourable thing and marry her but Ah didnae know whit tae dae, really. We wurnae even in love. In fact, we already hated each other by that time.

'In desperation, Ah went to see the parish priest and asked fur his advice. Ah told him aboot the wan shag Ah'd had in a midden and he advised me tae get married and love would grow fae there. But it didnae. We've got a grown-up son and we still hate each other. We've hated each other since day wan. It reminds me o' the story aboot the auld guy aged 98 who goes tae a lawyer and asks fur a divorce fae his 96-year-auld missus.

'"How long have you been married?" asks the lawyer.

'"Aroon 80 years. But after jist a few months married we hated each other," said the old guy.

'"But why get divorced now?" asked the lawyer.

'"Oh, simple: we decided tae wait until the children died."

'Ah want oot o' ma marriage as soon as possible. We jist don't talk. Last week, Ah wis readin' the *Daily Record* and she comes up tae me and says, "D'ye notice anythin' different aboot me?"

'Ah glances up fae ma paper. "New hairdo?" Ah says.

'"No," she replied.

'"New dress?"

'"No!"

'"New shoes?"

'"No!"

'"Whit then?" Ah said.

'"Ah'm wearin' a f***in' gas mask!" she shouted.'

Stuart was an extremely funny man and I could tell he used humour to brighten up his miserable life in a loveless marriage. But how did he end up in hospital? 'That's whit Ah'm tryin' tae tell ye,' he said. 'We wur havin' an argument and she was shoutin' that she wanted mair money. Ah called her an ugly cow and she kicked ma chair and Ah went flyin'. The next minute, the ambulance wis takin' me here wi a broken leg. But after the first operation, complications set in, so Ah've got tae go fur another wan soon. Ah've been here a fortnight and Ah don't care – the further and longer Ah'm away fae her, the better. She hisnae even been up tae visit me. That's fine, though. Ah jist don't care any mair. Ah hope she finds hersel a fancy man while Ah'm in here.'

There was a fairly rapid turnover and the patients on the ward were ever changing. As I lay in my bed, I thought that if you wanted to meet a true cross section of Glasgow people, this was probably the best place to be. After Paleface Peter went home, a man was rushed onto the ward and into the empty bed late at night. He was in a terrible state. His face was all bashed up and his body mangled. The nurses drew the curtains around him and he moaned as his injuries were treated. 'Car crash,' Stuart murmured to me in the darkness.

When I woke up in the morning, the man had gone. I presumed he must have died during the night. That morning, they put another badly injured man in the bed. 'Car crash,' Stuart said again. After a few hours, the man regained consciousness and was able to talk quite lucidly. One of the nurses told us that he was a builder and had been on an outing with his family when a drunk driver crashed into them head on. All his family were in hospital fighting for their lives; his wife, daughter and son were on life-support machines.

Stuart whispered to me, 'Remember that guy who wis in last night?'

'Aye,' I said.

'Well, he's the wan who crashed intae them. He's no deid but they've taken him tae another hospital tae get him oot the way o' this guy and his family.'

We tried to cheer the builder up with our patter and avoided mentioning the crash or his family's predicament. It would only have made things worse. He laughed briefly at one of Stuart's absurd jokes but then said to me, 'Get the curtains roon me, son.' We pulled the curtains around his bed and he began to sob loudly and uncontrollably. It was a primitive, high-pitched noise, the saddest sound I had ever heard in my life.

In that ward at the Royal Infirmary, I witnessed things that would influence me for the rest of my days. The main thing I learned was never to take good health for granted. I met one man from Possilpark who had only a few days left to live. He summed it up. 'Ye know, son,' he said, gasping for breath, 'Ah'd rather be oot dancin' tonight.' That was his dream: to leave the ward and go to the Barrowland and dance the night away 'wi aw the lovely lassies'. But the only dance he would be doing now was the dance of death.

After a week, my breathing had got better and, thanks to the magic of penicillin, I was able to walk around the ward. I watched how other people battled their illnesses. Some would be there for a short time and others indefinitely, while there were some who were destined never to leave at all.

One day, I noticed a beautiful dark-haired young woman bawling her eyes out in the corridor. A doctor had his arm around her and she had obviously been given some bad news. 'Oh, naw, doctor, naw. Me and Bobby wur due tae get married next week and the chapel and reception have been booked. Doctor, tell me this is aw a nightmare and Ah'm gonnae wake up soon.'

I quietly asked the matron what the score was with this beautiful crying woman. She replied, 'A motorbike accident. A tragedy, it is, and he's such a young fellow, only 21. If I had my way, I'd ban motorbikes from the roads. Over the past 30 years, I've treated so many people involved in motorbike smashes.'

This particular crash was pretty heartbreaking. 'That young lady and her fiancé were about to get married,' the matron told me, 'but what does the senseless young fool do? He buys himself a second-hand motorbike to save money on bus fares. He thought the money he saved would all go towards the new flat they'd got in Govanhill. He'd only had the bike one week when, after finishing work on a freezing rainy night, he skidded off the road and right into a brick wall. He's been unconscious ever since and he has severe brain damage. The consultant says he'll most likely remain in a coma. Another life down the drain because of a motorbike.'

I walked back along the corridor and the girl was still weeping outside a private room. Passing by the window into the room, I could clearly see the young man's face as he lay there. He had a big mop of curly red hair and a quiet, almost tranquil look on his face. I knew looking at that face that it would never be spotted on the streets of Glasgow again, that he would never stand in the wedding chapel with the love of his life.

A few days later, the consultant did his usual morning rounds and, after looking at my X-rays, he said, 'You're coming along nicely, young man. You still have some tiny patches of pneumonia on your lungs but they should clear up quickly with some more medication and rest. You have a choice: you can stay here for another week or so or you can recuperate at home. What do you want to do?'

'There's nae contest, doctor,' I said. 'Ah'd rather get better in the hoose wi ma family and pals aroon me. The staff here have been great but Ah think it's time Ah went hame, because hame is where the heart is, or so they tell me.'

The doctor laughed and replied, 'All right, you are free to go when you want but please remember to take your antibiotics when you're back home – and keep away from smoky environments.'

I was elated to be getting home. Two weeks I had been in that place and it seemed like two years. But I also had mixed feelings, as I was leaving my comrade Stuart behind and would miss his witticisms.

While I was packing my stuff, he couldn't resist leaving me with one last comic anecdote: 'The doctor came up tae me this mornin' and said he wanted a urine sample, a semen sample, a blood sample and a stool sample. Ah said, "Nae bother – jist look at ma underpants."' I laughed heartily. We shook hands and he added, 'They tell me Ah'm oan the mend as well. Ma leg is ten times better. Ah should be oot o' here by next week and Ah'll be be rarin' tae go. So we'll have tae meet up at Glasgow Cross fur a pint or two . . . or three . . . or four! See ya, pal! It's been a pleasure!'

An ambulance was waiting outside to take me back home. As I walked through the ward for the last time and along the hospital's corridors, more sick and dying people were being admitted. This was one adventure I had no intention of ever repeating.

6

RECUPERATION

BACK IN THE HOUSE, I DECIDED THAT THE BEST WAY to tackle my recovery was to spend minimal time in bed, instead spending the days lying on the couch in the living room. This proved to be an astute move. It was almost like having my own chat show! An assortment of friends and relatives would call in each day to see me and give me their stories and patter. My mother, a waitress, and my father, a chef, were out working most of the time and my brother was at school but my grandfather Dan, Uncle Mick the mad bus driver and a number of my old Gorbals pals would turn up for a cup of tea and the banter would flow. I noticed one thing during my illness: Glaswegians have a knack for cheering people up when they're down, seeing the bright side of even the bleakest situations.

Dan had been around a bit and had even served in the Second World War, so he had an abundance of weird and wonderful tales. He'd worked most of his life for the Royal Mail and loved recounting stories about his adventures as a Glasgow postman. 'Ah wis in the General Post Office in George Square sortin' letters,' he told me, 'when this other postman said tae me he had worked oot a plan tae recognise envelopes containin' money and postal orders bein' sent tae bookmakers. He said tae me, "Dan, we could make a right few bob oot o' this. Aw's we've got tae dae is be oan familiar terms wi the envelopes wi the money in them, then we make them disappear. It's as simple as that. They'll vanish intae thin air. Workin' together sortin' the mail, we'd be a great team. Naebody'd ever find oot. It's a foolproof plan, it cannae fail. Besides, the bookies have got plenty o' money, they'd hardly miss it."

'But Ah thought aboot it fur a few minutes and said, "Ur ye daft? We could both lose our jobs and end up in jail. It's a serious offence tae steal fae the Royal Mail and judges don't take it lightly. You go ahead and dae whit ye want tae dae. Ma lips ur sealed but if it aw goes wrang, the buck stops wi you. Ah want nothin' tae dae wi it."

'He carried oan wi his plan and Ah said nothin' tae naebody. He wis makin' bookies' envelopes vanish left, right and centre. Ah met him wan mornin' jist before Ah wis due tae start ma delivery and he wis flush wi money. He said he'd like tae buy me a drink and knew a pub that would open fur us early in the mornin'. Ah said Ah would have a quick hawf wi him before ma round. Ah had a bulgin' sack o' mail tae deliver. But he bought me mair drinks and the next thing Ah knew, Ah wis staggerin' aboot Central Station wi the heavy sack o' mail over ma shoulder.

'Well, a big polis spotted me, a steamin' postman wi a sack o' Royal Mail walkin' unsteadily aboot the station. He took me intae the wee polis office there and luckily Ah knew the inspector. They didnae even arrest me and Ah even got a ride hame, wi ma sack, in a Black Maria. But ye know somethin'? When Ah woke up the next day wi a terrible hangover and a worse conscience, Ah wis convinced that that wee bastard had slipped me a Mickey Finn tae take revenge oan me fur no joinin' him in his crooked plan. There was nothin' Ah could prove but it could have got me the bullet fae ma job, so Ah wis very careful fae then oan when Ah met him. Ah wis extremely wary o' takin' a drink fae him.

'Anyway, after a while Ah noticed that the Post Office had started tae employ a new lot o' windae cleaners. They seemed to be there aw the time, cleanin' the windaes as we sorted the mail. And that's how he got caught: they wur undercover polis and they wur secretly watchin' everybody. They soon huckled him and he got five years in jail. He'd underestimated the polis, never thinkin' they would pretend tae be windae cleaners tae catch him. The polis urnae daft – that's why they're the polis.'

Dan always injected a great deal of drama into the telling of his tales and I remember thinking that if I had recorded that story, it would have made a great item on the radio for thousands of listeners to tune in to. Lying on the couch recuperating, I reflected that I was lucky to be hearing this sort of anecdote from him. This was the old Glasgow, the Glasgow of the past, coming alive once again.

When he wasn't giving me his dramatic monologues, Dan usually banged on about how important it was to look after myself. The tone would be deadly serious at first but he usually ended by brightening up with another anecdote from his postie days.

'Yir doctor's right,' he might say. 'The way ye're goin', ye're no gonnae see 30. So be very careful. Keep away fae too much alcohol – whisky's the big killer – and remember if ye've got tae drink, always make sure ye eat. People who don't eat but carry oan drinkin' heavily don't last long oan this earth. Ah see them go every week. Ah buried two auld pals last week, wan in his late 50s and the other in his early 60s. It wisnae funny. The drink killed them. Drink ages ye, as well, makes ye auld before yir time.

'Ah wis deliverin' post wan day tae some posh hooses in Newton Mearns when Ah saw this wee auld geezer sittin' in a rockin' chair in his garden. As Ah handed him his letters, Ah couldnae help but notice how happy he seemed.

'Ah asked him, "Whit's yir secret fur a happy life?"

'He said, "I smoke a hundred fags a day, drink two bottles of whisky, hardly ever eat and I never take any exercise."

'"That's amazin', pal," Ah said. "Exactly how auld ur ye?"

'"Twenty-six," he replied.

'Yir typical Glesga guy disnae appreciate good health. Ye must have seen that in hospital. They drink like fishes and smoke like chimneys and they eat things like square sausage fried in lard. Ah wis talkin' tae a doctor the other week and he told me that, because o' the heavy drinkin' and smokin' and the fried food, the average age a man dies in certain parts o' Glesga is in his early 50s. That's worse than most Third World countries. That's why Ah've decided tae become a vegetarian. Nae mair fried food fur me. And Ah don't smoke so the best thing noo is tae cut back oan the drink, as well.

'Ah find, though, that when ye get tae ma age ye can get a bit depressed. A while ago, a wave o' depression came over me and, Ah'm no kiddin', Ah felt like throwin' maself aff a bridge. Ah bumped intae a doctor Ah know in the street and he told me, "Dan, if you ever feel depressed, go to a pub and order a large whisky. Only one whisky, mind you. Then drink it very slowly, over as long a period as you can. I am not advocating drinking but it works for many of my patients." Ah tried it and it does work. A real slow whisky. It cured me and noo Ah dae it every time Ah feel a wee bit doon. Another thing Ah dae is take regular exercise. Ah try tae hing fae the top o' the door frame and pull maself up. It make me feel ten times better.'

Dan obviously had it all worked out. He had become a strict vegetarian in his 60s and now he was doing tough-guy exercises. But why the change of habits at this stage? 'Listen, most people o' ma generation ur goin' downhill fast. They willnae gie up the drinkin' or smokin' or change their ways. That's why the best part o' ma social life is made up o' goin' tae funerals. Ye've got tae change yir ways tae survive.'

He looked serious for a minute and then brightened up, saying, 'Mind, sometimes it disnae matter whit ye dae. Some o' the guys Ah know have ended up wi Alzheimer's. They say that if ye're a Catholic and ye get Alzheimer's, ye forget everythin' . . . except the guilt! There wis a pal o' mine who'd gone doolally and he went intae a pub and said tae the barman, "Dae Ah come in here often?"

'Naw, aw jokin' aside, try tae keep as healthy as possible. That's the secret. And remember, live as long as ye can and only die when ye have tae.'

This almost preposterous pep talk made me feel a lot better, far healthier than I would have felt lying in a hospital ward watching people fighting for their lives. Dan was right about most of it and the expression 'live as long as you can and only die when you have to' has stuck in my mind ever since. I could feel myself on the road to recovery almost immediately. The influence of words on the mind and hence the body can be far greater than that of any medicine.

Just as that thought flashed through my mind, the doorbell went and it was Uncle Mick. He was a real wild guy. He wasn't my real uncle but my father and he had been close friends for years. They'd met in the early '60s when my father opened up a café called the High Spot in Clydebank. This business venture didn't last very long but for a while it attracted hundreds of teenagers who twisted the night away around the café's jukebox. Mick was one of those teenagers and my father took him under his wing. He had had a tumultuous childhood. At one point, he burned down the local cinema and was promptly sent to approved school, where he served time with young guys some of whom now made up the top echelons of the Glasgow underworld. Mick still had a wild streak and he was always full of stories and advice on how to survive on the streets.

Thickset, with dark curly hair, he looked every inch your Glasgow fly man and he had the patter to match, wild and fearless, full of bravado. Although I had been brought up in the notorious Gorbals, I knew very few people who could talk like him. He had a cavalier attitude to life that brightened up the atmosphere of any room he walked into. He reminded me of one of the characters who hung around with the Glaswegian comedy creations Francie and Josie, only Mick's over-the-top patter could be even funnier. He was absolutely fearless and if my father had to face a difficult situation with troublesome, aggressive or annoying bampots, he always called on Mick. Together, they were a formidable force.

Mick walked in with a bottle of Irn-Bru and some grapes for me, the recovering patient. 'Ah've had a helluva week,' he said, shaking his head. 'It seems naebody wants tae pay their fares. Ye get weans comin' oan and when the conductor comes up the stairs shoutin', "Fares, please," they're aw at the back o' the bus hidin' behind the seats. Then they rush doon the stair shoutin', "Driver, driver, stop the bus." Ah stop the bus and then they aw jump aff! Ah've got worse problems, too. The polis ur after me fur £150 in unpaid fines. So aw the time Ah'm drivin' roon Glesga, Ah've got tae keep ma heid doon in case Ah get noticed.

'There wis mair hullabaloo last week. Ah'd been in the pub wi a couple o' ma pals and when we came oot Ah noticed a bus lyin' empty. So Ah decided tae drive it hame but Ah ended up crashin' it intae a bridge. Luckily, Ah got away before the polis arrived oan the scene.'

Mick told me, 'When Ah'm drivin', Ah sometimes stop at Hurrel's pub in Oatlands and park the bus ootside. Then Ah go intae the off-licence there fur a carry-oot. Aw these people ur oan the bus wonderin' why we've stopped but Ah jist grab ma carry-oot and head back tae ma cabin, heid doon, before drivin' aff again.'

I knew Mick wasn't exaggerating because once when he'd had a bus in what was called 'full swing', jam-packed with people, he'd popped up to our flat in Crown Street for a cup of tea. He'd parked the bus outside and all the passengers were wondering where the driver was, shouting, 'Hurry up! We've got tae get hame!' while Mick was sitting in our house having his tea. That's the way he was and, as he admitted, 'Ah don't gie a f***! In fact, f*** them aw, especially the polis.'

When I was growing up in the Gorbals, Mick's weird and wonderful bus stories led me and my pals to make up a song called 'Jumpin' Aff and Oan the Bus'. Mick had advised me at the time, 'Ye don't have tae pay the fare. Jump oan the bus, go upstairs and head tae the back seat. When the conductor comes up towards ye shoutin' fur fares, jist brush past him, go doonstairs, ring the bell and get aff. Then get another bus and repeat the exercise until ye get tae yir final destination fur nothing.' The wee song we made up went like this:

> Jumpin' aff and oan,
> Jumpin' aff and oan,
> Jumpin' aff and oan the bus,
>
> If ye're ever skint,
> Ye hivnae got a hint
> And yir poor wee feet ur sore,
> Here's the thing to do,
> We're advisin' you,
> Go jumpin' aff and oan the bus.
>
> Jumpin' aff and oan the bus,
> Jumpin' aff and oan the bus,
> When the inspector came after us.

After Mick had finished recounting his exploits, he usually had a good shaggy-dog story to top it all off.

'The Pope arrives late at the airport fur a service at Glesga Cathedral. He goes ootside and his Popemobile has broken doon, so he hails a taxi and says tae the driver, "I've got to be at Glasgow Cathedral in 10 minutes." But the driver says, "No way, Yir Holiness, it's gonnae take at least 45 minutes and that's steppin' oan it." So the Pope says, "You get in the back seat and let me drive." The cabbie dis whit he's told and the Pope zooms aff at great speed, dodgin' in and oot o' the traffic. He whizzes past a polis oan a motorbike, who gives chase. The polisman eventually pulls the vehicle over. When the Pope pulls doon his windae, the polis clocks his face and gets oan the radio straight away tae polis headquarters.

'"This is road patrol. Ah need some advice," says the polis.

'"Whit's up?" asks headquarters.

'"Well, Ah've pulled somebody over fur speedin' and he's obviously very important. Whit should Ah dae?"

'"How important is he? Is it the Lord Provost?" asks headquarters.

'"No, bigger than that."

'"Is it an actor? Like Sean Connery?"

'"No, bigger than that."

'"It's no the prime minister, is it?"

'"No, even bigger than that."

'"Bloody hell!" says headquarters. "Who is it then?"

'"Ah don't know," the polis replied, "but he's got the Pope drivin' him aroon."'

The doctors, nurses and medication at the hospital had been first class but the laughter, outlandish anecdotes and patter back in the house were what really put me on the road to recovery.

7

STREET LIFE

A S I BEGAN TO FEEL BETTER, I DECIDED IT WAS TIME
to hit the wild streets of Glasgow again. I met up with my two
best pals, Wee Alex and Big Chris. Whenever we all got together,
anarchy tended to break out and an absurd adventure usually
unfolded. 'Every time we meet up, it's like they've let three lunatics
loose in Glesga,' Alex said to me. 'When Ah'm oan ma tod, nothin'
ever happens but when we team up it aw goes a bit mental.' He was
right: three Gorbals street boys together was not exactly a recipe for
a boring night out.

Alex had been a bit like the Gorbals' own Artful Dodger,
ducking and diving on the streets from a very young age. In an
attempt to reform him, the authorities had decided to send him to
approved school for three years. It was a change from his damp
single end in Thistle Street but it was a mistake. Alex mixed with
some of Scotland's most deviant criminal youths and learned a few
dodgy tricks along the way. 'They thought they'd turn me intae an
ordinary law-abidin' Joe but the truth is it had the opposite effect.
Ah'm worse noo than ever!' he said to me, chuckling at the irony
of it.

Chris was a product of a hard-working Irish family and was
renowned for his toughness. He had a typical Irish obstinacy about
him; he was never afraid and never conceded defeat. Indeed, at one
point in his childhood, he was known in the Gorbals as 'the boy
who never greets' because no matter how many fights he got into, no
matter how many bullies battered into him, he simply refused to cry.
One day, in the spare ground in Thistle Street, when Chris was about
ten, a big bully punched and kicked the hell out of him, shouting,

'Greet, ya bastard, greet! Ah'm gonnae make ye greet!' But Chris just took the doing and never shed a tear.

Whenever he'd been given a beating, he showed no sign of feeling any pain. He simply shrugged his shoulders and walked away, quietly vowing to sort the bully out when he was older and bigger. 'When Ah grow up, Ah'm gonnae get ma revenge. Don't worry aboot that,' he said to me. Years later, he made good on this promise, just as he'd said he would. To Chris, revenge really was a dish best served cold. The numerous bullies who had beaten him up were subjected to Chris's cool but violent retribution. In 1972, Chris was 17 and working as a labourer on the building sites. He'd developed a powerful physique. He was scared of no man and it showed.

One night, we were standing outside a fish-and-chip shop in Gorbals Street when Chris spotted the bully who had put him through hell years before. 'There's that bastard who tried tae make me greet when Ah wis wee. Well, we'll see who's gonnae cry noo.' He calmly walked up to the chip-shop queue and glanced at the bully. At first, the guy didn't recognise him but after a few seconds a look of fear came over his face. Unfortunately, the past has a knack of catching up with such people. 'Hey, you, ya f***in' dickhead, dae ye no remember me?' Chris said.

The bully feigned ignorance. 'No really. Where dae Ah know ye fae?' he said, clutching his fish supper.

'Ah'm the boy who ye beat the f*** oot o' years ago. Remember the boy ye tried tae make greet? Well, this is him, aw grown up!'

The colour drained from the guy's face and Chris punched him full on the nose; I heard the cracking noise of it breaking. Blood flew everywhere and the bully collapsed unconscious on the floor of the shop. His fish supper had fallen by his side and it was splattered with blood. It looked like tomato ketchup had been squeezed over it. 'Get the polis and an ambulance,' somebody shouted. It was time to disappear and we ran off. But Chris was adamant he had done the right thing. 'That bastard tried tae get me tae greet when Ah wis jist a wee boy. He's the wan that's greetin' noo.'

There was no doubt about it, I always felt safe on the streets of Glasgow when Chris was around; he was a powerhouse and he really knew how to handle himself. On another night out, he saw a guy who had been instrumental in his getting stabbed in the arm at school. 'Look,' he said, 'there's that bastard there. Ah've been waitin' years fur this.' The guy was with about ten other youths, all members of the notorious Cumbie gang. Chris walked over and said, 'You got me stabbed, ya c***.' Then, with one swift and effective movement, he knocked the fellow out. The others just stood there doing nothing. 'Dae any o' youse want it as well?' Chris shouted. But they were all frozen with fear. In fact, I noticed some of them shaking. Chris's reputation as one of Glasgow's hardest-hitting young guys had preceded him. 'They're aw cowards, these people,' he said later. 'When Ah wis wee, they thought they could dae whit they wanted tae me but look at them noo – aw shakin' in their boots when they see me comin'. Ah'm their worst nightmare, a nightmare fae their past.'

In fairness, Chris was by no means a bad guy. He simply believed in right and wrong. At the time, he was convinced that it was right to show certain people that their past actions had not been forgotten. He never used the cowardly form of vengeance – knives or razors – but let his hands do the talking or, on occasion, gave the bully a good old Glasgow kiss.

There were plenty of knife-wielding, razor-slashing cowards around. One day, I was standing at Glasgow Cross with two former school pals when a gang of about twelve young guys approached us. I had a dim recollection of one of the faces. He said to me, 'Eighteen months ago, Gorbals Cross. Remember, pal?' It all came back to me. This fellow had fallen out with one of my pals and tried to stab him with a commando knife. But I'd been quick off the mark and had managed to wrestle him to the ground and kick the knife along the street. We'd then taken great pleasure in giving him his just deserts by beating the living daylights out of him. So this was comeback time! I was determined not to back down to this mouthy coward and shrugged my shoulders saying, 'Aye, Ah remember ye. Ye tried tae stab Wee Joe and ye got a doin' fur it. Why? Whit dae ye want tae dae aboot it? You couldnae punch yir way oot o' a wet paper bag, ya tube ye.'

As I said it, I realised I had made a grave mistake. My friends had a look of fear on their faces and backed off. I looked down at the guy's right hand and realised he had an open razor in it. My first thought was, 'Surely he's not going to slash me in broad daylight at Glasgow Cross with hundreds of people milling round? There are too many witnesses here.' But I was wrong. He raised the razor and attempted to slash me on the right cheek. I put my left hand up to protect my face and the razor hit it, causing a nasty gash. I head-butted the guy full on the face and he fell to the ground moaning. We ran off, hotly pursued by the gang, some of whom were waving knives. They were shouting things like, 'Wait till we get ye, ya bastard! We're gonnae dae ye in.' But we were too fast for them and ran over the bridge to the Gorbals, where I was safe. I went to a local woman I knew and asked her to bandage up my arm. 'Oh my God,' she said, 'ye shouldnae be hingin' aboot that toon. It's jist no safe. There's too many bampots lurkin' aroon there. They'd dae ye in as soon as look at ye. Be mair careful in future.'

I recounted my harrowing tale to an older guy, a Gorbals gang member. He simply said, 'Ye wur lucky. It could have been yir face. A cut hand means ye got aff lightly. The first rule is if ye see somebody ye think is gonnae dae ye, don't even think aboot bein' game. Run like f***. There's an auld Glesga sayin': "He who fights and runs away lives tae fight another day." Don't be brave, be smart. Glesga is full o' so-called brave bastards who've got massive Mars Bars [scars]. They think havin' scars makes them look like fly men. But it's the guys wi'oot scars who're the real fly men.'

When I was fully recovered from pneumonia, Chris and I decided to follow a well-worn path for Gorbals boys: we got jobs as labourers at the Southside Sawmill. It had once been in the Gorbals but had moved to nearby Govanhill. It was a kind of tradition in the area: many local lads went to work at the sawmill while the girls took up jobs at the Twomax woollens factory.

Chris and I lasted only a couple of weeks. The job of humping wood around and stacking it up in piles was without a doubt mundane and very boring. I was no snob but I thought that I was cut out to do something better than be a low-paid labourer in a sawmill. Many of my old school pals worked there and most of them seemed to regard it as an excellent job; but as I queued up with them every morning to clock in, I just felt as if we had all been fooled into working-class slavery. One of the things that freaked me out was the fact that if you arrived even one second after the official start time in the morning, the printed time on your clocking-in card would turn red to signify that you were a latecomer.

Chris and I would join the other guys when they had their tea break in a little dilapidated hut in the warehouse. Some of the workers were dreadfully boring people, perhaps a reflection of the fact that they were stuck in dead-end jobs. Others used humour to try to make light of their situation. George had been at the sawmill for 30 years and he coped with his disillusionment by telling the most outrageous stories during the breaks. If he had had any ambition, he could probably have made it on the stage as a professional comedian.

'A fella walks intae a doctor's surgery,' he began one day. 'The receptionist says, "Yes, sir, may we help you?"

'"Aye, there's somethin' wrang wi ma dick," he replies.

'The receptionist, a wee posh woman fae Kelvinside, is clearly shocked and says, "You shouldn't come into a crowded doctor's surgery and say things like that."

'"Why no? Ye asked me whit wis the matter wi me and Ah told ye straight."

'"We do not use language like that here," she says. "Please go outside and come back in and say there's something wrong with your ear or whatever."

'The fella walks oot, waits a few minutes and goes back intae the surgery. The receptionist gies him a smug smile and says, "Yes, may I help you?"

'"There's somethin' wrang wi ma ear," he says.

'The receptionist gies him a nod o' approval. "And what is wrong with your ear, sir?"

'"Ah cannae pish oot it," he replies.'

Another fellow, Dan, was in his late 50s and had been there since leaving school at 15. He took great pride in the fact and he was an extremely dull, morose man. 'After leavin' school, there wis only wan place fur me – this sawmill. It's a job fur life and Ah'll be here until Ah retire, nae question. It's wan o' the best jobs in the world, workin' here. Ah've no gone hame wi a broken pay packet since Ah started aw those years ago and no many people can say that. Ah've been earnin' since day wan and ma missus knows she's guaranteed her housekeepin' money every week, wi'oot fail.'

These observations made me instantly depressed: a whole life spent working in this place! Surely I had to have a better future than that?

Chris and I soon got into a dispute with another older worker who took great pleasure in bossing the boys around. I thought he was like a cruel Dickensian character. He said things like, 'Hey, you! Aye, you! Get they planks o' wood and stack them up there, otherwise Ah'll stick the toe o' ma shoe right up yir arse,' or, 'Hey, bawheid! Get a move oan or ye're fur the tin-tack [sack].' I refused to take this man's impertinence, as did Chris, and we both threatened him with instant violence when he tried ordering us about. 'No,' I said to him. 'F*** off and stick this job right up yir arse.' He looked shocked at our insolence and made off rather quickly as we moved towards him, well prepared to beat him up. He couldn't talk to us game Gorbals street guys like that and get away with it!

Chris and I simply walked out the door and I felt as if we'd escaped from prison. Chris summed it up perfectly: 'Ah'm glad tae be oot o' that place. It wis a real sweatshop. Imagine workin' aw yir life in there – it would drive ye bonkers.'

'Mind you, we're bonkers already,' he added with a wicked smile.

8

CON MAN

WORK WAS NOT EXACTLY EASY TO COME BY IN Glasgow at that time, so, on reflection, I realised that giving up my lowly job at the sawmill might have been a bit rash. Act in haste, repent at leisure! However, I was confident at first that I would find something else. I trawled though job-vacant ads in the *Evening Times* and *The Citizen*. Then I went to the b'roo – the employment exchange – in an attempt to find a job. There were various employment agencies, too, so I put on my one and only suit and had a go at visiting them. It was a depressing experience. The jobs were mostly office based, poorly paid and with long hours. I also came across a serious hurdle to getting full-time employment: sectarianism. I spotted an advertisement for a job as store boy in the offices of a whisky distiller in the city centre, made a brief telephone call and promptly landed an interview.

When I got to the offices, the atmosphere was very stern and Victorian. I was shown into an inner office, where I met an elderly gentleman who was a director of the company. He looked half cut and reeked of whisky and cigars.

'What schools did you go to?' he asked.

'St Luke's and then St Bonaventure's,' I replied.

'Hmm. In the Gorbals, are they?'

'Aye.'

'Which team do you support – Celtic or Rangers?'

'Celtic, I suppose,' I replied rather nervously.

He looked me straight in the eye and said, 'Well, I suppose that was a foolish question because I can see you went to Catholic schools. Unfortunately for you, the people we employ here are all Protestants and big Rangers supporters, so I don't think you would fit in, if you know what I mean.'

He bade me farewell without so much as a (Masonic) handshake. As I walked through town, I weighed up my options. In future, I would be cautious about how I answered interview questions. I would modify the names of my schools slightly, not admit to supporting Celtic and lose the Gorbals tag.

The next interview I had was for the job of apprentice paint sprayer with a car-repair firm in Newton Mearns. When I met the boss, he seemed very upbeat and optimistic at first. Then it was down to the familiar questions: 'What schools did you go to?' I decided to drop the 'St' prefix from the names and replied, 'Luke's and Bonaventure's.' He looked puzzled.

'And where were you born and bred?' he asked.

'Hutchesontown,' I replied.

I was telling the truth, as Hutchesontown was an old-fashioned name for the Gorbals, although few people outside the area ever used it. He looked none the wiser at my reply.

Then he asked, 'Which team do you support?'

'Partick Thistle,' I replied.

But the man wasn't daft and when I said that he knew I was playing some sort of game. He at least shook my hand, saying, 'OK, we'll let you know by letter.' Of course, the letter never arrived.

My search for work took me to a catering-industry employment agency called Topstaff. In their city-centre office, I explained that I had a little experience as a commis chef. The woman shrugged her shoulders and said, 'Things are tough in the catering trade at the moment. In fact, it's tough everywhere. There's a recession going on. The problem is you've not got enough experience at the moment to fill any jobs we have, so we'll leave it there for the moment. But when you build up more experience, come back and see me.'

I thought this was a ridiculous situation. I mean, how could I get more experience if I couldn't get a job? I was pleased about one thing, though: she hadn't gone through all that sectarianism stuff, asking me what schools I'd gone to, what area I was from and what team I supported. I thought that in some ways Glasgow was not all that far behind Northern Ireland in terms of sectarianism.

It worked both ways, too. For example, jobs on the many building sites were dominated by guys of Irish Catholic descent.

As I looked all over the place for a job, I spotted other characters, young and old, in the same situation milling around the town. The competition was fierce and the vital thing wasn't what you knew but who you knew. I thought about a line my grandfather had heard during the Great Depression in the '30s: 'The geniuses o' the world ur aw hingin' aboot oan street corners daein' nothin'.'

Disillusioned after another unsuccessful morning, I found myself walking up Glassford Street towards George Square. I was passing by the Stepps Bar when a rather well-dressed fellow came out smoking a large Monte Cristo cigar. I immediately recognised him as 'Jack the Con Man'. When my friends and I were kids hanging around Gorbals Cross, he had often stopped to chat with us.

'What are you up to now?' he asked me.

'Oh,' I replied, 'lookin' fur a bloody job. They're harder tae get than rockin'-horse shite.'

Jack, who was in his late 40s, was dressed in an expensive-looking suit and a Rolex watch, which I suspected he had obtained by doing some con or other. A few years back, I had read about a job he'd done in the papers. The story said that he'd conned an elderly businessman out of more than £10,000. At the trial, the court was told that he drove a Rolls-Royce that didn't belong to him. He had taken it for 'a quick test drive' and never returned it. On that occasion, the verdict on the charge of fraud was not proven, while the charge of stealing the car was dropped because of a technicality. If Jack did appear in court, he usually got off with a not-proven verdict because, like all good con men, he was a brilliant liar. He had also cultivated an upper-class accent to impress judges and juries. What was more, he never skimped on lawyers and always hired the best. When he was in prison awaiting trial, he would read up on all the legal technicalities involved in similar cases and, with the help of his lawyer, he usually found a way to get off.

'I'll tell you what,' he said, 'join me for lunch.'

I replied, 'But Ah've no got any money, Jack. Ah'm skint. No got a bean tae ma name or a pot tae pish in at the moment.'

'Don't worry about that,' he said, quite confidently. 'Together, the two of us can go places. With my brains and your youthful looks, we'll be a winning team. The world is our oyster. First of all, we have to fetch a few items.'

We walked through the city centre and Jack stopped outside Tam Shepherd's Trick Shop. I'd used to go there as a kid to buy various comic toys with my pocket money. It was a brilliant place to buy a practical joke like a buzzer for your hand that would give someone a mild shock when they shook it, or a realistic plastic carnation containing a concealed water squirter. Tam Shepherd was a bit of a legend in Glasgow. When serving in his shop, he always wore a smart pinstripe suit and a dicky bow. When we went in, Jack turned on his poshest accent. 'Good day, my fine fellow! We are amateur actors and we require two moustaches: a large black one for me and a small brown one for the young man here.'

We left the shop clutching the fake facial hair in a paper bag. 'Watch and learn, young man,' Jack said. 'Just watch, listen and learn.' I didn't know what the hell he was up to but I just stayed quiet. We were embarking on an adventure and I certainly wasn't going to spoil it by asking too many questions.

Our next stop was a charity shop in Sauchiehall Street. Jack walked in and addressed the old woman behind the counter in a loud, plummy voice: 'Madam, we require two briefcases and a couple of cheap overcoats.' She quickly found two battered old leather cases and two dark overcoats that fitted us near enough. By the door, there was a cardboard box full of pairs of specs and Jack said, 'Choose a pair that suits you.' We bought a pair each and left the shop. The whole bill came to only around £1.50. The overcoats were around 40 pence each; the shop was almost giving them away to clear space for new stock.

We went to the Central Hotel in Glasgow and headed to the gentlemen's lavatory upstairs. There, Jack instructed me to put on my moustache, overcoat and glasses. We left the hotel clutching our empty briefcases, looking every inch like respectable Glasgow businessmen.

As we walked through the city centre, Jack quipped, 'Moustache you a question!'

I laughed and then asked, 'What's the next move?'

'Oh, simple,' he replied. 'We're going to the Rogano for a slap-up lunch, no expense spared!'

I was taken aback because the Rogano was one of Glasgow's best and most expensive seafood restaurants. Sometimes when we were kids we'd hang around outside and watch as people got out of their fancy cars – some of them even in Rolls-Royces or chauffeur-driven limos – to go inside. As far as we were concerned, this place was for the moneyed elite. I remembered saying to Alex when I was about ten, 'Wan o' these days, when Ah grow up, Ah'm gonnae eat in the Rogano.'

'Aye, if ye win the bloody pools,' Alex had replied. But here I was about to make my prediction come true.

We walked inside and the head waiter greeted us warmly. 'Hello, gentlemen. Have you had a good day? Business good?' As he said this, he took our overcoats and hung them in a little cloakroom by the door.

Jack replied in an extremely confident voice, 'Business has been very good today but, of course, when you're a broker, business is almost always good. Now, I want your best table.'

'Certainly, sir,' replied the waiter.

Meanwhile, I kept staring at the floor, frightened that the waiter might notice that my moustache was false or that my glasses were ill fitting. But Jack whispered, 'Don't worry. You look the part and to be the part you've just got to look it.'

The waiter took us into the dining room and the place was amazing. The wood panelling and art deco fittings had been modelled on those of the *Queen Mary* ocean liner. The restaurant was full of rich-looking people, all talking loudly about business and how much money they were making. We were given a table in a little private booth. The waiter came up and asked what drinks we would like to order. 'A bottle of your finest Dom Perignon,' Jack said. The champagne came in an ice bucket and we sipped it from chilled glasses as Jack ordered the food.

'What is your name, my fine fellow?' he said to the waiter.

'Peter.'

'Peter, what do you recommend?'

'Well, for starters, there is beautiful smoked salmon or you could have delicious escargots in garlic,' he said.

Jack waved his hand in an expansive gesture and said, 'I'll tell you what: we'll have both – two plates of salmon and two of escargots. And bring some caviar, as well.'

The waiter looked surprised but he must have decided that he was dealing with extravagant businessmen with generous expense accounts.

'And what do you recommend for the main course, Peter?'

'Well, we have some fresh lobster in.'

'That's fantastic,' said Jack. 'Two lobster thermidors. And when they arrive, would you bring another bottle of ice-cold Dom Perignon?'

'No problem, sir,' replied Peter.

'Oh, I almost forgot,' said Jack. 'Two large Monte Cristo cigars, as well.'

I was excited and a bit frightened, too. As I tucked into the escargots and salmon, I could feel my moustache slipping slightly but I gave it a firm press against my lip and luckily it stayed there. As we gorged ourselves on the finest food and champagne, the hubbub of conversation was loud enough that no one could hear what Peter and I said to each other.

'The first rule,' he told me, 'is that when you deal with someone like that waiter, you find out his name and keep repeating it. So, on this occasion, it's 'Peter this, Peter that'. You'll find that people like to hear their name being repeated back to them. Second, as you have discovered, you must always dress the part. Clothes maketh the man! Third, use the best accent you can muster up. As Shakespeare says, we are all actors on a stage and through our lives we've got to play many parts!'

By the time we were smoking our large cigars, my fears of getting caught had vanished. That morning, I had been at the employment exchange desperately looking for a job. Now here I was in one of the most luxurious restaurants in Glasgow breaking bread with one of Scotland's top con men.

'So, what's the problem?' Jack asked, blowing smoke rings into the air. 'Why can't you get a job?'

'Well,' I said, 'they say Ah hivnae got enough experience or qualifications. That's a big part o' the problem.'

'No problem, young man,' said Jack. 'Forge them.'

'Whit dae ye mean?'

'Counterfeiting is the greatest game in the world. If they want references, it's very easy to make them up. And if they want certificates, like O grades or Highers, fake them. All you need for the references is some headed notepaper. For the certificates, find someone who has them, photocopy them and, with a bit of glue, a typewriter and paper, you can put your own name on them. Look, it's all a con game. Life is a con game. How do you think all the people in this restaurant have got money? Because they conned their way to riches. They are no better than you or me. What they know is how to con people through so-called respectable business deals.

'There's an old Mafia saying: "Behind great wealth, there is a crime." Look at the banks. They con people all the time. Go into overdraft and they charge you. Getting a heavy fine in court for a minor driving offence is a con. Everything is a con and the sooner you wise up the better. Remember, I'm not trying to con other people; I'm just trying to stop them from conning me. Look at the prices in this place. It's all a con. But you can't con a con man!'

Suddenly, my employment problems were looking a lot less dire. Perhaps playing the game by the rules had been a waste of time. This lunch had proved that having a brass neck could get you anywhere. We rose from the table and left our briefcases on it as if we were going back.

'Do you require your overcoats now, sirs?' Peter enquired.

'No, I'm just going out to contact my chauffeur. Bring two coffees to the table,' Jack said.

We walked out the door and several blocks later I took my moustache off and threw it into a puddle. Jack bade me farewell. 'That bill must have come to hundreds of pounds and all they're left with is two old charity shop coats and a couple of empty battered briefcases. I told you life was a con!' He pressed a ten-pound note into my hand and we went our separate ways.

It turned out that the tenner was counterfeit. I shouldn't really have expected anything else.

9

SNAKEBITE

LATER THAT DAY, ARMED WITH MY FORGED TENNER and feeling the effects of my champagne lunch, I met up with Alex and Chris in a pub called the Lord Darnley in Pollokshields. We were starting our pub crawl there because it was the only place we knew that served snakebite. The drink – half cider, half lager – had been banned from many Glasgow hostelries because publicans believed it was too strong for the average drinker and that it transformed people into antisocial, aggressive creatures.

Although I'd never drunk it myself, I'd witnessed its effects in the Star Bar at Eglinton Toll a few weeks before. A man had come in, a Corporation bus driver who had just got paid at the local depot, and at first he seemed quiet and respectable. When I heard him say to the barman, 'Snakebite, pal,' I was intrigued. About six or seven snakebites later, the guy was like a different man. He began to shout, 'Bastards! Bastards!' But the worrying thing was he was shouting at fresh air. He had been sitting alone all night and had got into an argument with imaginary people. The next thing, he picked up a chair and threw it at the gantry, smashing all the liquor bottles and glasses. The bar staff were terrified. They ducked out of the way to avoid the madman and the police duly arrived to take him away.

The barman said to me, 'That's it! Snakebite is banned fae noo oan. People ur goin' crazy wi it. Last week, some guy went mental and tried tae smash up the toilets. Another guy pished himsel oan it, right here in the bar. It's too dangerous, no only fur the person who's drinkin' it but fur the folk who're servin' him.'

After hearing such stories, Alex, Chris and I, far from being put off, were determined to try out a few snakebites – a taste of the forbidden fruit, so to speak. After about four, I could certainly feel the effects. It gave you a strange feeling, simultaneously aggressive and happy-go-lucky. We left the Lord Darnley shouting, singing and bawling, and must have looked a right sight. People were crossing the road to avoid us. Three drunken Gorbals lunatics on the loose! Alex was shouting, 'Ah feel great, Ah feel like Superman, naebody can beat me noo!' By contrast, Chris was a lot quieter but I'd noticed that any time he had a few drinks he was very good at concealing the effects or, as they say in Glasgow, 'haudin' it well'.

We soon reached the Plaza Ballroom in Eglinton Toll and Alex shouted to a large fellow standing outside, 'Hey, Big Celtic, how ya daein'?' I had never seen this guy before but Chris said he was a friend of Alex's older brother. The man took great exception to what he saw as Alex's cheek. He said, 'Who you callin' Big Celtic?' and grabbed hold of him by the throat. The whole scene seemed ludicrous, slightly comical and slightly worrying. Chris intervened, running over to rescue Alex and punching the big fellow down to the ground. Suddenly, a weedy man wearing a pair of NHS spectacles appeared from nowhere, grabbed Alex's arm and shouted, 'Police! You're under arrest!' We could all tell straight away that he was bluffing. Alex punched him in the face, smashing his glasses, and shouted, 'You're no the f***in' polis!' The man ran off, leaving his smashed glasses on the ground. The snakebite had certainly turned Alex into a raving lunatic.

In our drunken haze, we all decided to go for a dance. The Plaza really was a relic from a bygone age but it was a wonderful place. It had a magnificent dance floor with a huge revolving glitter ball and the bar at the back was dimly lit, giving it a romantic atmosphere. At the side of the dance floor were little tables where couples chatted and new relationships often began. The two top places to meet a partner in Glasgow at the time were the Plaza and the Barrowland in the Gallowgate.

When we got inside, there were hundreds of women either dancing or sitting drinking at their tables. But they were a mixed bag: the good, the bad and the ugly. It was always interesting to listen to the bitchy comments between the women. The banter could be ferocious and very funny. Some of the best lines I heard were: 'Aye, hen, Ah love

the frock. Did ye have much bother sneakin' it oot the museum?';
and 'Hey, have youse two came oot fur a drink and left Cinders in
hersel again?'. The comments they made about the men on the dance
floor were equally interesting.

'Look at him, Ina. He thinks he's Omar Sharif. Ah widnae like tae
be kissed by a fella wi a moustache like that.'

'No, Agnes, Ah'll bet he's got a couple o' sparras nestin' in it!'

'And look at the state o' that wee bachle. He bought me a drink
last week and Ah ran ma hauns through his hair. Next minute, Ah
wis haudin' his wig.'

I struck up a conversation with a rather large lady who I'd
guess was in her early 30s. She was called Bella and she was from
Townhead. The first thing she said to me was: 'Ah only come here
'cause the telly's rotten at the weekend.' It wasn't exactly a romantic
first line but at least it broke the ice. She continued, 'Ah've got six
weans by five different faithers and Ah get the gossips criticisin' me
fur it. The thing is, every wan o' they fellas wis a waste o' time and
most o' them ur in jail. That's why Ah've come tae the Plaza: tae
meet a nice man, somebody like you.'

As she uttered that last line, she moved towards me and stuck
her tongue down my throat. It felt like a poisonous snake writhing
away. Meanwhile, Alex was near the bar, chatting quite animatedly
to a young blonde, giving her all the patter. Chris was milling about
the place with a smile on his face. I got the feeling that Big Bella
was moving in for the kill – she was obviously looking for her sixth
victim – so I decided to leave.

'Oh, ye cannae leave,' she pleaded with me. 'We could be an
item.'

'Aye, but what sort of item?' I thought. It was time to vamoose.

Outside, Alex spotted the frame of the man's glasses lying on the
pavement and picked them up. He stuck them on, laughing and
shouting, 'Police! You're under arrest!' Chris and I decided to leave
him where he was and jumped on a bus to the city centre. We soon
found ourselves in a pub just off Argyle Street and, for some mad
reason, I decided to reach behind the bar and pour myself a pint. We
were immediately ushered out of the bar by the angry manager and
his burly staff. Inevitably, a skirmish developed. But Chris spotted
a street cleaner nearby with a large sweeping brush. He grabbed it

and started wading into the manager and his cronies. A Black Maria arrived on the scene and Chris managed to make off while I was arrested – and all because of the evils of the dreaded snakebite!

The next morning, I awoke with a dreadful hangover in a cell at the central police station in St Andrew's Square. There was another man in the cell. He was wearing an expensive-looking grey suit and he too appeared to have had a night on the bevy.

'Whit happened tae you?' he asked.

'Bloody snakebite,' I said. 'It turned us aw a bit mad. Ah ended up tryin' tae pour maself a pint in a pub and the bar staff didnae like it wan bit. Ah ended up gettin' arrested. Whit aboot you?'

'Would ye credit it?' he said in astonishment. 'Ah wis oan the snakebite as well. Ah work as an accountant and we had a leavin' do fur wan o' the boys. It wis a men-only affair. It's aw a bit dim noo but Ah can recall gettin' intae a fight wi a cheeky bastard in George Square. Ah whacked him. Ah think Ah knocked him oot before the polis arrived.'

'Dae ye know whit ye've been charged wi?' I asked.

'No. It could be breach o' the peace, drunk and disorderly or common assault. Who knows? Whit aboot you?'

'Probably breach o' the peace: £25 fine and a slap oan the wrist,' I said.

A few minutes later, a turnkey opened the door and led us into a much larger cell, where about 30 men were waiting to hear what they had been charged with. They were a sorry and shabby sight and most looked as though they had dreadful hangovers.

The accountant looked at me and said, 'Ah want tae get the f*** oot o' this hellhole. Ah'll pay the fine aff straight away and keep it aw quiet. If ma employers find oot, Ah could get the sack. And heaven forbid if ma wife ever found oot. She comes fae a religious family and they'd be scandalised. Ah've got a cover story anyway. Ah'll say Ah stayed the night at ma pal's flat. As soon as Ah get oot, Ah'm headin' back tae ma wife and weans. Ah'm gonnae keep ma heid doon fur a while.'

A big police officer came in clutching a clipboard, which held the charge sheet.

'Mackintosh?' he shouted.

'Aye!'

'Common assault. Murphy?'

'Aye!'

'Drunk and disorderly. McDonald?'

'Aye!'

'Theft.' Then he shouted out my name. 'MacFarlane?'

'Aye!'

'Breach o' the peace.'

The next name to come up was the accountant's.

'Aye!' he replied.

'Murder,' the policeman said.

10

WHO WANTS TO WORK FOR A MILLIONAIRE?

NOT LONG AFTER MY BRUSH WITH THE LAW, MY father walked into the house and declared he had just landed 'a smashin' job' as chef on a millionaire's yacht. He wanted me to join him as a waiter; we would be a team. 'Ah told the staff at the employment agency that we wur a father-and-son team and they said that would be ideal.' The only problem I had was that I had never worked as a waiter before. However, my father was in a very confident mood. 'It's easy, man! We'll jist bluff it. This job is too good tae turn doon. The money's brilliant. Ye'll learn as ye go along.'

The millionaire in question was a Scotsman who had made his fortune importing foreign cars. He had a massive mansion outside of Gourock and a newly built million-pound yacht lying in the harbour. The papers estimated that he was worth at least £30 million but that figure was considered conservative. It was ironic: I knew of people in Glasgow, including me, who didn't even have 30 bob in the bank.

Arrangements were made for us to go to Gourock to meet his personal assistant and we were even put up in a three-star hotel. When the PA, a man with grey hair and an English accent, arrived for the initial meeting, he was very businesslike but friendly enough. 'As you know,' he said, 'your new employer is one of the richest men in Scotland and he expects the best. That is why he pays so well. He quite likes the idea of employing a father-and-son team. As a Christian, he believes in the power of the family. He is a great family man himself and he never lets business get in the way of his home life. He may deal in millions of pounds, but his wife and children always come first. We are willing to offer you a three-month contract on a very good salary. The plan is to cruise around the Scottish islands once the yacht is ready.'

He then told us that we would meet the millionaire and his family in the next few days. A dinner party had been arranged for later that week. Our boss would be entertaining Sweden's top car manufacturer – a multimillionaire himself. This news put the wind up me. I had no experience as a waiter and now I was about to be launched into a dinner party with a couple of tycoons and their families. Surely they would notice I was a chancer?

But my father was still totally unruffled. He always was. He had that Glaswegian talent for being gallus in even the most difficult of situations. 'Naebody knows where confidence comes fae and naebody knows where it goes tae. We're a couple o' game guys, so let's go fur it. Don't forget, it's aw an adventure – and an unusual wan at that.' With more than 20 years' cooking experience, he certainly had no doubt about his abilities and told me, 'Never lose yir self-belief, son. Ye'll sail through this nae bother.' I wasn't exactly won over by this argument. I had more self-doubt than self-belief. In fact, I thought I was more likely to sink than sail through.

To help my confidence, we even went to a second-hand bookshop where, for ten pence, I purchased a tattered old paperback called *A Beginner's Guide to Good Waiting*. I sat up all night in the hotel room reading it and studying the pictures showing how to lay a table for the perfect dinner party.

The next day, we met up with the millionaire at his grand house in the hills above Gourock. He was a small, skinny man, wearing glasses and with a high-pitched voice, nothing like the type I had pictured in my head. He was a self-made man and it showed in his friendly, easy-going manner.

'Right, boys, we have one of Sweden's most influential men and his wife coming for dinner tomorrow night. I was going to have the party on the yacht but it's not ready yet, so it'll just have to be here. Tell my wife what we need for the menu and we'll get it. It'll be a cinch for a couple of guys like you – a wee stroll in the park.' I felt my confidence coming back; this man had no airs or graces and he really made us feel at ease with his patter.

Later, we met up with his wife to discuss the menu for the following evening. She was a different kettle of fish: very cold, very arrogant. She put me in mind of a middle-class school matron with no sense of humour. She spoke to us as if she were addressing a public meeting: 'We shall keep the menu simple but very Scottish. I want home-made Scotch broth. I also want Loch Fyne herrings and smoked salmon. Then we'll have a touch of Braemar haggis and the best Aberdeen Angus beef. It's a little bit of a mixture, I know, but I wish to give our Swedish guests the most excellent that Scotland has to offer. They will also be served a selection of the finest cheeses and malt whiskies. Let's show the Swedes what a great nation we are.'

By this point, I was getting pretty nervous. The dinner party was the next night and all I had to go on was the guidance of an old second-hand book. But my father said to me later in the hotel room, 'Don't worry. Keep a grip. It's only waitin' at a table, fur goodness sake – nothin' tae it. Naebody'll notice if ye make the odd mistake. They'll be too busy havin' a good time.'

The ingredients were bought in and the evening came. My father and I were both in the mansion and I was all done up in my waiter's gear: dark trousers and jacket, white shirt and black tie. I had procured this get-up from a second-hand clothes shop the day before. I had a last look at the pictures of the table settings in my book, then went out and laid the cutlery and folded the napkins. The lady of the house came in a few minutes later and immediately said to me, 'That is not the way we lay cutlery or fold the napkins in this house!' Then she began to rearrange everything.

'Disaster!' I thought, but otherwise things were going all right. My father was getting on really well in the kitchen with the food. He was happy in his work and it showed. As he prepared the dishes, he sang the old country-and-western song 'Lovesick Blues'. It sounded great in a Glasgow accent. 'Ah've got a feelin' called the blues . . . since ma baby said goodbye . . .'

All the guests duly arrived, about ten in total, and then it was time to serve the soup. Our boss was sitting at the head of a long table, dressed in full Scottish regalia, kilt, sporran and all. Seated by him was the Swedish fellow, who was decked out in a dazzling pure-white suit. I had never seen one like it; it was immaculate. It reminded me of the film *The Man in the White Suit*, in which Alec Guinness invents a brilliant-white fabric that repels dirt.

As I approached the table with the broth, I could hear the two of them talking business, mentioning staggering amounts of money. 'I think we should do £20 million on that contract and leave another £10 million in a contingency fund,' Mr Sweden was saying to his host. I could feel myself trembling. These were big shots having conversations about big money and I was serving them. A few weeks before, I had seen a fight in a Gorbals pub over 50 pence.

As I went to serve Mr Sweden, I tripped, for no apparent reason, and soup splattered all over his immaculate jacket and trousers. 'You bloody fool,' he shouted at me. He soon calmed down, though, and left the table to get changed. The rest of the diners, including my employer and his wife, glared at me. If looks could kill!

I went back to the kitchen and tried to compose myself; I didn't tell my father what had happened. It would only have made things worse. Anyway, he had his own problems. He was having great difficulty working out the temperature levels on the brand-spanking-new oven that had just been installed in the kitchen. However, we managed to get the beef out, by which time the guest of honour had returned to the table in a new suit. From then on, everything went smoothly. The guests seemed to mellow out when they got their drams of malt whisky and by the end of the evening there was a lot of laughter in the air. However, I had a bad feeling that this was the calm before the storm.

I walked into the kitchen to find my father shouting, 'Oh no! Fur f***'s sake!' Flames were coming out of the oven and it looked like the kitchen was going to be burned down. We got a couple of pails of water and managed to douse the flames. However, the dishwasher then began to leak terribly and water flooded all over the floor. I managed to keep my composure and walked back into the dining room, where the guests were blissfully unaware of the drama that had unfolded in the kitchen.

Sweating profusely with fear, I served the distinguished party a selection of the finest of Scottish cheeses and then went back to my father. The place was like a bomb site and I knew we were for the sack once the owner found out. No sooner had I thought this than the wife walked in. She had just begun to congratulate us on the food when her jaw dropped and she screamed out, 'My God, what's happened here? This is a disaster area!' She walked back into the dining room in disgust.

We cleaned up as well as we could and in fact the kitchen didn't look that bad at all once we'd finished. But the cooker and the dishwasher were both badly damaged. When we were done, we headed off in my father's old Vauxhall Viva and I confessed to my father about the soup-spilling incident. We both knew the night had been a disaster. My father said, 'It wisnae really our fault. The cooker and the dishwasher had jist been put in and they wurnae installed properly – that's whit caused the problems. They cannae blame us fur that!'

'But whit aboot me landin' the Scotch broth aw over that guy's white suit?' I asked.

'Ach, don't worry aboot it. That happens every day in restaurants,' my father said as we sped back to Glasgow.

The next day, the PA was on the phone to my father. 'The lady of the house tells me the dinner party was an absolute disaster. How did you come to break their new cooker and dishwasher? Those two appliances had just been put in and they cost thousands of pounds.' My father explained that they had not been installed properly, as they would have been in a commercial kitchen, but nonetheless apologised profusely. He also said sorry on my behalf for spilling the soup, saying I had been nervous.

The PA replied, 'I wouldn't bother about that. They were all laughing about it afterwards and the Swedish gentleman said it would be a good story to tell his friends when he got back home. In fact, he was still laughing about it this morning. But, look, I think things haven't worked out the way we planned and anyway there's a problem with the yacht and it won't be ready for a while. So I'll have to lay you off. But, as a compromise, I will honour our three-month contract. So your pay cheques will be in the post tomorrow. Thank you for your service. Goodbye.'

What a nice bum's rush! When we got our three months' wages for one night's work, we couldn't stop laughing. My mother summed it up: 'That's whit Ah've been tellin' ye fur years: if ye work fur people who've got money, ye'll always have money yirsel!'

11

CRUISING FOR A PUNCHLINE

GLASGOW IS A GREAT PLACE IF YOU HAVE MONEY; IN fact, I suppose anywhere is a great place if you're flush. For a change, I was comparatively well off for a while. And what does a Glaswegian do when he has a few bob on him? He hits the pubs, of course.

I took some of the boys with me on a grand tour of the city's bars. Most of us were underage but we all looked older than our years. Our travels took us all over Glasgow, to the Saracen Head in the Gallowgate, the Shipbank in the Bridgegate, the Scotia Bar in Stockwell Street, the Victoria Bar nearby, the Dolphin in Partick, the Star Bar at Eglinton Toll and the Mally Arms in the Gorbals.

Glasgow's pubs are great for the patter merchants and I noticed that among the regular drinkers there were also well-known faces propping up the bars, most of whom had made their names as comedians.

Glasgow has always had a great comedy tradition and people like Stanley Baxter and Jack Radcliffe had put the Glasgow patter on the map, to be followed by Jimmy Logan, Chic Murray, Larry Marshall (who had his own lunchtime television show, *The One O'Clock Gang*, broadcast live from the Theatre Royal), Lex McClean, and Rikki Fulton and Jack Milroy, creators of Francie and Josie. The current generation included Billy Connolly and Matt McGinn, both of whom were also folk singers. We'd often seen Connolly standing outside the Scotia Bar telling his stories to a small gathering and McGinn could frequently be spotted in a Partick pub soaking up the patter and atmosphere.

It's no wonder so many great comedians have come out of Glasgow: the ordinary people of the city could easily provide a hundred of them with enough material to keep their acts going. On our extended pub crawl, we got talking to one old guy called Sammy in the Shipbank. His patter was very quick and he put it down to working for many years in the Clydeside shipyards. He took a sip of whisky and said, 'Aw the comedians come in here because they know they can pick up first-rate material fur their acts. Whit they dae is cruise the streets listenin' oot fur stories and punchlines. Ah would have loved tae have been a comedian but Ah freeze as soon as Ah go oan the stage. Ah tried it wance but the fear got the better o' me. It takes a brave man tae stand in front o' a hundred people or so and tell jokes. Ah can be funny wi you right here and noo but it disnae mean that Ah could dae it oan stage. There's a knack tae that. But whit annoys me is that the comedians come intae pubs like this and steal people's patter, includin' mine. But that's the way it is. There's nae copyright oan patter or jokes. If there wis, Ah would be fartin' pound notes.'

I thought it was a great idea – cruising the Glasgow streets looking for a punchline. If you were lucky, you might become famous and make a fortune, as well. But it really was amazing how much material was out there just waiting to be snapped up. I bought the old fellow a large Bell's whisky and said, 'Awright then, Sammy, gie's yir patter. Gie's a punchline that's worth repeatin'.'

The request and the whisky cheered him up and it was as if a different man had taken over. 'A big polis comes upon a terrible car crash in the Gallowgate where two people have been killed,' he began. 'A wee monkey jumps oot the wreckage and starts hoppin' roon the crashed car. The polis looks at the monkey and says, "Ah wish ye could talk." Well, the wee monkey looks at him and nods his heid. "Can ye understand what Ah'm sayin'?" says the polis. The monkey nods his heid again.

'"Well, dae ye know whit happened?" The monkey nods, pretends tae be haudin' a can o' beer and raisin' it tae his mouth. "Whit, they wur drinkin'?" asks the polis. The monkey nods. Then he pinches his fingers together and hauds them tae his mouth, suckin' deeply. "They wur smokin' marijuana as well?" asks the polis. Again, the wee monkey nods. Then he makes a sexual gesture wi his fingers.

"So they wur playin' aroon and aw?" asks the shocked polis. The monkey nods.

'"Noo wait a wee minute here. Ye're sayin' yir owners wur drinkin', smokin' and playin' aroon before they wrecked the car?" The monkey nods. "Whit wur you daein' durin' aw this time?" asks the polis. The monkey then hauds up his hands oan an imaginary steerin' wheel.'

Old Sammy had us all laughing and I must admit his patter was far superior to that of most of the comedians who were on television. It was unfortunate that nerves had kept him off the stage, as he had a really good comic face. He had a big red nose, a tartan bunnet and a range of facial expressions that had been carefully crafted over the years to accentuate his jokes.

He even joked about getting to an advanced age. 'Ye know somethin'? Whit you young guys will learn as ye get aulder is that there ur advantages tae gettin' auld. Fur example, by the time ye hit 70, naebody expects ye tae run intae a burnin' buildin' tae save people; yir joints ur mair accurate than the weatherman's predictions oan the telly; and aw yir secrets ur safe wi yir pals 'cause they cannae remember them either.'

As he talked, I realised that it wouldn't be long before all Sammy's great comic material, his jokes and stories, would disappear with him down the drain of time. We decided to move on to another pub but before we went Sammy insisted on reciting an old poem to us. It too was on the theme of old age:

> Ma nookie days ur over,
> Ma pilot light is out.
> Whit used tae be ma sex appeal
> Is noo ma water spout.
> Time wis when of its ain accord
> Fae ma troosers it would spring,
> But noo Ah have a full-time job
> Jist tae find the blasted thing.
> It used tae be embarrassin',
> The way it would behave,
> Fur every single mornin',
> It would stand and watch me shave.
> But as auld age approaches,

It sure gies me the blues
Tae see it hing its withered heid
And watch me tie ma shoes.

We headed off to the Victoria Bar and promptly bumped into another patter merchant, a guy called Tony. He was a teacher in his late 40s and an aspiring comedian. We told him about our encounter with Sammy and recounted his monkey joke. He laughed and said, 'That auld guy's patter is brilliant but ye'll find that in most Glesga pubs everyone has a story tae tell ye.'

Tony was a clever guy and I noticed that he often steered the conversation around to a subject he could tell a joke about. He started talking about drugs. The newspapers had recently been full of stories about an epidemic of addiction sweeping through the city. The school Tony taught at, in the rough area of Possilpark, had been particularly affected and he had seen a lot of young pupils go downhill because of drugs. Then he began his joke: 'Two young guys ur picked up by the polis fur smokin' dope and they appear before the sheriff. The sheriff says, "You seem like two nice young fellows and I'd like to give you a second chance rather than jail this time. I want you to go out this weekend and try to show others the evils of drug use and get them to give up drugs for ever. I'll see you on Monday and you can tell me how you got on."

'Oan the Monday, the two guys ur back in court and the sheriff says tae the first guy, "How did you get on over the weekend?"

'"Well, Yir Honour, Ah persuaded 20 people tae gie up drugs fur ever."

'"Twenty people? That's wonderful. What did you tell them?"

'"Ah used a diagram, Yir Honour. Ah drew two circles and told them, 'This big circle is yir brain before drugs and this small circle is yir brain after drugs.'"

'"That's admirable. And how did you get on?" the sheriff asks the second boy.

'"Well, Yir Honour, Ah persuaded 150 people tae gie up drugs fur ever."

'"That's amazing! How did you manage that?"

'"Ah used a similar approach. Ah said, 'This small circle is yir arsehole before ye go intae prison . . .'."'

Tony told us he was a divorcee and admitted that he was bitter about it. His only true joy in life was standing in Glasgow bars and telling stories. We were eager to continue our tour and had almost finished our pints when he said, 'Women, bloody women! They'll be the death o' me. But at least Ah've got a steady job in teachin' and at least Ah can go doon tae the pub fur a pint wi'oot anybody naggin' me. Here, Ah'll tell ye a quick wan before ye go.

'A teacher asks the children whit their dads dae for a livin'.

'Mary says, "Ma dad is a lawyer. He puts aw the bad guys in jail."

'Jack says, "Ma dad is a doctor. He makes aw the sick people better."

'Aw the weans in the class have their turn except wee Stevie. At last, the teacher says, "Stevie, what does your dad do?"

'Stevie says, "Ma dad is deid."

'"I'm sorry to hear that. But what did he do before he died?"

'Stevie turns roon and says, "Well, Miss, he turned blue and shat oan the carpet."'

On our punchline pub crawl, the jokes just kept on coming. We finished up in the Dolphin, which was full of old Glasgow characters. When we regaled them with all the funny stories we had heard, they couldn't resist having a go at doing better. A retired shipyard carpenter called Tam came up with the best one: 'A farmer goes intae the Central Hotel and orders a double malt whisky. An attractive woman sits doon next tae him and orders a cocktail.

'The man turns tae her and says, "This is a special day, Ah'm celebratin'."

'"Ah'm celebratin' too," she replies, clinkin' glasses wi him.

'"Whit ur you celebratin'?" he asks.

'"Fur years, Ah've been tryin' tae have a child," she answers. "Today, ma gynaecologist told me Ah wis pregnant!"

'"Congratulations!" the man says, liftin' his glass. "As it happens, Ah'm a chicken farmer and fur years aw ma hens wur infertile. But as o' this week, they ur aw finally fertile again."

'"How did it happen?"

'"Ah switched cocks."

"Whit a coincidence," she says, smilin'.'

Glasgow may well be a dark and dour place at times but the numerous pub comedians certainly bring warmth to the city. When God was handing out the senses of humour, Glaswegians were definitely at the front of the queue.

12

A TURNING POINT

IN DECEMBER 1972, I HAD JUST TURNED 17 AND I FELT
I was stuck in a rut. My father had once again worked his magic
for me and got me a job as a commis chef at a hotel in the South
Side. He had given the management the 'father-and-son' pitch and
they were happy to keep it all in the family. My father was employed
as a breakfast chef on £20 a week. I was on barely half of that.

On his days off, I would cover for him, doing up to 200 breakfasts
a morning with a small team of staff. It was actually quite a good job;
you started about seven and finished just after two in the afternoon.
Then you were free for the rest of the day. Getting up at around six
was a slight problem, though.

When I wasn't on breakfasts, the hotel employed me to do split
shifts, covering lunch and dinner. It was pretty exhausting but at least
the kitchen brigade was larger than at breakfast time. In any case,
I didn't mind, as I saw it as part of a learning curve. I knew I could
pick up cooking expertise that could be useful to me in the future.
In fact, I was surprised, as were the older chefs, by how proficient I
already was. I had picked up more in the way of culinary techniques
at the RSAC than I'd realised. It seemed to me that knowledge was
like riding a bike: once you learn how to do something, you never
really forget.

The thing that was slightly depressing about the job was that the
hotel employed mainly middle-aged and old people. For example,
Ted the grill chef was almost at retirement age and had been there
for donkey's years. He was Polish and had come to Scotland after
the Second World War. His catering abilities were questionable and it
was debatable whether any other restaurant in Glasgow would have

employed him but he'd been there for so long he was practically unsackable.

One day, I asked Ted where he had trained and he simply replied, 'The concentration camps.'

'Whit, under the Nazis?' I asked. 'That must have been bloody hard!'

'Bloody hard,' Ted replied in his half-Polish, half-Scottish accent. 'I had to cook for a couple of thousand people with almost no food. That was the most difficult thing – cooking without food. The Nazis were starving us yet it was my job to try to find something, anything, to fill their bellies.' At first, I wasn't sure if he was telling the truth but he showed me the tattooed number on his arm. 'At least I survived,' he said. 'Many of my family and friends did not.' From then on, I had the utmost respect for Ted.

The head chef was an Italian fellow who never seemed to smile and thought of himself as a strict disciplinarian, although in reality he was a real pussycat. The menu looked rather posh and some VIP diners frequented the place. On closer examination, however, the dishes were for the most part simple affairs given exotic or grandiose names. The other chefs were middle-aged Glasgow guys, most of whom seemed to have dubious kitchen experience. They were all taken aback when I told them I had started out at the RSAC, as that was premier division to them. One of the others had trained frying hamburgers in a Wimpy Bar. There were two waitresses who looked as though they had stepped straight out of an old-folks' home. Even the kitchen porter was ancient. One of the chefs said to me, 'The last time that guy had a birthday party, they had tae call the fire brigade tae put the candles oot.'

All in all, the staff members, aged as they were, were a likeable mob but it was not exactly the best place for a young man like me to be. When I complained, Ted told me, 'I have been through the horrors of the war and I know what hardship is. This is a secure job for life. Keep your head down and stay out of trouble and you will be here until you retire.' I knew he meant well but those remarks only put me off the job even more.

By this time, I had stopped frequenting what was left of the old Gorbals, as I found that any time I hung around there I usually got into some sort of skirmish. My life now was living in ever-so-middle-class Shawlands and commuting to my work at the hotel just a few miles up the road. But on my days off, boredom would often set in and I would find myself with my pals roaming about the city centre or, on the odd rare occasion, the Gorbals.

One day, on my day off, I was sitting on a Corporation bus heading for town when an old drunken guy sat next to me. He said nothing for a while but just before he was due to get off he looked at me, reeking of wine, and said, 'Ye know, young fella, Ah'll gie ye some advice. There ur three things that get ye intae trouble in yir life.'

'Aye and whit's that?' I enquired.

He sighed heavily and replied, 'Yir mouth, yir knob and yir signature.' Then he got off the bus without uttering another word. I thought nothing of it at the time but I was soon to find out just how true the maxim was.

First, your mouth. A week later, I made one of my rare excursions to the notorious Portland Dance Hall in the Gorbals. Me and a few of the boys had been consuming Lanliq, a cheap wine, in a spit-and-sawdust pub in the Gallowgate. Later we went into the dance hall, which was a well-known hangout for major IRA guys and Gorbals gang members. I soon got into an argument with a young fellow known as 'Mac the Knife'. He was beginning to make a name for himself in the area as a violent guy. He had stabbed or slashed several people. However, I had known him at school, when he had been a rather weak-willed character – certainly no fighter – and I didn't rate him as a hard man at all.

Drunkenly, I taunted him, 'Ye're no a real hard case. Ye're whit we call a cardboard hard case and Ah could bend ye nae bother at aw. Ye're jist a wee bampot kiddin' oan ye're a game guy.' He looked angry and I thought he was going to go for me but the dance floor was jam-packed and the place was swarming with big burly Irish bouncers, so he decided not to retaliate there and then. However, he did say rather menacingly, 'Aye, we'll see the morra when ye sober up. Ah'll show ye whit the score is. Ye'll no be boastin' the next time we meet up. Ah'm gonnae gie ye a lesson ye'll never forget.'

Later, a few of my drunken comrades got mouthy with a couple of the huge bouncers. I said to one of them, 'Ye're jist a big balloon. Don't even think o' messin' wi us, ya big Irish tube ye.' At this, he and his pal grabbed me by the arms and ushered me down the front steps of the building into the street. It was the classic drunken bum's rush; I fell onto the wet pavement. My face was all bruised, bashed and bloodied, and there was a steady trickle of blood coming from my head. My first painful thought was that they could have killed me.

Second, your knob. As I sat up, a heavy-set woman appeared from nowhere and began to tend to my cuts with some paper napkins she had in her handbag. She then went inside the dance hall and came out with some wet paper towels and cleaned me up. I could tell she fancied me. 'Oh, ye seem like such a nice guy,' she said. 'Why dae ye put yirsel in these situations? Ye need somebody like me tae look after ye.' My cuts had stopped bleeding and she took me by the hand into a dark lane nearby, where we began what Glaswegians euphemistically call 'a real winchin' session'.

Finally, your signature. Afterwards, I drunkenly wrote my name, address and telephone number on a scrap of paper and half-heartedly told her to give me a ring so that we could meet up again.

The next morning, I awoke with a terrible hangover – death by wine. Oh no! Did I really insult Mac the Knife, that young psychopath? Oh no! Did I really call that big monster of a bouncer 'a balloon'? Oh no! Did I really have a winchin' session with that big ugly woman in the dark lane and then give her all my details? Oh no, no, no, no, no!

I decided to keep away from the Gorbals from then on, at least for a couple of months anyway. About six weeks later, Alex phoned me one night and said, 'Hey, watch it when ye come back here.'

'Why?' I enquired.

'Well, Mac the Knife is goin' roon sayin' ye've got a big mouth and he's gonnae chib ye if he ever sees ye again.'

Needless to say, this had me worried.

A couple of days later, the phone rang and there was a woman's voice on the line: 'Hi, it's me, Tina.'

'Tina who?'

'Tina who ye met ootside the dance hall a few weeks back. Remember?'

I tried to conceal my shock. 'Oh, aye, how ye daein'? Awright?'

'No really. Ah think Ah'm pregnant,' she replied.

We carried on the conversation for a few minutes more and I said

I was busy working at the moment but added that we could meet up for a talk as soon as I had time.

This was definitely a turning point. I had a mad hard case after me and a woman I barely knew saying I might be the father of her child. It was time to get out of town – fast!

I remembered what Jack the Con Man had told me, took some headed notepaper from the hotel and quickly forged a glowing reference:

> To whom it may concern:
> Mr MacFarlane is an outstanding young chef, one of the best of his generation. During his time here, he has excelled in all departments and is no stranger to long hours and hard work. We will be sorry to see him go but he has a desire to move on to build on his already considerable experience. We wish him all the best in any future employment. He will be welcome back here any time.
> Yours sincerely,
> The manager

A printer pal of mine kindly made up some counterfeit culinary certificates for me at the last minute. As soon as they were ready, I walked into a catering employment agency in Renfield Street, rather smartly dressed, and said in my best accent that I was looking for a new opportunity. The office manageress was clearly impressed with my references and certificates, and she said, 'We have just the job for you: head grill chef in an Oban restaurant. The money is very good, £25 a week, and you will have free board and lodging.'

Twenty-five quid with free board and lodging! This was a better deal than my father was on and he had more than 20 years' experience. Bullshit baffles brains!

Later that night, in the spring of 1973, I headed by train from Queen Street to Oban, leaving the madness, badness and sadness of Glasgow behind.

13

OBAN

WHEN THE TRAIN PULLED INTO OBAN STATION IT was after 10 p.m. and pitch black. A man directed me to the restaurant. A member of staff led me through the dark streets to the staff boarding house. I was given a large room and, as I lay on my double bed, I felt anxious about the next day and how I would fare in the new job. However, I also felt a great sense of relief at having left Glasgow and my problems there behind.

When the morning came, I walked down the main street and was astounded by how beautiful everything looked. The town seemed bright and dazzling compared to the near-constant greyness of Glasgow. On the front, the scenery took my breath away. There were fantastic views over to the nearby island of Kerrera and to Mull in the distance. Dozens of picturesque fishing boats were moored in the harbour. 'Man,' I thought, 'I've hit the jackpot!'

In the restaurant, I met my colleagues. They all looked surprised at how young I was: 17 with the title of head grill chef! The other chefs all had a great deal of experience. Most of the brigade were from Germany. There was Friedrich, the executive head chef, who was the boss and hailed from Berlin; Oskar, the head chef, from Stuttgart; Paul, the pastry chef, from Austria; Franz who was from Nuremberg; Helmut from Frankfurt; Kurt from Dresden; Lars from Sweden; and Danny, who, although he was from Glasgow, had worked all over Europe. I knew straight away that they were a great bunch of fellows and they all seemed to take to me, too. To me, in defiance of the stereotype about their over-seriousness, the Germans seemed very similar in temperament to the Scots and had the same sense of humour, especially those from the south, who tended to have an air of wildness about them.

The waitresses at the restaurant were largely beautiful Swedish women, long-legged blondes from Stockholm. One of them, Ingrid, was so good-looking that we were all convinced that if she'd entered Miss World she'd have won it outright. Most of the German chefs were going out with one of these beautiful girls, who were in a different league from most of the girls I'd met back home. Other members of staff included kitchen hand Gerry, from Glasgow, who was also a cabaret singer; Hamish, the kitchen porter, an amazing raconteur; and Charlotte, a pretty 18-year-old local girl who worked part time as a waitress. When the summer season came, hundreds of students from all over Britain would descend on Oban to work in the town's hotels, restaurants and bars.

The restaurant itself was a busy affair with several dining rooms serving traditional Scottish fare such as haggis and neeps, mince and tatties, and Aberdeen Angus steaks to the tourists.

As I got to know my colleagues better, I realised that most of the people I was working with were half mad. The boss, Friedrich, was an extremely funny man but woe betide you if you got on the wrong side of him. He came into the kitchen one day shouting and bawling. 'You bunch of useless bastards!' he cried. 'If you served food this bad in Germany, I would have you dismissed immediately!' We all bowed our heads in fear and mock shame. Friedrich proceeded into the restaurant, sat down at a table and ordered a well-done sirloin steak.

Franz was a friend of Friedrich's and he said to me in broken English, 'He's a nice guy but he does have a terrible temper. It's time he was taught a lesson.' I was a bit nervous about this remark, as I had only been in the job a couple of weeks at this point and I didn't want to do anything that might get me the sack.

I cooked Friedrich's steak to perfection and added chips and salad as requested. Everything had to be perfect for the boss with the bad temper. But just as the waitress was ready to take the plate away, Helmut rushed over to the hotplate and shouted, 'Let me check that everything's OK.' I saw him fiddle about a bit with the presentation and then the meal was sent out.

A few minutes later, Friedrich rushed into the kitchen, his face red with anger. 'Who are the bastards who did this?' he shouted, and threw the plate onto the hotplate. I could see what the problem was all right. Helmut had placed a condom under the steak. At first, I was terrified but then Helmut owned up and everyone in the kitchen burst out laughing.

Friedrich just laughed and said to Helmut, 'You are a no-good scumbag! I'll get you for this!' It was then that I realised that the two men were always playing practical jokes on each other. This time, Helmut was well ahead of the game. He said to me, 'I have known Friedrich since I was young. He loves playing jokes on people but when he's on the receiving end he sometimes finds it not so funny.' The practical jokes were one way of dealing with the stress and pressure of a busy kitchen.

One day not long after I'd started, Franz, who had only a smidgin of English, approached me and asked, 'Will you teach me how to speak English?' I agreed to give him lessons as we worked in the kitchen each day. After two months, Franz was speaking in a Glasgow accent and saying things like, 'how's it gaun?' and 'nae bother at aw'. Indeed, some of the newer staff who joined were convinced that he was actually from the Gorbals.

Over time, the other chefs' personalities began to emerge. Paul, the pastry chef, was a good-looking fellow and very much the ladies' man. He had several beautiful girlfriends, some Swedish, some Scottish. I asked him the secret of his success and he simply shrugged his shoulders, saying, 'It is all in the eyes, my friend, all in the eyes.'

Head chef Oskar was of the same ilk. He drove a Porsche and was married to a beautiful Englishwoman, a former model. But when his wife was out of town, he had a string of beautiful women to keep him company. Helmut was a big fan of beer, Scottish and German, and he too had an eye for the ladies, especially once the beer had taken its effect. Lars, the Swede, did not drink and was a bit of a trainspotter type who was more interested in talking about engines than about women.

Kurt from Dresden spoke no English at all. He had a habit of going out and causing anarchy, getting arrested for smashing up pubs. The rest of his German workmates told me that they reckoned that Dresden's near-total obliteration by the Allies in 1945 had left its mark on the city's inhabitants. 'The people of Dresden are all round the bend because of the bombardment. Kurt is a reflection of that,' Helmut said to me. Helmut's father had been in the SS. He was always telling anti-Semitic jokes, which didn't seem too surprising to me, given that he'd been brought up by a Nazi.

By contrast, Danny, the chef from Glasgow, was into peace and love. He was a dope connoisseur and one night he said to me, 'Ah'll let ye intae a wee secret. If ye want tae get stoned quickly, take a spoonful o' ground nutmeg and ye'll get as high as a kite.' Ground nutmeg was freely available in the kitchen so it was no wonder Danny always seemed a bit out of it. He wasn't a big drinker but he invested some of his money in Red Lebanese hashish, or 'Red Leb', which he had sent to him by an Arab pal in Morocco. 'When Ah finish work, Ah don't go oot much; Ah jist sit in ma room and get stoned oot ma tiny little mind,' he confessed. 'After the season's over, Ah head tae Morocco fur the winter. But whit Ah dae is, Ah take a load o' *Broons* and *Oor Wullie* books and back copies o' the *Sunday Post*. Then Ah spend aw winter gettin' stoned while readin' them and killin' maself laughin'.' *Oor Wullie* and *The Broons* with hashish and Morocco sounded an odd combination but I suppose it was a case of whatever gets you through the night, or rather the winter.

The maddest character in the kitchen was Gerry from Glasgow, the porter cum local cabaret star. By day, Gerry cleaned the kitchen; by night, he stood on stage in the local pubs, clubs and hotels telling jokes and singing songs. His real name wasn't Gerry but, working with the German guys, he sometimes used a fake German accent, which had led to his nickname. When he wasn't walking around being as daft as you like, he could be a bit of a sad character. He had never really recovered from his divorce. The marriage had produced one child, who was now living with Gerry's ex-wife.

Gerry used the kitchen staff as a sort of sounding board to try out his new material. One day when he had a show in the evening, he came up to me and launched into one of his jokes: 'A guy walks intae a shop tae buy a Barbie doll fur his daughter and asks the shop assistant how much they are. "Which one?" the woman asks. "We have Barbie Goes to the Gym, £10, Barbie Goes to the Ball, £10, Barbie Goes Shopping, £10, Barbie Goes to the Beach, £10, Barbie Goes Nighclubbing, £10, and Barbie Gets Divorced, £150."

'The guy asks her, "Why is the divorced Barbie £150 when all the others are a tenner?"

'"Well," the woman says, "that one comes with Ken's house, Ken's car, Ken's boat and Ken's furniture."'

Gerry then looked me in the eye and, in a serious tone, said, 'Ah like tellin' jokes aboot divorce. Ah've been through a terrible time and it makes me feel a wee bit better.' Then he asked me, 'Listen, why don't ye come tae ma show tonight? Hamish is goin', so tag along wi him if ye want.'

After work, Hamish and I went along to the hotel where Gerry was performing. Another of the kitchen porters, Hamish was a Highlander through and through. He didn't tell jokes like Gerry but he was full of philosophical stories and quotations that made you think. We arrived just after eight and Gerry was on the small stage. I was surprised by the size of the crowd. The place was packed with locals and tourists.

Gerry had a manic grin on his face. He started off by singing 'Bonnie Mary of Argyll' and 'Okie from Muskogee'. The crowd loved it and they gave him rapturous applause. Then he shouted to them, 'Knock, knock!'

The audience shouted back, 'Who's there?'

'Aardvark.'

'Aardvark who?'

Gerry began to sing, 'Aardvark a million miles for one of your smiles, my mammy!'

The audience lapped it all up. You would never have thought watching Gerry that he was a lowly kitchen cleaner by day. He worked the audience well and I thought that, with a lucky break, he could have been star material. I had seen much worse acts at Glasgow's Pavilion Theatre.

The audience was full of American and Canadian tourists who loved jokes about the Scots. Gerry gave them what they wanted: 'A Scotsman returned hame fae the doctors and said tae his wife, "There's good news and bad news."

'"Tell me the bad news first," his wife says.

'"Ah've got sugar in ma urine, so there's a strong chance Ah'm diabetic."

'"And whit's the good news?"

'"Think o' the money Ah'll save by pishin' oan the cornflakes."'

Another of his Scottish jokes went: 'Did ye hear aboot the Scotsman who got intae a taxi tae take his bird hame? The girl was so beautiful he could barely keep his eyes oan the meter.'

This kind of material might not have gone down so well in Glasgow but the tourists lapped it up, giving Gerry a rousing standing ovation at the end of his act. 'Bravo! Bravo!' one visitor was shouting.

Later on, Gerry, Hamish and I ended up back at the staff accommodation. At first, Gerry was on a high, excited about how successful he had been that night. Then, as we drank some wine, his mood began to change; he was on a downer. He started to talk about his estranged wife and child. 'Ah cannae live wi'oot them. Ah've near enough lost the will tae live. Whit is the point o' this life? It's aw a mess. Everythin' is a bloody mess.' He was sobbing and the tears dropped into his wine glass. I had never seen a man's mood change so dramatically.

Hamish sat sipping from a small bottle of whisky. He said, 'Listen, Gerry, don't worry about the past. It's all over. The only time that counts is this very minute, this moment. Remember this: yesterday is history, tomorrow is a mystery and today is a a gift; that's why we call it the present.'

After Hamish said that, we all cheered up a bit. He was a kitchen-porter philosopher who knew how to say the right thing at the right time. 'If only we all had that talent,' I thought.

14

ALL YOU NEED IS LOVE

HAMISH HAD HAD A PRETTY INTERESTING LIFE. He was in his 60s and had worked for a long time as a fisherman in Oban, Benbecula, Mull and Stornoway. At the same time, he had become a successful preacher, specialising in fire-and-brimstone sermons. He had also been a big hit with the girls and had been married three times. When I asked him how many children he had, he just laughed, saying, 'One for every month of the year – twelve!' His children were scattered around the Highlands and he still kept in touch with them all. 'Five boys and seven lassies, and all bloody great Highland people. They must be great people because I'm their father!'

In his mid-40s, he gave up fishing to study philosophy at Aberdeen University and for a decade he became a teacher. But he said that he woke up one day and decided to give it all up to become a bit of a drifter. 'I realised that, although I was Scottish, I didn't really know Scotland as well as I should, so I vowed to travel round and see as much of the country as I could before I got too old. For the past ten years, I've been working on my biography, which is really a book of Scottish philosophy. I usually work as a kitchen porter in hotels and restaurants to make sure I have the lodgings and money I need to keep on writing. While I'm cleaning the pots and pans, I get plenty of time to meditate on the absurdity of life.'

His patter was certainly different from the kind I'd been used to back in the Gorbals. He wasn't a wiseguy who simply told jokes but a smart man, a truth-seeker, who recounted parables rather than funny stories.

One morning, I walked into the pot-wash room to hand him a

dirty tray and he looked me up and down, laughed and then said, 'You know, you don't have to be like this.'

'Whit dae ye mean?' I said.

'Well, you walk like a Gorbals hard man, you talk like a Gorbals hard man and you act like a Gorbals hard man. But you don't have to do that any more. Here in Oban, you can reinvent yourself. You can become whoever you want to be. Forget the Gorbals and Glasgow for a while and try becoming a different person. It'll do you good.'

He continued, 'There's an old story. A lion cub says to his father, "Dad, why have I got such big ears?"

'The father lion replies, "So that when you're in the jungle, you can hear other creatures coming for miles."

'"Dad, why have I got such big teeth?"

'"So that when you go hunting in the jungle, you can make a kill easily and devour your prey."

'"Dad, why have I got such big eyes?"

'"So that you can see other animals coming through the jungle from miles off."

'"Dad, one last question."

'"What's that, son?"

'"What am I doing in London Zoo?"

'The point of that story is that you are just like the lion cub. You don't have to do all that Gorbals stuff any more because you're not in the jungle any more. If you change, you'll feel ten times better. And do you know what my advice to you is?'

'Whit's that, Hamish?'

'Find someone to love, find something to do and find something to look forward to. You already have something to do here in Oban, so see if you can find the other two things. They are the essential ingredients of life. People say there's no love in the world any more. But you go to any railway station or airport and look at people coming and going. Watch them crying as they say goodbye to their loved ones and see how happy they are when they come back. It's then you realise that there's still a lot of love in the world.'

A few hours after my conversation with Hamish, it was time for my afternoon break. The weather was wonderful: clear blue skies with not a cloud in sight. Oban, with all its natural beauty, looked wonderful, almost magical. It was a sharp contrast to the filthy streets and run-down tenements I had been used to growing up. I walked along the seafront and decided to lie on the grass outside the Corran Halls and soak up the sun. I dozed off briefly and woke to find someone standing above me. 'Hello. Enjoying the sun?' It was Charlotte, the 18-year-old local girl who waitressed at the restaurant. She was beautiful, with long, flowing blonde hair and perfect pale skin.

Much to my amazement, she sat down beside me and we struck up a conversation. She revealed she was a vet's daughter. She lived with her family in a big house outside of town. She was obviously intrigued by me, having seen me prancing about the kitchen in my gallus Gorbals manner. Although I fancied her a lot, I secretly felt unsure of myself. I mean, what was she doing talking to a scruff like me? She was obviously well brought up, with her beautiful soft Highland accent. She was a complete contrast to all the wild, foul-mouthed herries I had known back in Glasgow.

However, we got on very well and I made her laugh with my sharp patter. Before we headed back to work, we agreed to meet at the same spot the next day 'for a good laugh and a talk'. As I walked back to the restaurant, I had an incredible feeling inside of me. But what was it? I had never felt it before. Could it be love, the very emotion that Hamish had been harping on about? 'Ain't love a wonderful thing!' I thought as I strolled past the harbour.

Back in the restaurant, Gerry was crying his eyes out in a little office, 'Ah've jist had a lawyer's letter sayin' Ah cannae see ma wean any mair. She claims Ah'm a bad faither. They've barred me fae seein' ma ain child,' he sobbed.

Hamish was trying to reassure him and give him some more philosophical advice. I thought the advice had better work quick, as Gerry was due on stage at a local hotel in just over an hour's time.

'Look, Gerry,' Hamish said. 'It's no good worrying about it. The problem will sort itself out at the end of the day. They can't bar you from seeing your child for ever, so keep calm and stop worrying. Worry ends up killing people; it's the most dangerous of diseases. Worry gets you nowhere at all. It's all ifs and buts. What is it they say? "If your auntie had balls, she'd be your uncle." So forget about the ifs and buts and carry on with your life.'

Gerry wiped his eyes with a kitchen towel and, when he looked up, I thought he looked like a little boy who had just thrown a tantrum. 'But how can Ah stop worryin', Hamish? Ah've got a lot oan ma plate and it seems noo that the whole world is against me. It's a good job ma audience ur behind me every night, otherwise Ah'd crack up wi aw this worry. Ye're right: it's gonnae end up killin' me, Ah'm sure o' it.'

Ah! This was the perfect cue! I waited to see what parable Hamish had about worry. He didn't disappoint: 'There was a big oak tree in the forest and it had stood there for more than 200 years. Every year it stood there and every year it was hit by terrible snowfalls. Every year it was hit by heavy rain. Every year it was hit by lightning. But the big oak tree still stood there. Do you know what killed the big oak tree?'

'No, whit?' Gerry replied.

'It was the little beetles gnawing away at it. That's like worry: don't let it gnaw away at you.'

At this, Gerry perked up a little and headed off for his show. That night, he got another standing ovation. Hamish's philosophising had succeeded yet again.

Over the next few weeks, I followed Hamish's advice on love, and Charlotte and I became an item. She introduced me to her many friends in Oban, who were mostly hippy types. The women were all stunningly beautiful, wearing long floral dresses as if they had stepped out of some hippy commune in San Francisco. The men all had beards and used phrases like 'heavy vibes, man' and 'cool, dude'. These people were the complete opposite of the hard cases I had hung around with in Glasgow. I was impressed by their peace-and-love attitude. It was a refreshing change to talk about harmony and tranquillity rather than street gangs and razor slashings.

I would meet up with Charlotte and my new-found friends high above the town at McCaig's Folly, which had been modelled on the Colosseum in Rome. The hippies said it was a magical place because it had been built on a ley line. Someone usually brought a tape recorder and we'd play Bob Dylan albums. Most of them smoked dope as we sat in the ramparts of the folly looking down at the beauty of Oban harbour and the Western Isles in the distance. I was not a great dope smoker but, in an attempt to be part of the gang, I did take a few puffs. As Dylan sang 'It Ain't Me Babe' or 'Positively Fourth Street', I'd look at all the wondrous natural beauty around me: the dazzling young women like Charlotte and the breathtaking Highland scenery. I felt as if the freshness of the clear Highland air was having a revitalising effect on me. The atmosphere was never like this in Glasgow and I felt as though I had thrown a heavy, dark cloak off my back. This was peace, man!

15

A TALE OF TWO CITIES

'**P**ISS IN THE TOMATO JUICE!' FRANZ SHOUTED AT me.

'Whit?' I asked, bewildered.

'Piss in the tomato juice! Now, before she comes!'

All the chefs were laughing. They were involved in an act of revenge against a new manageress who had recently started, a young woman from Perth who had not long graduated from catering college. Although she was lacking in experience, she had a very hands-on management style and had had the impertinence to start ordering some of the chefs around. These were talented European chefs who had worked all over the world and they would not be talked to like idiots. But each day, she'd come into the kitchen, look around and, in a condescending manner, say things like: 'That table needs to be cleaned. And please keep your chefs' hats on while you're preparing food.' She talked as though she owned the place. I didn't think she was any too bright. I got the impression that she only appeared intelligent because of her well-spoken voice and alert manner.

Every morning, she poured herself a large glass of tomato juice before going through to the restaurant. That day, Franz, Paul and Kurt had all urinated in the juice. I did as I was ordered and then Franz put it into the fridge to cool down before she arrived.

About an hour later, she turned up, took the juice from the fridge and poured herself a large glass. She seemed in a good mood; for a change, she didn't have any complaints for the chefs. She drank the tomato juice down in one go. 'Mmm, lovely! You can't beat a nice glass of tomato juice. It sets you up for the day,' she declared, before heading into the restaurant.

We were all cracking up. This was a prank that had been played many times before in restaurants all over Europe. It was a common way of exacting revenge on domineering managers or anyone else kitchen staff didn't particularly like. After that, I never touched the juice from the fridge just in case someone had it in for me.

Lars, who was usually so quiet, said to me, 'You find that all the time in the catering business. Someone leaves college, like that silly cow, gets a job as an assistant manager, then starts to lay down the law to the real workers. Bastards! Pissing in their fruit juice is too good for them. They think they're winning but there's an old American saying: "Some days you eat the bear and some days the bear eats you." Today, the bear is eating that bitch.'

On my break that afternoon, I picked up a copy of the *Daily Record*. The headlines were about gang warfare. Numerous stabbings and slashings were taking place in my old haunts. The influx of drugs into the city had a lot to do with it. I recognised the names of some of the victims – old acquaintances and school friends. I breathed a sigh of relief, glad to be out of it all.

Reading between the lines, I reckoned Mac the Knife must have been behind at least some of it. He was going all out to make a name for himself. I still thought he was a coward. He knew that if he slashed or stabbed someone they wouldn't reveal anything to the police. It was against the underworld code to grass on someone, so, in a way, he had a free rein to do what he wanted. I was 100 miles away, so it was of little concern to me.

But the next day, a note arrived at the restaurant's office addressed to me. It was from one of the Gorbals boys, Andy. 'Contact me on this number urgently,' it said.

I did so and an anxious-sounding Andy said, 'That wee nae-good bastard Mac is runnin' amok. He stabbed two o' the boys last week and slashed another wan this week.'

'Ah know,' I said, 'Ah saw it in the papers yesterday.'

'The problem Ah've got,' said Andy, 'is Ah've got tae get oot o' toon fur a while until aw the madness dies doon a bit. Can ye get me a job in Oban fur at least a couple o' weeks?'

'Aye, nae bother,' I said. 'There's plenty o' work in the hotel game.'

'Great. Then Ah'll see ye the morra at Oban station, aboot 8 p.m.,' Andy said before hanging up.

I felt a bit deflated because things had been going so well for me in Oban. I didn't really want him turning up and ruining it all. He was known as a bit of a wild bastard, especially when he had a drink in him. Over the years, I'd witnessed him getting into too many fights to mention. I decided that the best course of action was not to have him working with me. That could have been a recipe for disaster. Instead, I had a word with an acquaintance who worked in the kitchen at a hotel on the seafront. He said it wouldn't be a problem, as they were looking for cleaners and porters. The money wasn't bad and accommodation and food were thrown in.

When I saw Andy getting off the train, I was struck by how incongruous he looked in Oban. He was dressed in real Glasgow hard-man gear, a smart suit with a hankie protruding from the pocket. No one looked like that here. I realised that that was what I must have looked like when I'd first come to town several months before. Now, I had longish hair and was wearing flares. Andy shook my hand. He looked me up and down and said, 'F***in' hell, pal, ye've gone fae hard man tae hippy within a few months!'

We went to the Clarendon Hotel for a pint and Andy explained his situation: 'There's a lot o' drugs flowin' intae Glesga – hash, heroin, cocaine, you name it. That wee tube Mac is heavily involved. He's sayin' the Gorbals is his patch and has got a heavy team together. Anyway, like you, we aw got intae an argument wi him and it ended up wi three o' the boys gettin' stabbed. Ah jist want tae keep a low profile fur a wee while and then Ah'll make a comeback.' It was the same old Glasgow garbage. Where had all my peace and tranquillity gone now?

I gave Andy some advice: while in Oban, he ought to change his appearance – lose the big-city hard-man look – and try not to be aggressive with the locals. The indigenous population did not take too kindly to loudmouthed Glaswegians. Then I told him about the job I'd found him and took him to the hotel.

We agreed to get together a few days later but when we did meet up, he was more than a little disheartened. 'Ah don't think Oban's fur me. It's too quiet here. Ah'd prefer tae be havin' a pint in the Turf Bar. That's where Ah feel at hame, wi aw ma pals.'

I knew what he meant; I liked the Turf as well. But there was no way I would have given up Oban to have a pint there. He said he'd give it another week, to let things cool down a bit, before he made his mind up whether to return to Glasgow.

A week later, I bumped into him outside the restaurant. He was in a panic. 'Ah've got tae get the f*** oot o' this toon,' he said. 'There wis a new woman handin' oot the wages at the hotel and Ah told her Ah wis the head chef, so she gie'd me his bulgin' pay packet. Ah'm offski back tae Glesga and Ah'm gonnae have a good drink tonight in the Turf wi aw this money.' You can take the man out of the Gorbals but you can't take the Gorbals out of the man.

I walked with Andy to the railway station and when he climbed aboard the train to Glasgow, a sense of liberation came over me. I felt as if Glasgow was a great theatre where I had been a major player; but, for the time being, I was happy to play a smaller, quieter role here in lovely Oban.

It wasn't all plain sailing, of course. Sometimes I had to let my Gorbals character emerge again. A few days after Andy left, for example, a big fisherman came into the bar I was sitting in and gave me a dirty look. I had come across him before but we had never really talked. He had a reputation around town as a bully and someone had told me that he was extremely jealous that I was taking Charlotte out. He had asked her out several times but she had always turned him down.

He had been drinking heavily and he said to me, 'Who're you f***in' lookin' at?'

'An ugly fat bastard who stinks of fish!' I replied.

As soon as I said it, he lunged at me and tried to choke me. I saw a big heavy glass ashtray, grabbed it and hit him over the head with it, knocking him out cold.

Afterwards, I was worried for a few days in case he and his fisherman pals were looking for me, so I kept a low profile. Just by luck, Big Chris and his pal John turned up, completely out of the blue, and we met up at the harbour. I felt safe now that some of my Gorbals pals were around. We were having a bit of Glasgow banter when the big fisherman came towards me with one of his pals.

'Hey!' he shouted. 'You knocked me oot wi an ashtray.'

I was well-handed and completely unafraid. 'Whit aboot it? Dae ye want it again, ya tube?' I said.

Realising that the three of us were ready to go ahead, he backed down and said there had been a misunderstanding. We eventually shook hands.

I really preferred my new hippy way of life to all this aggressive baloney but I realised I would sometimes have to revert to my old Gorbals-style behaviour to survive. And as Chris said to me, 'It's a sad fact o' life but, unfortunately, if ye want tae get yir message across, some people only understand the threat o' violence.' He was right. In fact, he was preaching to the converted.

16

METAMORPHOSIS

AT THE HEIGHT OF THE SUMMER, OBAN WAS THE place to be in Scotland. I had never had such a good time in my life. Students and real characters from all over Europe were turning up to work at the restaurants and everyone had a story to tell. It really was an education in itself. There were at least three staff parties every week and most nights we just drank until the sun came up in the morning. Then we'd have a couple of hours' sleep before heading to work.

At the parties, you'd get all the astoundingly good-looking Swedish women, the German chefs, getting drunk on beer they had imported from Hamburg or Berlin, the British and foreign students, and, of course, great Scottish characters like Gerry and Hamish. The parties were completely different from the ones I'd experienced as a boy in Glasgow. At those, people would gather in someone's front room and get stuck into the bevy before having a sing-song. Someone usually shouted, 'Order! Order! One singer, one song!' Then the air would be filled with old-time standards like 'I Belong to Glasgow' or Al Jolson's 'April Showers'. But these staff parties were a different kettle of fish. Everyone stood around chatting over a few bottles of wine and there was hardly ever any singing, although a record player would blast out the hits of the day in the background.

At one of these parties, I got chatting to a guy called Douglas, one of the seasonal workers. He was a real toff, doing law at Edinburgh University. He planned to be an advocate, even a High Court judge. Meanwhile, he had taken up a job as a kitchen hand for the summer. He was a remarkably bright fellow who talked in the sort of upper-middle-class accent that can instantly make you feel inferior – or set your teeth on edge.

'You know something,' he said, 'I've been watching and listening to you as you go about your work and I can tell one thing.'

'Oh aye, whit's that?' I said.

'You're a bright fellow. Instead of working in a mediocre kitchen, sweating your bollocks off, you should be at university like the rest of us, doing a degree. You have the communication skills to do well in life. So don't waste it. Go to college as soon as you can. Once you're educated, nobody can take that away from you. I'm at Edinburgh University with a lot of so-called bright people but many of them have had the advantage of going to fee-paying schools or having private tuition. Unlike you, they have been spoon-fed through life. You, on the other hand, have been to the school of hard knocks in the Gorbals. But that won't stop you getting a degree. You're destined for something far better than being a chef in an Oban restaurant. You're young enough to catch up, so don't delay.'

'But Ah left school at 15 wi nae qualifications. How the hell am Ah gonnae end up at university?' I asked him.

'For God's sake, it's simple: go to further-education college and do your O grades and Highers. You're a lot brighter than most of the dim bastards on my course. It'll be a cinch – no problem to a man of the world like you.'

This piece of astute advice had me thinking. Months before, I had been mixing with some really rough characters in Glasgow. I'd been on a downward slope. But now that I was interacting with people who had different aspirations, I could feel my mentality changing. I was going through a metamorphosis.

I glugged from my wine bottle and said to him, 'But, Douglas, if Ah follow yir advice and go tae college, whit dae ye think Ah should study?'

He thought for a moment and then said, 'Well, you like being around people and you love good conversation; it's as if you're working out how people tick. So I would suggest you do psychology. You like hearing and telling stories, too, so maybe a job in journalism might suit you.'

He was right. I had always been fascinated by how people react in different situations and the way people's minds worked had always interested me. Journalism wasn't a bad idea either, as I had been good at writing essays in school. Perhaps this conversation was fated to be. However, it was too late to apply to a further-education college that year, so I decided to wait until the time and my circumstances were right. I laughed to myself, thinking of the daft Glaswegian line: 'Ah wis edumacated in Sauchiemahall Street.'

Gerry always arrived at these parties after his gig and, if he wasn't crying about his ex-wife and child, he was excellent company, walking around telling jokes. When he turned up that night I told him about my conversation with Douglas and he said, 'Aye, a guy like you is as bright as f***. Some o' these students ur dull bastards – if their brains wur TNT, they widnae have enough tae blow their hats aff – but they manage awright at university. Ye'll dae well if ye go tae college, nae bother at aw.'

Then he launched into storytelling mode. 'There's a fella lyin' in bed and his maw says, "Come oan, it's time tae get up fur school!"

'"But, Mammy, Ah don't want tae go tae school."

'"Why no?"

'"Because the teachers aw hate me. The pupils aw hate me. Even the jannie hates me."

'"But, look, son, ye've got tae go tae school. After aw, ye're the headmaster."'

A little while later, Hamish walked into the party. He was soaking wet, absolutely drenched. For a change, he was the one with a worried look on his face. He was definitely on a downer, while Gerry, by contrast, was on a high.

'Whit happened tae you? It's no rainin' ootside, is it?' I asked.

'No, I got to drinking a fair bit of whisky and it got me thinking about how futile life is. How f***in' daft we all are,' he replied.

'So whit did ye dae, Hamish?' I said.

'Well, I was in the pub and I shook everyone's hand, telling them this was the end. I told them I wouldn't be seeing them again as I intended to drown myself in the harbour. They all came out of the pub and watched as I walked up to the harbour wall. I climbed up onto it while the tourists looked on, shouted "Cheerio to you all!" and then leapt into the water. I'm a strong swimmer, so I'd decided to keep on going until my arms went weak, and then I'd drown. "What a glorious way to go!" I thought.

'As I was swimming further and further away from the harbour, I looked back and saw all the people watching me. I swam even further out, still thinking, "This is a great way to die!" But after a little while I suddenly realised it was the whisky that had fooled me into thinking I should put an end to myself. As the cold water sobered me up, I suddenly saw the faces of my 12 children and thought how they would miss me. I panicked, turned myself round and swam for my life, as quick as I could, back to the harbour and safety. That was a lesson for me never to touch the whisky again. I'm lucky to be standing here talking to you right now.'

The roles were reversed. For a few brief moments, Hamish was the depressed victim and Gerry the philosopher.

Gerry said, 'Ah've thought aboot daein' maself in many a time. In fact, Ah went tae Oban Library last week and asked where Ah could find books oan suicide. "First on the left," said the librarian. Ah went and had a look but the shelf was empty. Ah told the librarian and he said, "I'm not surprised. They don't often bring them back."

'No, aw jokin' aside, ma auld maw told me somethin' no long ago. She said that if we aw had a chance tae parcel up our problems, tie them up wi a fancy ribbon and take them intae a room where we had the opportunity tae exchange our parcel o' problems fur somebody else's, we'd aw walk back oot wi our ain parcel.'

17

MON AMOUR

'**D**O YOU WANT TO COME TO PARIS WITH ME AT the end of the season?' asked Charlotte.

'Paris? Sure!' I said.

The furthest I had been from Glasgow was London, so it would certainly be an adventure. Charlotte was the love of my life and there was no better place for lovers to go than Paris. However, I had one problem: I couldn't speak French; indeed, some British people could barely understand the form of English I spoke. Luckily, there was a Frenchman working at the restaurant and he always seemed to be broke.

He was a fellow called François, who thumbed his way around Europe every summer. Just before coming to Oban, he had spent three months in Amsterdam getting stoned out of his mind in the cannabis cafés. He told me all his money went on dope and that he never even spent money on food when he was on the road.

'How come?' I asked.

'It's simple. I find out where the nearest supermarket is and I wait until night. Then I go through the bins to find the food that is just past its sell-by date. In Amsterdam, I have dined on the best salmon, in Paris I have eaten pâté de foie gras, in London steak pie, in Edinburgh haggis – all from a bin! If you go through a supermarket's bins, you can eat like a king, as long as you don't mind the food being out of date by a day or sometimes just a few hours.'

This guy was not daft; in Glasgow, he would have probably earned the title of fly man. What was more, he was a proficient speaker of not only English and French but also German, Dutch and Italian.

'Can ye teach me how tae speak a wee bit o' French?' I asked him.

'Of course I could. It would be a pleasure. Which part of France are you going to?'

'Paris,' I replied. 'Ma girlfriend wants tae go at the end o' the season and it's only a few weeks aff. Whit Ah want ye tae teach me isnae the schoolboy stuff but phrases Ah know Ah'll use.'

'Gay Paree!' François chortled. 'The Parisians are arrogant bastards but if you make an attempt to speak French to them, they do appreciate it. They hate the British going over there and not even trying to speak their language. So I think it is a good idea for you to learn a little French. Besides, you will feel a lot better on your travels if you can actually speak the native language to people.'

I said I'd give him a couple of bob for his trouble and he was delighted. 'Now then, what sort of stuff can I teach you? Describe the kind of situations you may find yourself in and then we'll proceed from there.'

'Well,' I said, 'Ah want tae know how tae order a couple o' beers, how tae order a bottle o' white wine; how tae ask whit the price is and how tae say it's far too expensive. Ah also want tae know how tae thank the waiters and how tae book accommodation. And perhaps ye could tell me a short joke in French that Ah could use in company.'

'Excellent idea!' he said. 'You have picked the essentials and I will even tell you how to say "f*** off", as that can be useful when you're dealing with the high-and-mighty Parisians. But Paris is a wonderful place and the food is unparalleled. You will find restaurants there that would make this place look like a soup kitchen. All the countries of Europe have their advantages; I know because I have been in them all. First of all, I'll teach you the joke you require.'

François then taught me to say: 'In heaven, the cooks are French, the policemen are British, the mechanics are German, the lovers are Italian and the bankers are Swiss. In hell, the cooks are British, the policemen are German, the mechanics are French, the lovers are Swiss and the bankers are Italian.'

Over the next couple of weeks, he taught me enough French to get by and it cost me only a tenner and a half-bottle of whisky.

At the end of the season, I was offered an extended contract to stay on during the winter to do functions. But there was no way I was going to accept it. I was going on a French adventure with a beautiful blonde-haired woman, and only a fool would turn that opportunity down. Besides, there was always next season.

Everything was changing so quickly. One good thing was leading to another and the shadow of my wild past in Glasgow seemed to be fading by the minute. One day, I looked in the mirror and was surprised by my physical transformation. I had hippy-style long blond hair and a slight bum-fluff beard and I was wearing flares, a flowered shirt and an Afghan coat. My new look did mean I had to put up with some ridicule, though. The manager of the restaurant said to me, 'You're a different guy from when you arrived at the start of the season. Then you looked like a razor king from the Gorbals, now you look like Shirley Temple. That's your nickname from now on: Shirley Temple.' Then he laughed and walked off. I wasn't that annoyed about his observation or the nickname. In fact, I was pleased that I had managed to change so much over the course of the summer. From a character out of *No Mean City*, I had become a long-haired hippy with a beautiful girlfriend. If my friends could see me now, they'd never believe it! On the other hand, I wouldn't have wanted them to see me; they'd have thought I'd lost my balls.

Charlotte and I travelled down to Southampton, where she had a wee Glasgow auntie who had a gigantic house. The auntie was as mad as a hatter. At first, I could tell she was wary of me but I thought the best way to charm her was to turn on the patter and keep her laughing most of the time. I found that she always laughed hysterically at naughty jokes involving men's private parts so as part of my charm offensive I laid them on for her.

'A Gorbals pub owner has a look at his accounts and decides he needs tae have mair drinkers comin' intae his bar. So he hauds a competition tae find the toughest man in Glasgow. He puts posters up aw over toon and even advertises in the *Daily Record* and the *Evening Times*. The night o' the competition comes and the bar is jam-packed. The first contestant is a giant o' a man haudin' a snappin' turtle. He jumps oan the bar and whips oot his large penis. Then he picks up the snappin' turtle and hauds it right in front o' his dick. With unbelievin' eyes, the onlookers gasp as the turtle bites doon oan the man's penis. The big fella lets go o' the turtle and starts swayin' his body. The turtle bounces fae side tae side aff the man's hips. After aboot 30 seconds o' this, the man pokes the turtle in the eyes and it drops to the floor. "Now," shouts the big fella, "is there another son o' a bitch in here who thinks he's tough enough tae dae that?" A wee fella at the back o' the bar raises his hand and shouts, "Ah'll dae it . . . if ye promise no tae poke me in the eyes."'

It was an old joke but it worked and Charlotte's auntie laughed uncontrollably. She reminded me of the 'Bingo Bellas' we'd often told such jokes to when I was a kid in the Gorbals. 'Oh,' she said, 'you should be oan the stage. Ah've never laughed so much in ma life. Ye've really cheered me up wi aw the auld Glasgow patter. The people here jist hivnae got that great sense o' humour. At first, Ah didnae like the look o' you but noo Ah'm jist glad that Charlotte has found somebody like you who's a good laugh. The world is full o' miserable buggers.'

I got the impression that she was extremely homesick for her native Glasgow and that I had reminded her of her younger days, when she had laughed all the time and 'didnae have a care in the world'. We spent around two weeks with her in Southampton and she looked rather sadly at me one day and said, 'Look, ye don't have tae go tae France. Stay here instead and we can aw have a good laugh.' I explained to her that we had to go to Paris and that it was all part of the great adventure. But I promised that we would look her up again if we ended up back in Southampton. On the day we headed for the boat to Calais, she cried her eyes out. 'Oh, please come back and see me,' she pleaded. As I looked at her tearful face, I just thought that there must be millions of Scots like her all over the world. They have great, prosperous lives away from their native country but inside the homesickness gnaws away.

Charlotte and I got the boat over the Channel to Calais and then the train to Paris. We arrived at the Gare du Nord and there were plenty of little hotels and *pensions* (boarding houses) nearby. We quickly found a room at the Hôtel du Nord. The man at the reception desk, who had a large handlebar moustache, looked at the beautiful Charlotte and said, '*Oh là là! Quelle belle femme!*' He gave me a naughty wink and handed over the keys to the room.

Paris was indeed the city of love – *la ville d'amour* – and now I had a beautiful woman on my arm and a bedroom in the heart of it. *Que la vie m'est douce!* Ain't life sweet!

18

GAY PAREE

ONE OF THE FIRST THINGS I SPOTTED WHILE WALKING up the Champs-Elysées towards the Arc de Triomphe was a man with a long white beard wearing a leather miniskirt. As he walked along, *camionneurs* (lorry drivers) were beeping their car horns at him, laughing and waving. They were shouting things like, '*Quel beau mec!*' (What a beautiful bloke!) But he took it all in his stride, smiled and waved back, shouting, '*Foutez-moi le camp!*' – in other words, 'f*** off'. When I saw his face close up, I got the shock of my life because he was almost the exact double of a notorious Glasgow gangster I knew.

It was the first time I had seen a transvestite but the ordinary Parisians on their way to work barely batted an eyelid as they passed him by. One of them did remark to her friend, '*Un homme barbu qui porte une mini-jupe! C'est épatant! La France, qu'est-elle devenue?*' ('A bearded man in a miniskirt! It's crazy! What is France coming to?') My thoughts went back to Glasgow and I wondered how people there might react seeing a man in a skirt walking up Sauchiehall Street. I imagined one gossip saying to another, 'Would ye look at the state o' that, Maggie? Whit in the hell is the world comin' tae? Auld men wearin' leather miniskirts. They'll be wantin' tae give birth next.'

Paris was certainly very different from any other place I'd been. My friend François in Oban had been right: the people did seem rather aloof and arrogant, what they called *orgueil*. The place oozed sex and the Parisian men were not backwards in coming forwards when they saw a beautiful young woman like Charlotte. They acted as if I wasn't there and made direct approaches to her.

One middle-aged man walked up to her in a shop, looked her in the eyes and said, '*Voudriez-vous passer une folle nuit d'amour avec moi?*' I didn't have a clue what he was talking about but when I asked Charlotte she merely shrugged her shoulders and said, 'It meant he wanted to go to bed with me.' I felt like going back into the shop and giving the man a good old Glasgow kiss but I had to remind myself that this was, after all, not the Gorbals but Paris, so there had to be a bit of give and take where the locals' behaviour was concerned.

Everything on the Champs-Elysées was very expensive, especially compared to Scotland. I remember that for the price of two coffees – '*deux grands crèmes*' – I could have got four fish suppers in Glasgow. However, the boulevard was an exceptional location for people-watching; everyone, young and old, appeared to have made an effort to be stylish. People took great pride in looking elegant and they all gave the impression they were inspecting one another and expected to be looked at in turn. To them, life was theatre. They were all living in the public eye and I thought it was a compelling spectacle – and free, too! What would these well-dressed people have made of the scruff-bags who hung around Paddy's Market in Glasgow? They would probably have been traumatised by the sight of them.

I also noticed that, even in the poorest areas of the city, the food shops were always sparkling clean and the merchandise displayed beautifully. The French were definitely into the pleasures of the palate, from fine dining to the simplest picnic of a crusty baguette with ham and cheese washed down with inexpensive red wine. They also had the most delicious takeaway food in the world, available from charcuteries on every corner: quiche lorraine, *saucisses* (salami) and *jambon cuit* (cooked ham). In the restaurants, they had amazing dishes like cassoulet and the Provençal speciality bouillabaisse. For dessert you could order such things as crêpes, extravagant pastries and refreshing sorbets. In the restaurants and brasseries, the best thing to do was go for the *plat du jour* or the *menu touristique*, which meant that you paid a set price without fear of being ripped off.

A bottle of wine here was within everyone's budget. For a few francs you could buy a bottle of red for a fraction of the price you would pay for the ever-popular El Dorado wine in Glasgow. I had read somewhere that the French suffered more from cirrhosis of the liver than any other country in the world, including Scotland. I thought it was no wonder; they seemed to love their bevy all day long. Strong drink was consumed as early as 5 a.m. as a pre-work fortifier and then at any time during the day. The workers drank brandies and liqueurs, including Poire William (pear brandy) and marc (a spirit made from grape pulp). Pastis (Pernod or Ricard) served with water and ice was also very popular. I was surprised to see many of the cafés advertising Lipton's tea. Sir Thomas Lipton originally came from the Gorbals, from where he built up a massive worldwide business empire.

One afternoon, after leaving our café on the Champs-Elysées, we walked up towards the Arc de Triomphe. The roads around the monument were teeming with chaotic traffic. It was a sweltering day and I decided to take my shirt off and lie on a grass verge just across from the Arc de Triomphe. I often did this on Glasgow Green without any aggravation. But the next minute, a big French policeman was waving his baton at me and shouting hysterically, '*Quittez la pelouse et remettez votre chemise!*' ('Get off the grass and put your shirt back on!') I wondered what the matter was but Charlotte said, 'He wants you to put your shirt back on. It's a sign of disrespect in France to take your shirt off near a national monument and particularly in the vicinity of the Eternal Flame. The Arc de Triomphe was built as a homage to the armies of Napoleon Bonaparte; they don't want a wee Glasgow chancer showing disrespect. If you don't put your shirt back on, you'll end up in jail.' I just thought that it was no wonder the French prison service was bursting at the seams. I'll bet you the food was good, though.

Later, as we strolled in the Place de la Concorde, Charlotte said, 'You'd better start behaving yourself. I remember they told us at school that 1,300 people died here during the Revolution.'

'What did they die of?' I asked her.

'The guillotine,' she replied. 'So you'd better keep your shirt on or you'll be for the chop next.'

We also went to the Louvre to see the *Mona Lisa* by Leonardo da Vinci. You can't go to Paris without visiting the *Mona Lisa* or the Eiffel Tower; as my father used to say, 'It's not to say that you've seen, it's to say that you've been.' Inside, it was a bit of a rammy as crowds of tourists vied to get as close to the painting as possible. I thought it was ironic that the other da Vinci paintings, including *Virgin of the Rocks*, were almost totally ignored by the tourists. I was impressed by the *Mona Lisa* and the Louvre but I thought the Kelvingrove Art Gallery in Glasgow was just as good and Dalí's painting there, *Christ of St John of the Cross*, ranked alongside or higher than the *Mona Lisa*. That's the great thing about us Glaswegians: rightly or wrongly, we always think we're better than everyone else.

After we left the museum, I almost got arrested again. We were at the Louvre metro station and a policeman asked me where my ticket was. I couldn't find it and he fined me 50 francs – £5 – on the spot. And, you guessed it, if I didn't pay up he was going to arrest me. I had never had this sort of problem on the Glasgow underground system, even though I had dodged the fare many times when I was skint.

My favourite thing about Paris was the thousands of cafés there, full of characters waving their arms wildly and telling stories, and because the Parisians loved their Gauloise cigarettes, there was smoke in the air everywhere we went. In Glasgow, the only real café I frequented was the Queen's Café in Victoria Road. Here, it was a different ball game. Cafés came in all forms: big ones, small ones, scruffy ones, stylish ones, snobby ones and arty-farty ones. All the main squares and boulevards had cafés spreading onto the pavement and these establishments were always more expensive; but if you went off the beaten track, it was easy to find inexpensive cafés where the locals hung around. Cafés in the tourist spots charged an arm and a leg, and after a while we tended to avoid the Champs-Elysées. On the Left Bank, we went to famous cafés like the Deux Magots and the Café de Flore, where Picasso, Hemingway, Sartre and de Beauvoir had been customers. And, now, of course, a Gorbals guy and his Oban bird could be added to the list! The cafés in the St-Germain and the Latin Quarter were supposed to be full of literary-intellectual types and big names in arts and letters, cinema, politics and philosophy, as well as hangers-on.

In one such Left Bank café, I noticed a waiter going about his work at terrific speed. He was a proud-looking fellow, a typical Parisian, I thought, arrogant but highly proficient. I ordered two coffees and he said to me, 'Ur ye fae Glasgow?'

I was a bit taken aback. 'Aye,' I replied.

He said, 'So am Ah, Ah'm fae Bridgeton. Came here 30 years ago as a French student, met a local girl, fell in love and never went back.'

'Ah thought ye wur French,' I said.

'Aye, well, Ah speak French and ma young family ur French. Ah rarely speak English noo.'

'Dae ye ever go back tae Glesga?' I said.

'Whit, that dump? No, never. Ur ye daft? When ye live in a magnificent place like this, ye don't want tae go back tae somewhere like Bridgeton. Everythin' is better here. Ah'm here fur life.'

I asked him what cafés he would recommend and he said, 'As a fellow Glasgow boy, Ah'd recommend headin' fur the university. The cafés ur good there and they're reasonable, too. Keep away fae the Champs-Elysées. They jist rip ye aff there.'

We took up his recommendation and found ourselves in a packed café in the Boulevard St-Michel, where a fat British man, quite drunk, was telling a series of jokes about the French to his cronies: 'Where's the best place to hide anything from a French woman? Under the soap! Why are there so many tree-lined boulevards in Paris? Because the Germans like to march in the shade!' I didn't think his jokes were funny but his cronies hee-hawed at all his witticisms. I thought they must be laughing because he was a powerful man.

He heard our Scottish accents and struck up conversation, saying how beautiful Charlotte was. She blushed with embarrassment. It turned out he was originally from South Wales and was now a millionaire, living a champagne lifestyle across Europe.

I had the audacity to ask him how he made his money and he said, 'I was a young guy in the Valleys and I was skint, out of work. I had just married a local businessman's daughter but he was a mean old bastard and wouldn't give us any money. So there I was, tramping through the streets of Cardiff with a hole in my shoe and it was tipping down. I was soaking wet when I saw this Rolls-Royce. An old guy was sitting in the back smoking a big cigar. I tapped on the window and, like you, I asked him how he had got so rich. He said he had been just like me, young and skint, but then one day he bought an apple for a penny, gave it a polish and sold it on for tuppence. Then he bought two apples, did the same and sold them for fourpence. It went on and on until he ended up a millionaire.'

'Is that what you did?' I said.

'No. That old bastard of a father-in-law died, leaving us two million quid,' he said.

With the money, he had started up a mining-equipment company and he now had factories all over Europe. 'I suppose I've got it all. I drink champagne and eat in the best restaurants. I have an apartment in Paris, a luxury yacht moored in the harbour at Monte Carlo, a villa in Cannes. I have two Bentleys and a Rolls-Royce. I'm on my second marriage and I married a former beauty queen, the most beautiful woman in the world. But do you know what I sometimes long for?'

'What's that?' I asked.

'A pint of Welsh bitter, ten Woodbine and a good shag in a Merthyr Tydfil back lane.'

A few hours later, Charlotte and I found ourselves beneath the Eiffel Tower. The sky was pitch black and the tower, 300 metres and 7,000 tons of steel, stood majestically above us in the darkness. I was overawed by how gigantic it looked. It had been the tallest building in the world when it was first erected in 1889.

Nearby there was a sad sight. A dead dog lay on the road near the pavement. There was thick red blood coming from its mouth and, to me, it looked like a painting that might have hung in the Louvre. I had seen dead dogs before but never one like this. 'Paris even does dead dogs better than Glasgow,' I thought.

19

THE LAST LAUGH

WHEN OUR HOLIDAY WAS OVER, CHARLOTTE WENT back to Oban. She said she'd wait until I got myself a job and then come down to Glasgow and join me. However, jobs were about as scarce as one-legged men at an arse-kicking competition. The economy was in a state, with Ted Heath's government having trouble with the miners and introducing a three-day week. There was an energy crisis resulting in a hike in petrol prices and blackouts all over Britain. The news was full of images of bank clerks working by candlelight.

At home, my father, like millions of others, was in and out of work, although my mother held down a steady job as a waitress at the nearby Newlands Hotel. My brother Ross was proving to be a fine musician and his songwriting and guitar playing had improved immeasurably since I'd left on my adventures. If my father wasn't working, he would hold court in the evenings, chatting with me and my brother and giving us lessons in confidence. These nights were full of banter and patter, and after talking to my father for a few hours, I always felt full of bravado and as if I could take on the world.

One night, around midnight, my father, Ross and I were all sitting in the living room. My mother had gone to bed, as she had to be up at 7 a.m. for the hotel's breakfast service. My father announced, 'Ah'm fed up wi people singin' "I Belong to Glasgow". Surely we could write somethin' better? We're aw good wi words and Ross is great oan the guitar, so let's have a go.' Over the next few hours we put a melody and words together:

Wish I was back again in Glasgow,
With all the friends that I once knew.
Your city lights and all your Saturday fights,
Glasgow, I belong to you.

So I think I'll go, take a train,
Without a ticket once again,
To be in Glasgow, my home town.

Down the Gorbals into Benny's Bar,
Buy some cider and some wine,
Your uncle Jimmy doesn't drink there now,
The barman says he's doing time.

We added another couple of verses and the song sounded wonderful but, around three in the morning, there was a loud banging on the wall. It was my mother. My father burst out laughing: 'Here we ur, aspirin' poets and songwriters, tryin' tae write a new melody fur Glasgow, and the only sensible wan is lyin' in bed attemptin' tae get a kip before her work in the mornin'!'

It really was hard work looking for work. But we were all in the same boat. I met up with Wee Alex at a bookie's near the Bridgegate and he filled me in on all the latest news. It had been almost a year since our last conversation. 'Man, ye look like a hippy,' was the first thing he said to me, and he added jokingly, 'Get a shave, get a haircut, get a job, get a life.' Back in Glasgow, I was becoming used to people taking the mickey out of my appearance. In fact, earlier, when I'd gone to visit Chris in his Govanhill flat, his father, a burly Irish building-site worker, looked at me and said, 'Mr MacFarlane, ye look like an auld poof sittin' there.' However, I wasn't going to make any drastic decisions about my appearance just yet.

Alex told me, 'That wee Mac the Knife is still runnin' wild, stabbin' and slashin' people. He asked me a few weeks ago where ye wur and Ah told him ye wur workin' up in the Highlands. He said tae me, "Well, tell him Ah'm still after him."'

This had me slightly worried but Alex had another piece of news that put Mac out of my mind. 'Ye remember that big bird, Tina, who said she might be expectin' by you?'

'Aye,' I replied with a degree of trepidation in my voice.

As a boy in the living room of our Gorbals tenement.

Norfolk Street, not far from our flat, in 1969. Even then there were few cars on the road (© Michael Martin, courtesy of Jean Doig).

Gorbals Cross: if I hung around here for ten minutes, I was bound to meet someone I knew (© Michael Martin, courtesy of Jean Doig).

Glasgow Green, with the People's Palace in the centre and Templeton's carpet factory in the background (© Michael Martin, courtesy of Jean Doig).

Paddy's Market: a legendary place full of life, characters
and patter, where there was never a dull moment
(© Michael Martin, courtesy of Jean Doig).

The old Gorbals overshadowed by the new: St Francis Church and the new tower blocks (© Michael Martin, courtesy of Jean Doig).

Growing up, my brother Ross and I played football in the street all the time. But when we were rehoused in Shawlands, we found that football wasn't allowed in our new back yard (© Michael Martin, courtesy of Jean Doig).

Having a laugh with Mam and Dad
during our Shawlands days.

A young aspiring chef in 1971, helping my dad (left)
out at a function.

How I looked in 1971: notice
the black buttons on my
tailor-made Arthur Black shirt.

With my best pal Big Chris as
we get stuck intae the bevy
in a Gorbals drinking den.

Sunny Oban! Outside the Corran Halls, wearing flares and
letting my hair grow in the sunshine.

Dressed as a Glasgow wide boy with a large knot in my tie and, in
later days, looking every inch the serious student.

The author today
(photo by Philippa MacFarlane).

'Well, she had a baby a couple o' months ago.'

'Oh aye?' I said, giving nothing more away until Alex continued.

'But Ah'll tell ye whit, it's definitely no yours.'

'Aye, and how dae ye know that?' I asked.

'Baby boy, she had . . . as black as the ace o' spades!' Alex laughed as he saw a look of relief appear on my face.

I bade him farewell and said we would meet up again soon. At a loose end, I decided to go into Paddy's Market. I watched as hundreds of people stood in the rain and wind selling what looked like bundles of rags. This was real poverty and as far removed from the glamour and sophistication of Paris as I could imagine. At the back of one of the market's small arcades, there was a shabby restaurant that sold the best Glaswegian food: home-made ham-and-lentil soup, steak pie, mince and tatties, and ham ribs with cabbage and mashed potato. But you didn't go there only to eat: the conversations you overheard were always entertaining. I ordered a plate of ham ribs and sat near two old men who were deep in conversation.

'Aye, they buried Wee Jimmy last week. Eighty-three, he wis, so he had a long run. But ye know whit happened when Ah turned up at his hoose fur his wake?'

'No, whit happened?'

'Well, they had Wee Jimmy laid oot in the back room and ye know whit some stupid bastard had done? They'd stuck his false teeth in!'

'Whit? They new teeth he always hated?'

'Aye. Jimmy hated wearin' them. He said they stuck oot so much they made him look like a donkey. Anyway, he looked great apart fae his donkey gub. The teeth wur stickin' oot and they made him look embarrassin' tae aw the people who turned up tae say farewell. They should have left the teeth oot.'

'Aye, ye're right. Ah bet he looked like a right bampot. Ah hope that disnae happen tae me when Ah go tae meet ma maker.'

When my plate of ham ribs arrived, it tasted delicious and I tucked in, thinking to myself that even in Paris they would have been hard pushed to have matched the taste of this.

I was about to finish when half a dozen young guys came into the restaurant, all laughing, joking and swearing loudly. They were a rough mob but all comparatively well dressed; it was obvious that they were gangsters. One of them shouted, 'Right, whit ur ye havin', boys? Ah'll square it up because we've done a good wee bit o' business the day . . . Right, missus, six soups, two steak pies, two mince and tatties and two ham ribs.' He pulled out a large wad of money and put it on the counter. 'Drug dealer,' I thought. Then he turned round and a wave of shock came over me. It was Mac the Knife. I knew that if he recognised me, I was going to be slashed or stabbed. I had visions of myself lying dying in a gutter at Paddy's Market.

He glanced briefly over in my direction and I thought, 'This is it. I have no chance against six of them but I'll put up a fight to the death.' He said nothing, though, just went over and joined his criminal pals at their table, where they carried on with their wild banter. He hadn't recognised me! The hippy long hair, bum-fluff beard and Afghan coat had done the trick. The last time he'd seen me, I'd been dressed as a Gorbals hard man: Arthur Black tailor-made shirt and flash two-piece suit with protruding hankie. My metamorphosis had worked in my favour. In fact, when I look back, I'm sure that becoming a part-time hippy saved my life.

I made my way out of the Bridgegate towards Glasgow Cross and then headed for Renfield Street to catch a bus home. I decided to get out of the city centre fast, as I might bump into Mac the Knife and his pals again and next time he might recognise me. Better safe than sorry. Strangely, as I stood at the bus stop, a car was stuck in a traffic jam and Bobby Darin singing 'Mack the Knife' boomed out from it. If this wasn't an omen, then what was?

The next morning, I bought a copy of the *Daily Record* and the headline said, 'Gorbals Man Stabbed to Death in Gang Fight'. Underneath the headline was a photo of the now deceased Mac the Knife. It turned out he had met an untimely end after he got into an argument over drugs with rival gang members near Paddy's Market. In the photograph, he had a manic grin on his face, the sort of grin I'd seen appearing just before he slashed someone. But now he would grin no more. Death had had the last laugh.

20

DOMINOES

WITH THE DEMISE OF MY FRIEND MAC, IT WAS NOW safe for me to hang around the Gorbals and the city centre once more. While I'd been away, for some reason incomprehensible to me, Chris and some of the boys had become addicted to playing dominoes, or 'doms' as they were called. So when I went to Govanhill, met up with Chris and asked him what he fancied doing, 'a game o' doms' was usually the reply. Sometimes my heart sank when he said this, as dominoes was an old man's game, as far as I was concerned, and everyone took it very seriously.

My first experience of the domino subculture was when I was 14. With a couple of the boys, I'd gone into the Clydesdale Bar in the Gorbals and the place was so rough that the barman didn't even ask us our age. A group of about 12 old men were gathered round a table. They had an air of quiet concentration reminiscent of chess grandmasters and were using unfamiliar phrases, including 'Ah'm chappin' [knocking]', which was followed by tapping the table with a domino. This meant you didn't have a domino that matched one on the table and couldn't play. When I looked at their faces, they all had scars. These were the hard cases of Glasgow past, relics of the 1930s when the Gorbals really was as it was portrayed in *No Mean City*.

A pal and I sat down to join in one game. This was unusual, because the men took their dominoes so seriously that they rarely let strangers join in, especially young guys like us. But my pal's grandfather, an ex-Merchant Navy sailor and old jailbird, persuaded the other older fellows to let us play. 'Gie the young fellas a chance. Let them in fur at least wan game and they can listen and learn.

They've got tae start learnin' tae play doms somewhere and it might as well be here.'

I asked him how he had learned the game and he said, 'Ah trained wi the best domino players in the world. We'd play night and day in the Gorbals pubs and these guys wur the grandmasters o' the game. They wur very hard tae beat unless ye wur very lucky. But after a while, it's a bit like poker: ye get tae readin' people's faces and ye can usually tell by their expression whit sort o' hand they have. The thing aboot this game is ye've got tae be a good actor.'

This man talked as if he were a high-flying poker player in Las Vegas. In a way, he lived in a fantasy world. Every night, he would play dominoes for a few pennies in the Clydesdale Bar. He was known as one of the best players there and always kept his hand close to his chest as though the next deal could be worth millions.

'Never, ever let your opponent have an idea of whit ye have in yir hand. Always keep yir dominoes close tae yir chest. The best player in the world told me that,' he said.

'Where did ye meet these people, in the Merchant Navy?' I asked rather naively.

'No, ya daft bastard, Barlinnie Prison. Some o' the best domino players in the world ur there. They play as much as they can tae make the time go faster.'

I put in my tuppence, which, strangely, felt like a lot of money all of a sudden, and proceeded to play. However, I was soon chapping and a few moves later I was out. The other players gave me smug grins; I had only wasted tuppence but I felt as if I had lost a fortune. Chris, though, was a much better player than me and held his own. If dominoes had ever become an Olympic sport, he would certainly have been a contender for a medal.

A while later we were sitting at another table as the old fellows continued with their games when one guy, who looked really ancient, shouted to another, 'Ya cheatin' bastard ye! Dae ye think ye can con me? Ah f***in' know whit ye're up tae!' He began grappling with another old man and the table overturned in the ensuing brawl. The two men fought as though they were 19-year-olds, punching and kicking until the burly barman intervened. 'Hey, youse two auld bastards better start behavin' yirselves,' he said, 'otherwise ye're oot the door and that means nae mair beer and nae mair dominoes here. So square it up noo, or else ye're barred.' The two elderly gentlemen looked at each other, shook hands and then went back to the table to play a new game. It was as if nothing had happened. The threat of being banned from playing their favourite game had brought them back to their senses. Dominoes, after all, was their life.

These days, Chris played a lot and when he found himself in a game with strangers, he would sometimes turn on his fake German accent. This was very funny.

'Where dae ye come fae, son?' one player might ask.

'Düsseldorf, Germany,' he would reply in a German voice straight out of a war film.

'Oh aye? Ah heard Düsseldorf is a very nice place.'

'Yes,' Chris would reply, 'my father hanged many British from Düsseldorf Cathedral.'

The other players were usually too shocked to reply until Chris burst out laughing and said that he had only been winding them up.

During these evenings sitting with Chris and a load of old guys, I often thought, 'I've just been in Oban and Paris having an exciting time. What the hell am I doing here with a bunch of old men in a Glasgow pub playing dominoes?' As I chapped yet again I'd get the feeling that life was passing me by.

The old men would often joke about their advanced ages. 'Three things happen when ye get as auld as me,' said one. 'First, ye start losin' yir memory . . . and Ah cannae remember the other two!'

Another responded, 'Ah said tae ma wife the other day, "Why ur ye readin' the Bible aw the time?" And she said, "Ah'm studyin' fur ma final exams."'

'Aye,' said another, slightly younger fellow, 'ye realise ye're gettin' oan a bit when ye start havin' dry dreams and wet farts.'

Unlike Chris with his obsession with dominoes, Wee Alex preferred going to the bookie's and sticking a bet on. One of the domino players, who had once been a bookie's runner in the Gallowgate, said to him, 'Bettin' is a waste o' time. Ah mean, have ye ever seen a bookie oan a bike? They've aw got big flashy motors. They're aw loaded. When Ah wis younger, a wee fella came intae the shop and stuck a pound oan an accumulator. And every wan o' his horses came in until he had only wan tae go. Ah said tae the wee bookmaker, "Boss, if that last horse comes in, ye're gonnae owe that guy thousands o' pounds." But he said to me, "Ah'm away doonstairs tae make a cup o' tea. Come doon and see me as soon as ye know whit the result is." He was sweatin' buckets because he knew a big win like that could wipe him oot. In those days, aw the races wur oan the radio, so Ah listened in, jist as nervous as ma boss. Anyway, the horse wis leadin' aw the way when suddenly it fell at the last fence. Ah went doonstairs tae tell the boss and he breathed a sigh o' relief, stirred some sugar intae his tea and said, "Well, that's another pound we've got oot the bastards!"'

Alex nodded his head. 'Aye, too right, the bookies always win. Ye can try tae beat them but ye willnae. How dae ye leave a bookie's wi a small fortune? Ye go in wi a big wan!'

Another one of the old domino players joined in. 'Ye're right, ye cannae win. At the end o' the day, the bookie always comes first. Ah heard that archeologists recently found the mummified body o' a 3,000-year-auld man who had died o' a heart attack. He had a piece o' parchment in his hand. It wis a bettin' slip that said "5,000 on Goliath".'

In the Clelland Bar one of those nights, I got bored of doms and bet a guy about the same age as me that I could beat him at pool. 'Ye've got mair chance o' beatin a carpet,' he said to me in a gallus manner. I beat him easily but he laughed, saying that he wouldn't pay up. 'Ye've got mair chance o' screwin' the Queen than gettin' a pound oot o' me,' he said. In refusing to honour the bet and using the cheeky patter on me, this guy was showing extreme signs of disrespect. He would never have tried it in my pre-Oban days. I looked like an easy touch because of my bohemian style. We ended up violently fencing with our pool queues. It was like a duel from an Errol Flynn movie. I came out of it the victor but with a small gash on my head.

After I'd got home and stuck an Elastoplast on my forehead, I had a sudden realisation: I couldn't dress as a hippy in Glasgow any more than I could dress as a hard man in Oban. They were two distinctly different arenas. I had to find a balance. The best bet was: when in Glasgow, dress as a tough guy; and when in Oban, dress as my friends there did. I remembered one of the older Gorbals guys I knew advising me, 'Tae be the part, ye've got tae look the part. Ah mean, when ye go tae a bank fur a loan or tae invest money and ye meet the manager, he isnae dressed in a Mickey Mouse T-shirt and jeans, wearin' a beard. He's got a nice pinstripe suit oan and he's clean-shaven. The point is that the bank manager dresses like a bank manager because that's the way ye expect him tae dress; that way, ye feel safe wi him dealin' wi yir money. If he wis dressed in a T-shirt, ye widnae be so confident. It's the same wi the polis. Dae ye think they would have the same power if they didnae have a uniform?'

The next day, I had a shave, went for a short back and sides, and stuck on a flashy suit that had been sitting unworn in my wardrobe for months. When in Rome, do as the Romans do.

21

SHOWBIZ

My **FATHER FLITTED FROM JOB TO JOB AND PICKED** up some marvellous anecdotes along the way. He was a tremendous raconteur and would come back to the house and regale us with stories about the people he had met – many of them quite famous. Because he worked in the hotel trade, he often bumped into celebrities who were on the cabaret circuit, which was booming in the '70s, and after work he sometimes got the chance to sit down and have a drink with them.

When I came back to Glasgow, he was working in a hotel on the Ayrshire coast where comedian Tommy Cooper was performing for a few nights. After Cooper's show was finished, my father would join him for a drink. One night, our phone rang and my mother picked it up only to find, much to her surprise, that it was Tommy Cooper on the line saying he wanted to talk to her. My father had put him up to it during one of their late-night drinking sessions.

'That guy really is as mad as a hatter,' my father said. 'Tommy told me that, because he's always usin' taxis and hotels, he used tae tip aw over the place, which wis provin' very expensive. So he came up wi an idea tae save himsel money. He went oot and bought a packet o' tea bags and noo every time he has a taxi ride or goes tae a restaurant, he pulls a tea bag oot o' his pocket, puts it in the pocket o' the taxi driver or the waiter and says, "Have a drink on me." They laugh so much they forget aboot the tip. Whit a brilliant idea! He says they tea bags have saved him a fortune over the years.'

He said that Cooper was a great psychologist when it came to dealing with other acts. 'When somebody else oan the bill comes tae join us fur a drink, Tommy'll say tae them, "What happened to your act tonight?" They usually get aw self-conscious, sayin' things like "Oh, the drummer wasn't in time," or "My voice was a bit out of tune." And aw the while they don't realise that there wis nothin' the matter wi it and Tommy's jist takin' the mickey. It's hilarious.'

Because I was still looking for full-time work, I sometimes went down to Ayrshire to help my father out part-time in the kitchen. He was right: the place was crawling not only with singers and comedians but also with well-known footballers.

Bernard Manning, the outrageous and controversial Manchester comedian, was there one evening. He had been booked to host a dinner, appearing before and after a live televised boxing match between two black heavyweights. He was making racist jokes about the sportsmen and I thought his patter was scandalous. He would never have got away with it today. In the '70s, though, even mainstream television was full of xenophobic jibes, with programmes like *Love Thy Neighbour* and *On the Buses*.

After the show, I asked Manning why he did so many bigoted jokes and he shrugged his shoulders, saying, 'I'm not racist or bigoted. We all tell jokes about the Scots, the English, the Irish, the black people and the Jews. We all make fun of one another. Most of my so-called critics are dumbwits. I don't listen to them. I just carry on making people laugh, no matter what colour or race they are.'

At the time, he had a massive following and was a wealthy man. He owned his own club, the Embassy in Manchester, and he turned up for the gig in a Rolls-Royce with a personalised number plate: 'COM1C'.

One Friday night, a First Division football player joined us for a drink just after the cabaret ended. He was drunk and still knocking back large whiskies, and he told us he had problems with his marriage. I was surprised by the state he was in because he was a great player and due to take part in a big match the next day. Referring to his estranged wife, he bellowed, 'That f***in' bitch is tryin' tae take me tae the cleaners fur the whole lot: the house, the cars, the bank account. It's puttin' me aff ma fitba.' This was a side to football stars I had never seen before. I had read about them in the newspapers and the glossy magazines, seen them perform on the pitch and on television and I'd assumed they lived glamorous, uncomplicated lives. Here was the proof that fame and money couldn't buy you love and happiness.

A fairly well-known Scottish comedian was with us and, although he was extremely funny on TV, in reality he was a bit of a depressive. Offstage, he rarely told jokes and moaned most of the time. 'It's aw a game, keepin' the punters happy. Gie them whit they want and most importantly gie them value fur their money. Yir typical Scottish guy works hard fur 40 hours aw week and wants a laugh at the weekend. That's where guys like me come in. We cheer them up.'

The football player chimed in, 'Aye, we're aw in the same f***in' boat. After workin' aw week they come tae see me playin' fitba and it makes their lives aw worthwhile. We're like the Roman gladiators: we gie the workin' classes entertainment. It keeps their minds aff o' revolution. There'll never be a revolution in Scotland as long as we've got fitba.' I thought that this was an astute observation: bread and circuses and all that.

The cabaret star responded, 'Aye, ye're right there. We gie aw they stupid bastards whit they want, we cheer them up and there'll never be another Scottish uprisin' as long as guys like us ur aroon.'

Then, suddenly, he looked at the football star and said, 'Hey, ye're knocking back the whisky awfy fast. Ye're playin' the morra, ur ye no? It's time ye got the f*** tae yir bed, otherwise ye'll be fit fur nothin'. Besides, if the big man, yir manager, hears that ye've been drinkin' like this oan the eve o' a big game, there'll be murder.'

At that, the player went beserk. 'Who ye talkin' tae, ya f***in' fat tube. Mind yir ain business. Ye're aboot as funny as a burnin' orphanage.'

Before I knew what was happening, the table was overturned as the footballer lunged at the cabaret star. Glasses, ashtrays and alcohol went flying everywhere. We managed to hold him back and I helped him up to a hotel room. He was in a hell of a state and I wondered how he was going to be able to play the next day.

The following morning, I banged on the door of his room to wake him up. When he answered it, he looked like death warmed up. The previous night's actions came back to him. 'Oh no! Did Ah really say aw that shite? Did Ah really go fur him? F***in' drink again! Ah'm gettin' as bad as George Best.'

He thanked me for looking after him and then, much to my surprise, handed me two tickets for the match that day. They were like gold dust and I was over the moon. I rushed back to Glasgow by train and met up with one of my pals at George Square. We headed off to the match and the atmosphere was electric, with thousands of supporters chanting and singing.

The player and the comedian had been right: there would never be a revolution in Scotland as long as there was an atmosphere like this at the football. It was enough to take your breath away. What's more, the player was indeed a modern gladiator: when he came out of the tunnel, there was no sign in his face or in the way he played that he had been on the large whiskies or involved in a fight the night before. After a few minutes, he scored one of the most spectacular goals I have ever seen. The crowd went mental. Bread and circuses!

Later on, my friend and I got rather drunk in a Gallowgate bar and a full-scale brawl broke out between supporters of the two teams. I was stuck in the middle of it and got a bit of a kicking. The next day, my face was in a hell of a mess. I was in the green room backstage at the hotel when the cabaret singer Vince Hill came over to me. He was immaculately dressed in a black tuxedo and deeply suntanned, just like a star should be. He asked in a chirpy manner, 'What happened to your phizog?'

'Oh,' I said, 'Ah wis at the fitba. Ah got a bit of a kickin' yesterday. But Ah suppose we expect that; it's part and parcel o' goin' tae a big match and, like the game o' fitba, some days ye win and some days ye lose. Yesterday, Ah lost big time.'

'My goodness,' Hill said, 'I've heard about how ferocious football fans can be up here but I didn't really believe it. Now I've seen the evidence!'

The comedian I'd been drinking with the night before joined in and, for once, he told a joke off duty. 'Aye, Vince, this young fella looks like the punchline fae a Celtic and Rangers joke. Here's wan: a guy goes tae a Rangers–Celtic match fur the first time and is a bit worried because there ur beer bottles flyin' over his heid.

'He says tae another supporter, "Ah'm gettin' a bit frightened in case wan o' they beer bottles hits me oan the heid."

'The other supporter says, "Don't worry aboot it. It's like the war: if yir name's oan the bullet, ye're gonnae get it!"

'"Ah know that," he says, "but ma name's McEwan."'

Vince and I laughed heartily, me complete with my grazed mouth and two black eyes. To cheer you up, there's definitely no business like showbusiness.

22

LANDING ON MY FEET

BACK HOME IN SHAWLANDS, THE PHONE RANG. IT was Franz. Because of the Gorbals elocution lessons I had given him, he sounded more Glaswegian than German.

'Colin, dae ye want a job?'

'Course,' I replied.

'Well, Ah've fallen oot wi Paul aboot a woman. So we're no talkin'. Ah'll meet ye in Glesga and we'll discuss a battle plan.'

A German meeting up with a Gorbals guy to discuss a battle plan – now that should be interesting! I had an inkling what Franz wanted me for. He had told me at the end of the season in Oban that he and Paul had landed very well-paid jobs running a posh restaurant in the Home Counties. I'd also heard on the grapevine that Paul had got involved with Franz's girlfriend and that it had almost led to World War Three – Germany against Austria.

A few days later, I met up with Franz in a café in Byres Road. 'Paul and Ah ur no talkin' and there's no way Ah want him tae join me doon there. The wages ur almost double whit ye got in Oban and as usual yir food and accommodation is free. Ma plan is tae dae the job until early summer and then we'll go back tae Oban. But who knows? If we like it enough, we might stay. The guy who owns the restaurant is a multimillionaire, drives a Bentley, aw that. He wis wantin' two European chefs but Ah've told him ye're jist as good as Paul, if not better, so ye can have his job as second chef. Ah'll be head chef and Ah'll be responsible fur drawin' up the menus and the general runnin' o' the kitchen, so ye'll have nae problems wi yir boss!'

I had certain misgivings. I was nowhere near Paul's league when it came to cooking. Not only was he a tremendous cook, he was a brilliant baker as well. It would be hard to match his standards. But when I voiced my fears, Franz said, 'Don't worry aboot that Casanova bastard. Let's take the money and run!'

Within a few days, we were on a plane flying from Glasgow Airport to Heathrow. I felt like a pop star. I had never been on an aeroplane before and, as we sat there sipping some chilled Chablis that the hostesses had kindly brought us, I thought, 'I could do with more of this lifestyle.' Everything was being paid for by the restaurant's proprieter, a former City trader called Henry. *La dolce vita*!

We landed in London and a taxi was waiting to chauffeur us to the restaurant. I was a bit disappointed: I'd imagined this fellow Henry would be picking us up in his Bentley.

We got stuck in a massive traffic jam and everything looked dark and grey. The driver, a real Alf Garnett type, turned the radio on. The news was full of gloomy stuff about Britain's economic situation. It was depressing to listen to. But then a programme came on about a man who communicated with a trumpet to flowers. To make them grow and stay healthy, he played his trumpet to them every day and, as a result, he'd won prizes in numerous flower shows with his blooming plants. 'Would you believe it!' said the taxi driver. 'We've got all this trouble in Britain with the three-day week, the miners on strike, the power cuts and there's some f***in' idiot out there playing a trumpet to his plants. It could only happen in Britain. This country is going round the bend by the sound of it.' I found this extremely funny. There was plenty of doom and gloom in the air but a man with a trumpet playing to his flowers could change the atmosphere, for a short time at least.

We were driven to the restaurant, which had recently been refurbished at a cost of millions of pounds. A member of staff showed us around and the restaurant was at least as plush as the Rogano in Glasgow. The various bars were luxurious, all decked out in oak, and the place had a dance floor that put the Plaza's to shame. We had definitely landed on our feet.

Henry, a gentleman in his 50s, met us in the restaurant and we sat down for an initial meeting. 'As you can see,' he said, 'this place is intended to cater for the elite and only the best will do here. Of course, we serve beer but champagne is more popular with our guests. These are stockbrokers, lawyers, successful businessmen, football stars – and they all have one thing in common.'

'Whit's that?' Franz asked.

'They like to spend money, plenty of it. And that is why I've brought you two guys in: to provide the best food that money can buy.'

Henry was dressed in a Savile Row suit and had a cut-glass public-school accent. His air of prosperity and entitlement immediately intimidated Franz and me. For his part, he could hardly understand a word we said to him.

After the meeting, he took us to an annex that housed our accommodation. I was given a large suite with views overlooking the countryside. Franz had a similar one just down the corridor. We were told that if we were hungry, the kitchen was at our disposal. We were being treated like royalty. Not bad, I thought, for a German chancer and a kid from the Gorbals.

We went down to the kitchen and helped ourselves to the best grub: smoked salmon, fillet steaks and ice-cream gateau. Suddenly, a worried look came over Franz's face. 'Ah jist hope Ah'm up tae the job,' he said. 'Ah don't want tae blow it. This is a marvellous place and the money's too good tae be true. We cannae mess aboot here. We've got tae make an effort and make sure everythin' is done tae the highest standards. In Oban, we could get away wi murder but no here – it's a different kettle of fish.'

However, Franz had nothing to fear. Over the next few weeks, everything went swimmingly. His menu, which was full of classic European dishes with rich sauces, went down a storm with the well-heeled locals and, most of all, Henry was pleased with us, so much so that he often sent a bottle of champagne into the kitchen to congratulate us. In fact, we were starting to get accustomed to getting drunk on champagne and swore that if ever we got rich we would drink it all the time.

The staff were a mixed crew. The manageress, Selina, was a beautiful, posh woman in her late 20s or early 30s, who we suspected had a thing going with Henry. The restaurant manager, Gomez, was from Sicily and claimed he had been in the Mafia at one stage. Abdul was an African Muslim who cleaned the pots and pans, and Madri was a chancer from the Indian subcontinent who had landed the job of dessert chef.

Gomez, a stout man with a goatee beard, claimed to be in his 30s but he looked more like he was in his 50s. However, Madri said, 'He's not kidding about his age. When he was younger, he had too many women, too much alcohol, too much gambling, too much wacky backy; that is why he looks so old. He's a young man in an old man's body.'

Madri, who was in his 40s, had dubious catering skills. He was neither a baker nor a proper chef but he was pretty good at opening packages and tins. I found out that he was on the same money as me but I just thought, 'Good luck to him!' We were both chancers, although I was a slightly more talented chancer.

Abdul was a middle-aged guy who had fled his country for political reasons and found asylum in Britain. He was also on good money for a lowly pot washer and he didn't drink or smoke. I asked him where his wages went. 'I am saving up to go to Mecca,' he replied.

I was completely ignorant about Islam and said, 'Dae ye play bingo much?'

He laughed. 'No, my young friend. Mecca is in the Middle East. It is a sacred place where every Muslim must go before he dies.'

'When dae ye plan tae go?' I asked.

'I have enough money to go now but first of all I must make friends with my enemies. I have two. I also have some debts to clear before I go. You see, I wish to make peace with my enemies and be free of debt before I visit Mecca.' I thought that this was a great idea; if everyone in Glasgow made up with their enemies and cleared their debts, it would be a much safer and happier place.

One night, while we were busy serving a packed restaurant, a fight broke out between Abdul and Madri. They had never liked each other and someone told me that it was because Madri was Hindu and Abdul Muslim. Apparently, this was like a fervent Catholic working with a staunch Protestant. 'You bastard,' Abdul was shouting, 'you put bacon in my soup! I'll kill you!' He lunged at Madri with a large carving knife. Madri maintained that he hadn't touched the soup but Franz and I didn't know what to believe. Franz said it was too dangerous for them to be working together in the kitchen and promptly sacked both of them.

I met Madri the next day when he came to collect his wages. 'That stupid son of a bitch says I gave him soup with bacon in it,' he said. 'I didn't know anything about it. Now he's got the both of us the sack. I will never work with a Muslim again.'

Later, Abdul came in to fetch his final pay packet. 'That no-good bastard! He would be hanged for that where I come from. I will butcher him if I ever see him again.'

I don't know if Abdul ever made it to Mecca but he had at least one more enemy to make amends with before he set off.

23

THE DANCER

AFTER ABDUL AND MADRI LEFT, WE HAD TO FIND some new staff. The most difficult task was getting a half-decent kitchen porter – someone who could wash up properly. In some ways, this job was almost as important to the kitchen as the chef's. So we advertised and attracted the usual sort of deadbeats and alcoholics, which we expected. Much to my surprise, I was given the task of interviewing the potential candidates. Aged eighteen, I was quizzing guys some of whom were three times my age about their suitability. I felt like a big shot but a sense of mischief told me I should hire a character: someone who had been round the block and had a sense of humour; and if he was Scottish, all the better.

The first few candidates were a bit of a disappointment. One fellow from Africa spoke very little English and just nodded his head to all my questions. When I asked him his name he nodded his head. When I asked him if he had ever worked on the moon, he nodded his head. Another fellow, a fat man from Essex, had just been released from a mental institution, having tried to murder his wife and her lover. 'I'm all right now,' he assured me. Then he showed me a letter from his psychiatrist verifying that he was perfectly normal, although it also mentioned that his crime had involved a machete. Another fellow turned up so full of booze he didn't know whether it was New Year or New York.

Finally, enter Pat from Govan, Glasgow. He was a wiry man in his 50s and his red, bloated face told me that he was a bit of a drinker. However, he had an air of shrewdness that the other candidates certainly hadn't possessed.

'So, Pat, whit have ye been daein' recently and why dae ye think ye should get the job?' I asked him.

'Well, Ah've been workin' as a kitchen porter in London, at the Dorchester and the Park Lane Hilton and, as ma references state, Ah'm very good at ma job and a very hard worker,' he replied.

Taking advantage of my new position of power, I thought I would be slightly cruel and asked, 'Ur ye a big drinker? Because big drinkers ur nae good tae us. We need somebody reliable.'

'Well, Ah'm no gonnae tell ye a lie, Ah dae like a drink – but oan ma day aff. Ah never drink when Ah'm workin', Ah jist get stuck intae ma pots and pans,' he said.

Pat then handed me three references, one from the Dorchester, one from the Hilton and one from a dance-band leader. I had a close look at the references and I could tell he was up to the same game I had been playing a few years ago – the references from the hotels were obviously forged. These phoney testimonials gave glowing reports, saying he was the best pot washer they'd ever seen and that he was a dutiful and extremely honest employee. The only thing that let down the counterfeit references was the fact that they were all littered with spelling mistakes. For example, 'accommodate' was spelled 'acomadate' and 'definitely' was spelt 'definatly'. I had left school at 15 but I could spot a spelling error a mile off. Pat might have been a bit of a patter merchant but he certainly couldn't spell to save his life.

The third reference was several years old and looked more authentic. It was from the leader of a dance band in London. It said:

> Pat McDonald is one of the best male dancers I have ever had the pleasure of coming across. He is extremely proficient at the foxtrot, tango and waltz. I have had the wonderful experience of working with him for several years now and in that time he has won an array of prizes for his dancing skills. Without a doubt, he is one of the finest dancers in Britain, if not the world.

'Whit happened? Why ur ye no dancin' professionally?' I asked him.

166

'Ah fell in love wi a woman Ah used tae dae the tango wi. Ah wis besotted wi her and we travelled aw over Britain as dancin' partners. But she ended up trottin' aff wi a wee greasy Italian and Ah wis left oan ma tod. Well, much drink followed and Ah jist gave up the dancin' game and ended up workin' in kitchens.'

It was an amazing story! I had to hire this man. I offered him good money, with accommodation and food thrown in. Initially, Pat seemed to be an inspired choice. When he wasn't cleaning the pots and pans, he would give us waltz and tango lessons in the kitchen. They would have cost a fortune if we'd paid a dancing instructor for them. Sometimes Pat would waltz around the kitchen pretending to be Yul Brynner in *The King and I*. 'Wance, Ah wis the best damn dancer in Britain and noo Ah can still dance better than hawf o' they bampots oan the telly!' he'd boast.

He was also full of jokes that he'd tell as he tangoed with an imaginary partner around the kitchen. 'In Glesga, Ah grew up in an auld tenement wi six brothers and three sisters. That's how Ah learned tae dance – standin' ootside the stairheid lavvy waitin' tae get in fur a pish.' Other favourite lines were: 'Did ye hear aboot the big fat ballerina fae Govan? She had tae wear a three-three,' and 'Ma faither wis a tap dancer until he got injured. He slipped and fell in the sink.'

Pat was certainly an entertaining guy and Franz congratulated me on my choice, even though I told him I hadn't checked his references. But after a few weeks, Pat began to turn up late for work in the mornings. I'd go to fetch him and find him lying in a drunken stupor in his room. One morning, Franz shouted, 'Where is that lazy bastard? We didnae employ him tae be an alcoholic dancer. His job here is tae wash pots and pans.' He filled a champagne bucket full of ice and water and we went up to Pat's room. He was lying face up on his bed, snoring loudly. I shook him and shouted, 'Wake up, Pat, time fur work!' but there was no reaction so Franz threw the bucket of icy water over him.

Pat leaped out of bed shouting, 'Whit the f*** did ye dae that fur?'

Franz shouted back, 'Get tae work, ya lazy bastard, or ye're sacked.'

Pat did what he was told but over the next few days he was very subdued and rarely talked. One day, he didn't turn up for work at all and again we went to check his room. Pat and all his stuff had gone. We went back to the kitchen and Henry rushed in looking extremely flustered. 'The takings have gone. More than £5,000 has disappeared from the tills in the restaurant and the bars. We didn't lock them all last night and someone has taken the lot.' It didn't take a genius to work out that Pat had waltzed off with the takings.

Franz shouted at me, 'That nae-good bastard might have been a good dancer but he's a bloody thief and a useless alcoholic. Why did ye choose scum like that tae work in this kitchen? Now we're aw in the shite because of yir stupid decision tae hire that layabout. He must be laughin' aw the way tae the pub wi that money. Ye should never have hired him. Ah blame maself. Ah should have done the interviews and we widnae have had aw this trouble.'

Of course, an investigation was launched and I got the blame. Henry said, 'This reprobate has run off with a lot of money. He's been caught on the hidden camera in the restaurant, which clearly shows him taking cash from the till. The CID have been called. He's obviously a cunning thief who takes up a job and then cases the place, waiting until the time is right. I believe it was your choice to hire him, so I have a few questions I'd like to ask you.'

Had I bothered to check his references? 'No,' I replied. Was I not concerned that this man appeared to have a drink problem? 'No.' Did I know where he was now? 'No.' Did I know if he had any relatives in Glasgow or London? 'No.'

I tendered my resignation that morning and flew back to Glasgow that night. I wasn't that depressed; Henry had given me a month's wages. I just hoped Pat would do well with his new-found wealth. And me? Well, I was looking forward to my next adventure.

24

A FIRST STEP

THE GREAT THING ABOUT GLASGOW IS THAT YOU see and hear things on the streets that'll stand out in your mind for a lifetime. I had been back in the city for only a few hours and was standing at a bus stop in St Enoch Square. Two mounted policemen were riding past nearby. A sudden frost had come over the city and the streets were covered in treacherous black ice. I slipped once and thanked goodness that I wasn't drunk; if I had been, I'd probably have broken a leg.

As the two police horses passed by, I could hear the loud clip-clop of their hooves. The officers looked grand on their steeds and had an air of self-importance about them as they rode past. A little old woman, complete with floral headscarf, was standing in the long bus queue. She said to me, 'Look at them! A pair o' big-heided polis who think they're better than us because we've got tae catch a Corporation bus hame while they're ridin' aboot the place oan their daft horses. But it's us that ur payin' fur their horses and they shouldnae forget that.'

Just as she said that, one of the horses slipped on the icy road and hurtled the policeman into the air; he crash-landed in the road. The other guy got off his horse to help his colleague back up and he slipped on the ice. The whole thing was absurd. Then the old woman began laughing hysterically and started to sing, 'Did you think I would leave you crying, when there's room on my horse for two?' The whole queue joined in, myself included, singing Rolf Harris's 'Two Little Boys'. The expressions on the policemen's faces had changed from conceited to humble. The woman shouted, 'Aye, serves ye right, ya pair o' big imbeciles! Get yirselves a decent job instead o' thinkin' ye're Glesga's versions o' Roy Rogers.'

Later that day, I met up with my girlfriend, Charlotte. It was winter and there were months to wait until the start of the season, so she'd come down to be near me. She was staying with relatives in Carfin, near Motherwell, until we made alternative plans.

A few days later, I was passing by a restaurant in the South Side and saw a little sign in the window: 'Part-time night chef required'.

'Perfect!' I thought, and I went in to see the owner, who reminded me of the Penguin character from the *Batman* TV series. He was dressed in a suit and tails, complete with black bow tie. His apparel looked a bit out of place in a small restaurant – more appropriate for the Savoy, I thought. But he explained to me, 'I've invested a lot of money in this venture and I want it to be the best little gourmet restaurant in Glasgow. We've built up a following of regular customers already and they appreciate good cuisine. I have a woman who runs the kitchen service during the day and I need a young guy like you to run it at night, when we can get very busy.'

He then showed me the menu and it took me aback because it was full of cordon bleu dishes that would be difficult for one man to prepare if the restaurant got busy.

I said, 'This menu is a lot fur wan guy tae knock up oan his tod. Ah think ye'll need at least three people in the kitchen at night if ye're goin' tae be busy.'

He just laughed and shook his head. 'No, times are changing,' he said, 'and this is a restaurant that has changed with the times. Come through and I'll show you.'

In the kitchen, there was a large pot of water and a microwave, the first I had ever seen. On the work surface was a pair of scissors. 'Pick something from the menu,' he said. 'In fact, pick two dishes.' I chose beef stroganoff and lamb on the bone in mint sauce. He switched the heat on under the pot, went over to a large fridge and brought out two plastic bags, one containing the lamb and the other the stroganoff. He threw one bag into the boiling water and the other into the microwave. After a few minutes, the two dishes were cooked. He then cut open the plastic bags and arranged the contents on plates. I had to admit, they looked magnificent.

'We are a boil-in-the-bag restaurant,' said the owner. 'I buy in all the food in frozen plastic bags and all you need to do is use your scissors once they're cooked. Even the starters, things like pâté, come in ready-prepared tubes. You just have to squeeze them onto a plate.'

I had to pinch myself. All this time I'd spent trying to be a half-decent chef and now all I needed was a pair of scissors.

'But dae the punters not know that aw these gourmet dishes ur boil-in-the-bag?' I asked.

'No, of course they don't – and they pay top whack for it. The food is as good from frozen as it would be freshly prepared and what they don't know won't hurt them.'

The owner then said that my wages would be cash in hand at the end of each night. The rates he was offering were better than those that were to be had in other 'proper' restaurants, so, armed with my scissors, I took up the job.

During my time at the restaurant, I decided to follow up possible routes to university. I set up a meeting with a lecturer who dealt with admissions at Langside College, a further-education establishment in Glasgow. They weren't taking new students until September 1974 but I thought I'd apply early and get my oar in. The lecturer was a history buff who specialised in the causes of the World Wars. I was surprised by how down to earth he was. He said to me, 'I had the same sort of upbringing you had and around about your age, at 19, I decided to get myself educated. I came here first of all then went to Aberdeen University. I did a history degree and I've ended up back here as a senior lecturer.'

'Dae ye think Ah'll be able tae fit in as a student?' I asked.

'You'll have no problem,' he said. 'You've been around the block a few times and guys like you often make the best students. You've not come straight out of school and you know what the real world is like.'

We decided that I would start that September and would initially study for O grades in English, history, economics, biology, modern studies and Latin. I didn't really want to do biology or Latin – they both kind of frightened me – but the lecturer explained to me that they would be useful if I wanted to get into university.

He told me that I wouldn't get a student grant for the first year. I wasn't too worried about it, as I could always get part-time work as a chef. In the second year, when I would do Highers or A levels, I would be eligible for financial help.

We shook hands on the plan, with the lecturer saying to me, 'Do you know what the Chinese say?'

'Whit's that?' I said.

'"A journey of a thousand miles starts with one step." This is your first step.'

As I left the campus and wandered into town, I still felt a bit apprehensive about how I would get on. But I remembered my pals in Oban telling me that I would be fine, that the majority of students weren't all that bright, anyway. And then I thought of some of the stories Hamish had told me from his days as a teacher. One of his pupils had asked him what a comet was and he'd said it was a star with a tail. When he asked the kid if he could name a comet, he'd replied, 'Mickey Mouse.'

Some of the answers he got back on test papers were totally stupid, too. To the question 'When did Julius Caesar die?' a student had responded, 'A few days before his funeral.' Another was 'Where was the Magna Carta signed?' to which some idiot had replied, 'At the bottom.'

These thoughts cheered me up. I figured that, with people like these around, no matter how tough I found it, I wouldn't be the daftest person in the class.

I decided it was time to celebrate and that afternoon I met Chris in Eglinton Street. As we were walking past the Kiloran Bar, a large lorry was unloading crates of beer. A sudden urge came over us and we grabbed a case of 24 cans of Tennent's lager from the lorry. We ran off, chased by the driver, who was red in the face with anger and exertion, waving his fists and shouting hysterically, 'Come back, ya bastards! Drop they cans or Ah'll kill ye!' We soon lost him in the back streets and we headed off to Pollok Park, where we sat with our free carry-out on a grassy hill. It was a beautiful day and we bathed in the sunshine, laughing and joking and supping our beer. Chris said, 'Ah've been thinkin' – there's 24 cans in this case and there's 24 hours in a day – coincidence? Ah don't think so!' Then he asked me, 'Whit's the difference between a drunk and an alcoholic? A drunk goes tae work! Ach, ye cannae beat havin' a good laugh. It's the cheapest and best way tae improve the appearance o' yir face.'

I laughed out loud but a nagging worry was getting to me. Would I still be up to outrageous antics and adventures when I was educated? Only time would tell.

25

CONNOLLYMANIA

WHEN I WAS OUT SEEING CHARLOTTE IN CARFIN one day, she said to me, 'There's a new Glasgow comedian performing at a hotel just up the road. Do you fancy going?'

'Whit's his name?' I asked.

'Billy Connolly.'

The answer took me aback, as I remembered thinking after bumping into him that he was destined to be a superstar. An article in the local newspaper said that he was to perform at the Tudor Hotel in Airdrie and that the gig would be recorded for a live album. When we turned up at the hotel the following night, the place was jam-packed and the performance was a sell-out. I approached the organiser and gave him a bit of patter, telling him my story about meeting Connolly in London, and he agreed to let us in.

That night, there was an absolutely incredible atmosphere. Even before Connolly appeared, it was electric and when he arrived on stage he did the most hilarious sketches I had ever heard. One of them, about the Last Supper taking place in the Gallowgate rather than Galilee, had everyone falling about laughing. When I listen to the album, I can distinctly hear my own laugh during a couple of the sketches. Connolly's use of real Glaswegian speech was brilliant and very exciting, and when he stood on the stage that night everyone in the audience knew they were experiencing something magical.

The *Solo Concert* album went on to sell more than a quarter of a million copies. After its release, Connolly's rise to superstardom began in earnest. He even had his own comic strip in the *Sunday Mail* called *The Big Yin* written by him and artist Malcolm McCormick. It was an instant rival to *Oor Wullie* and *The Broons*. In one such strip, Billy's uncle comes down from Uist and is told, 'If ye're jist gonnae sit scrounging bevy, ye can away back where the animals run aboot an' streams run doon the slopes.'

'Ye mean Hampden?' he replies.

Connolly's big achievement was to make the Glaswegian dialect something that people loved, appreciated and found hilarious not only in Scotland but the world over. Some people, though, were not amused by his strong language and sketches about religion. Connolly recorded a religious-affairs programme for BBC Scotland in which Moses said things like, 'Nip hame and get yir people . . .' And short jokes like the following did not exactly endear him to the Christian fundamentalists: 'What are the three most unnecessary things in life? A nun's tits, the Pope's balls and a round of applause for the band.'

Religious zealots such as Baptist minister Pastor Jack Glass started to mount demonstrations outside his shows. Connolly wasn't surprised, and shrugged, 'Ah, well, it's not every day you get a demonstration in your honour,' adding that the pastor was 'an ass'.

He had other detractors as well. Tony Blackburn, a Radio 1 DJ at the time of *Solo Concert*'s release, told his millions of listeners that he couldn't see anything funny about the Glasgow patter merchant. But Connolly's management said that Blackburn slagging off the album was one of the highest recommendations a comedy record could get. Others found Connolly's humour too lavatorial for their liking, while many people in Glasgow believed that their patter was just as good and that Connolly had made it big only because he was lucky and had a pushy manager. He even got poison pen letters.

Connolly mocked the typical Scottish reaction to success in a joke about the Second Coming: a man rushes down the street to tell his neighbours, 'He's here! He's here! He's come!'

'Who has?'

'Jesus Christ!'

'Aye . . . Ah kent his faither.'

But Connolly was quite adept at dealing with hecklers during his shows. He'd say things like, 'The last time I saw a mouth like yours, pal, Lester Piggot was sitting behind it,' or 'The more I hear of you, the more I believe in birth control.' When one heckler shouted 'IRA!' in Dublin, he replied, to rapturous applause, 'Aye, you're very brave down there in the dark, pal. Try shoutin' that in the middle of Ibrox Park some time.'

Connolly was slightly different from the other Scottish comedians around at the time as he had been influenced by the outrageous storytelling of American comics like Lenny Bruce. A story that had a big impact on Connolly was about Lenny Bruce on stage in San Francisco. There were policemen in the audience waiting to arrest him for using obscene language. Bruce got up on the stage and explained to the audience that because the police were there, he'd use alternative words. For example, when he wanted to say a four-letter word that started with C and ended with T, he'd say 'tulip'; when he was going to say a word that started with F and ended with K, he'd say 'daffodil'; and the word that started with B and ended with D would be 'rhododendron'. He checked with the audience to see if they had got the code – tulip, daffodil, rhododendron. Then he started off, 'There was this Mexican c***s****r . . .'

Connolly had broken the mould for Scottish comedians. His many put-downs to hecklers and critics were based on the patter he had heard in the Glasgow pubs and streets but the so called 'Mr Glasgow' at the time, the comedian-singer Glen Daly, would never have dared use such patter. I had heard many of Connolly's lines before in the streets of Glasgow but somehow he made them sound funnier.

He regularly used an old Glasgow joke that I had heard my father tell years before at a party: a magistrate says to his wife, 'This drunken hooligan came up to me in the street and was sick all down my jacket. It was disgusting. But when he comes into the court in front of me, I'm going to fine him £20 and teach him a damn good lesson.'

He comes back from court the next day and his wife brings him his sherry. 'You know that man you were going to fine £20 for being sick all over your jacket?' she says.

'Aye?'

'Well, you'd better fine him another £20 – he's shat in your trousers.'

Another typically Glaswegian joke about a wedding was considered by some to have crossed the line. There's a big reception in somebody's house after a wedding and everyone's having a great time, getting into the bevy and dancing. Then, suddenly, someone rushes into the room and shouts, 'The party's over. On your bikes! Somebody f***ed the bride!' Everyone starts to get their coats on, the music stops and they're all about to go. Then the same guy comes running back into the room: 'It's all right! Don't go away! He's apologised!'

When I saw Connolly record his album, he seemed so original that I thought he represented a completely new beginning for Scottish comedy. However, older people pointed out that he was part of a tradition of Glaswegian patter merchants like Stanley Baxter and Tommy Morgan.

Baxter, like Connolly, had a great knack for capturing the Glasgow banter. One of his jokes went: 'They put a poster outside of a Glasgow police station saying "Wanted for murder" and 200 men applied for the job.' His command of language was verging on genius. One of his stories concerned a young woman and her parents who were walking home after visiting friends when the father sat down suddenly on the pavement. His daughter inquired of the mother, 'Heh, murra, whit's the marra wi ma farra?' Her mother informed her, 'Yur farra canny go nae furra.' She points to an abandoned wheelbarrow and suggests that they put the overtired gent in it and wheel him home: 'Erra barra owererr. We'll pirrim oan an' hurlim hame.'

Unlike Connolly, however, Baxter never swore or cracked sexual jokes; his humour was based on old music-hall routines he had witnessed at the Empire or the Pavilion: 'That Bella McLeish gies her man the life o' a dug. She gies him Pal Meat and eggs fur his breakfast and Pal Meat sangwidges fur his dinner and tea. Aye, they say he ate that much Pal Meat he couldnae pass a lamppost.' He specialised in jokes about 'wee baldie bachles' and bourgeois Kelvinside women having tea. One such character was 'Wee Baldie Bain': 'His wig blew aff in Sauchiehall Street. He ran after it and he wis hawfway tae Edinburgh afore he found oot he wis chasin' a Pekinese dug.'

He often told the story of the two ladies from Kelvinside in a downmarket Glasgow café. As soon as they entered, they started up with imperious and impatient calls of 'Miss!' The girl ambled over to them and was told by one of the ladies, 'Bring us a pot of tea for two and make sure I get a clean cup.'

The waitress gave her a glare of hatred and sauntered off. Some twenty minutes later, she was back with a tray on which were a tin teapot and two cups and saucers. 'Here ye ur,' she rasped, 'Which wan o' youse wanted the clean cup?'

His put-downs were also brilliant, lines such as: 'Her spuds [feet] wur that big she got a job in the Ministry o' Agriculture stampin' oot the forest fires,' and 'She's that bowly, she can walk on both sides o' the street at the same time.'

Chic Murray was in the same mould but his patter was a lot more surreal and bizarre. He recounted a story about a man knocking on the door of his flat and asking to see Chic Murray. Chic turned on his poshest accent and said that Mr Murray wasn't at home and asked if the man would care to wait in the library. The visitor beamed, impressed that there was such a facility in the flat. He made to step over the threshold but a large hand stopped him, as Chic said, 'Fine, if you go back downstairs, turn left at the close, you'll find it on the corner of the next street. A lovely big sandstone building, you can't miss it.' The door was then closed.

Murray also specialised in short jokes.

'What's your problem?' asks a doctor.

'I've got butterflies in my stomach,' says Chic.

'Have you eaten anything recently?'

'Butterflies, actually.'

Another favourite was: 'I walked into the bedroom. The curtains were drawn but the furniture was real.'

Before Baxter and Murray there was Tommy Morgan. If Connolly learned something from some of Baxter's jokes and techniques, then Baxter did the same from Morgan.

Tommy Morgan, a big moon-faced man from Bridgeton, was regarded by many as the greatest ever exponent of Glaswegian humour. He was immensely popular and played to packed houses at Glasgow's Pavilion Theatre each summer season for 19 consecutive years. Favourite targets of his rough-and-ready patter included councillors, snobs, football teams and misers. His comedy was broad but never malicious and, unlike some comedians at the time, he rarely made jokes about people with physical disabilities. He was mortified once when a cross-eyed man confronted him outside the Pavilion and complained about a gag in the show. By modern standards, though, the joke was mild: 'This wee fella had such a bad squint that nae lassie would look at him. He was that depressed he decided tae droon himsel in the Clyde. He went doon tae Jamaica Bridge, climbed ontae the parapet and jumped. But him bein' squinty-eyed, he jumped the wrang way. He landed flat oan his back oan the pavement, "Ma God!" he says. "Jist ma luck! The Clyde's frozen over in June!"'

There is a poster that hangs in the People's Palace museum on Glasgow Green that sums up the city's attitude to its comedians:

> When Connolly was at the peak of his fame, a survey revealed that 74 per cent of the population of Glasgow thought that they could be funnier than Billy Connolly given the chance, while 17 per cent thought they were already funnier than Billy Connolly. The other 9 per cent thought that they were Billy Connolly.

26

COUNTRY LIFE

I'D DECIDED THAT THE BEST THING TO DO WAS TO accumulate as much money as I could so that when I started at Langside at the end of September I would have enough to survive. I worked most nights at the little restaurant and I was proving to be quite proficient with the scissors. When I did have a couple of nights off, I would catch the train to Motherwell and then a bus to Carfin to visit Charlotte and her relatives.

Whereas, back in Oban, Charlotte lived in a grand house, her cousin lived in a shabby council estate. The place was really run-down and impoverished looking but who was I to complain? I had been brought up in one of the scruffiest places in the country. I had witnessed almost every image that poverty could offer but in Carfin I saw something new: two local boys, aged around ten, were playing football in the street . . . with a boxing glove. I asked them where their football was and one said, 'We burst it oan some railings last week and ma maw and da hivnae got the money fur another wan. We looked roon the hoose and the only thing we could find wis this auld boxin' glove. But ye get used tae playin' fitba wi it. Ah think it's made us better players.'

A strange image came to me of someone else in the area boxing with a deflated football on his hand. Strangely enough, years later I recognised the boy's name and face in the newspapers. He had been signed up by one of the top London football clubs as a striker. So perhaps he'd been right about it improving his game. Over the years, I've discovered that life is full of surprises; that's what makes it so enjoyable.

In the council house with Charlotte, her cousin, the cousin's husband and their children, it reminded me of the old Gorbals. 'Aye, we might struggle fur money but, by God, we still know how tae enjoy ourselves,' the lady of the house said to me. 'Ye know, ye see aw they toffs goin' aboot wi their fancy motors but ye never see them smilin'. After aw, whit's the use o' bein' the richest man in the graveyard? Ye cannae take it wi ye. We might be poor but we're a lot happier than most.'

She was a thin, pale woman in her late 20s who managed to bring up her three children on a tight budget. Like millions of others, her husband was in and out of work. He was accustomed to living on the breadline. He told me, 'Ah wis brought up in a poor family. We wur so poor we used tae go tae the fish-and-chip shop tae lick other people's fingers.' Like his wife, he had a great sense of humour and made light of their situation. 'If ye want tae know whit God thinks aboot money,' he said, 'jist look at the people he gave it tae.'

On one visit, I felt so sorry for the family and so affectionate towards them that I went to the local supermarket and bought them a pile of food. I also got the alcohol in so that we could have a wee party. Later that night, as the wine flowed, we all had a sing-song and I was urged to give them at least one number. I was reluctant but the alcohol had given me enough courage to sing 'Bye Bye Blackbird'. I thought my voice didn't sound too bad at all and tears, no doubt helped along by the consumption of cheap wine, flowed down most of the partygoers' cheeks. It was a great night, just like old times.

The next day, I caught the train back to Glasgow and by early evening I was back in the kitchen of the restaurant. The owner and the day cook were there.

'We have a VIP wedding party coming in tomorrow,' said the wee man, 'and they have insisted on roast duck, so, for a change, we won't be doing boil-in-the-bag for them. We have 20 ducks roasting in the ovens. Just make sure you take them out when they're done.'

'Nae problem,' I said. I had roasted ducks before so I knew what I was doing. Anyway, it would be a nice change from using the scissors.

That night, we were extremely busy. My scissors were doing double time. I was rushed off my feet and exhausted when I finished around 10 p.m. The party in Carfin the night before hadn't helped and when I left the restaurant I headed straight for my home and my bed. I fell asleep straight away but I woke at about 6 a.m. and a cold sweat came over me. I realised I hadn't remembered to take the ducks out of the oven. They would be burned to a cinder. What about the wedding party that day?

Later that morning, I went into the restaurant shamefaced and the owner was none too pleased. 'You've managed to cremate 20 ducks! I think you were better with a pair of scissors. How the hell did you forget all those birds roasting in the oven?' I explained how hectic the service had been and that the ducks had completely gone out of my mind. I tendered my resignation immediately – another day, another job down the drain.

I wasn't that bothered, anyway. It was only a few weeks until I would be starting in Oban, so perhaps it was time for a short holiday. 'Do you want to go with me to Forfar to visit my other relatives?' Charlotte said. 'They live in the countryside and it should be a good break before we start work in Oban.' I agreed straight away. I was eager to see another part of Scotland. When we got there, I was not disappointed. The area was beautiful. Charlotte's relatives, a young-ish couple, lived in a lovely cottage with wonderful views.

After a few days taking in all the scenery and visiting the local villages, the man of the house, a sturdy farming type, said we were going down to the local hotel that night for a knees-up and a bit of a session. In the lounge bar of the hotel, there was a cabaret singer with a guitar playing country-and-western numbers like 'Tie a Yellow Ribbon' and 'Help Me Make It Through the Night'. There was a great ambience and a real community atmosphere as all the farmers, young and old, sang along and consumed vast amounts of beer and spirits. The tables were all littered with empty glasses. The older farmers seemed friendly but the younger ones a bit less so. When they heard my accent, they started to act in a more aggressive manner, as if they wanted to show that they were harder and smarter than any Glaswegian.

It got very late and when I asked one of the older guys what time the place shut, he said, 'It's open until everybody gives up and goes home.' The barman then appeared and handed everyone a Forfar bridie, a Scottish pasty, free of charge. When I asked my host if this was a local tradition, he laughed, saying, 'Oh, no, it's to cover themselves if the police raid the place in the early hours. Under local by-laws, as long as people have been provided with food, they can drink. That's not just a bridie, it's a legal loophole.'

The farmers began a rousing sing-song, warbling favourites such as 'The Northern Lights of Old Aberdeen' and 'Bonnie Wee Jeannie McColl'. Then, all of a sudden, several fights broke out. My host said, 'It happens every weekend. They fall out during the week, at the weekend they punch hell out of each other and by the Monday everything's forgotten about and it's back to work as normal. Now that's a tradition!' I thought that it was certainly different from Glasgow, where a punch-up was rarely forgotten and could result in a dispute lasting months or even years.

The dust settled, things quietened down and I joined a few of the older guys who were sipping from their whisky glasses and telling jokes and stories. One old fellow began, 'A man sees a farmer walking a pig and he notices the animal has a wooden leg. He asks its owner how the pig lost a limb.

'"Well," he says, "one night the wife and I were asleep when the pig spotted that the house was on fire. It broke the door down, ran up the stairs and dragged me to safety. Then it went back and carried out my wife, then it went back again and rescued my four children. We'd all be dead if it weren't for this pig."

'"So did the pig get its leg burned in the fire?" asks the man.

'"Oh, no, it was fine," said the farmer, "but when you've got a pig like this, you don't eat it all at once."'

Later on, a few of us ended up back at the cottage with a carry-out of whisky, beer and cider. I immediately noticed some danger signs. One of the young farmers began to make a play for the wife of another guy. She was a respectable married woman and this was definitely going to lead to trouble. The young guy tried to kiss her, her husband saw it and he went berserk, shouting, 'You wanker! How dare you make advances to my wife!' He lunged at the young farmer and a fight developed but the farmer's friends joined in and gave the fellow a kicking.

Bloody, battered and bruised, he staggered outside into the darkness. I tried to see if I could find him, shouting his name from the door, but there was no reply. The farmer had taken a liberty but there was nothing I could do as I was vastly outnumbered by his pals. Inside, the guests were still very aggressive, with one of the young farmers saying to me, 'Do you think you're a hard man just because you come from Glasgow?'

I was ready to give a smart reply, and to get stuck into him if necessary, but just then the front door burst open and it was the husband. He was carrying a shotgun, which he must have produced from his car. 'You bastard,' he said, 'you tried to take advantage of my wife. Well, take this!' I was standing up near the fireplace when suddenly he pulled the trigger. Bang! The bullet missed me and the young farmer by inches and blew a large hole in the living-room wall. Someone managed to grapple the gun from the irate husband and he was given another kicking, after which he ran off again into the darkness of the countryside.

Early the next morning, I decided it was time for my girlfriend and me to get out of town fast. As we sat on the bus back to Glasgow, I reflected on what had gone on. I had come through the wild streets of the Gorbals without any harm but, ironically, I could have ended up getting shot in a sleepy Forfar village where they handed out free bridies in the pub. That really would have been a strange way to go.

27

HIGHLAND FLING

CHARLOTTE AND I RETURNED TO OBAN FOR THE summer season and it was great to be back, meeting all the new characters who were hitting town to take up work in the restaurants and hotels. As before, many of them were highly intelligent students from universities including Oxford, Cambridge, Edinburgh and Aberdeen. A lot of the time, I felt that I was learning something just by talking to them; it was my run-in to becoming a full-time student.

Take, for example, Peter, an English language student from Oxford who was working in the kitchen with me. He was a wild aristocratic fellow who drank like a fish and had an astounding ability to recite poetry from memory even while totally blootered. When we first met at a party in our staff accommodation, one of many that year, he said to me in a condescending but humorous tone, 'Mr MacFarlane, are all you working-class Glaswegian bastards as tough as you say you are?'

'Tougher!' I replied. 'In fact, Ah'm so tough, Ah'm havin' a heart attack noo and it disnae even affect me!' We both laughed.

Peter and I continued to chat and, in his abrasive way, he told me: 'I have been reading up on the poet Robert Service and he stayed in that stinking hole you call Glasgow. He even mentions it in one of his poems.' He was right. My father was a big fan of Robert Service and had often recited 'The Cremation of Sam McGee' and other poems by him. Peter began to recite the poem 'Bindle Stiff', in which Service describes himself as 'to Glasgow gutter bred', off the top of his drunken head.

'Burns is another one I admire,' he continued, and began to quote 'A Red, Red Rose':

O my love is like a red, red rose
That's newly sprung in June;
O my love is like the melody
That's sweetly played in tune.

As fair art thou, my bonnie lass,
So deep in love am I;
And I will love thee still, my dear,
Till a' the seas gang dry.

Till a' the seas gang dry, my dear,
And the rocks melt wi the sun;
I will love thee still, my dear,
While the sands o' life shall run.

And fare thee weel, my only love,
And fare thee weel, awhile!
And I will come again, my love,
Tho' it were ten thousand mile.

His drunken reading was very impressive; he had a fine speaking voice, to say nothing of his memory. It looked like his expensive education had paid off. Hearing him recite these poems, I thought to myself, 'I want to be like that: educated and interesting. I want to start behaving and talking like an educated person.'

When he'd finished his recital, Peter shouted, 'Now, you Glasgow bastard, fetch me some more wine and I'll give you a couple of Scottish ditties.' I went and found some more booze because I didn't want to miss the chance of hearing him reciting more poetry. As the old Glasgow saying goes, 'Kid oan ye're daft and ye'll get a hurrel fur nothin'.'

When I returned, Peter continued. 'This one is by the brilliant and highly underrated poet William McGonagall,' he said. It was called simply 'Glasgow':

Beautiful city of Glasgow, with your streets so neat and clean,
Your stateley mansions, and beautiful Green!
Likewise your beautiful bridges across the River Clyde,
And on your bonnie banks I would like to reside.

> . . . 'Tis beautiful to see the ships passing to and fro,
> Laden with goods for the high and the low;
> So let the beautiful city of Glasgow flourish,
> And may the inhabitants always find food their bodies to nourish.

> . . . Beautiful city of Glasgow, I now conclude my muse,
> And to write in praise of thee my pen does not refuse;
> And, without fear of contradiction, I will venture to say
> You are the second grandest city in Scotland at the present day!

It was the first time I had heard any McGonagall and I laughed heartily, thinking that it sounded like a poem written by one of my old schoolmates in the Gorbals. As Peter glugged from a newly opened bottle of red wine, he began to recite the nursery rhyme 'Wee Wullie Winkie', which he described as 'the best little Scots poem I know':

> Wee Wullie Winkie rins through the toun,
> Up stairs and doon stairs in his nicht-goun,
> Tirlin' at the window, cryin' at the lock,
> 'Are the weans in their bed, for it's noo ten o'clock?'

Finally, slurring his words now, Peter quoted a few lines from, appropriately enough, Burns' 'A Bottle and a Friend':

> Then catch the moments as they fly,
> And use them as ye ought, man:
> Believe me, happiness is shy,
> And comes not aye when sought, man.

As he spoke this last line, he collapsed onto a bed and within a few minutes was snoring loudly. 'These educated posh boys,' I thought, 'they even know how to get drunk with class!'

Before long, Gerry the mad cabaret singer appeared. It was the first time I had seen him since the previous year and he looked fit and well. So what had he been doing all winter?

'Oh, ye know – showbiz. Daein' gigs here, there and everywhere, mostly pubs and clubs but it keeps the money flowin' in. Fur the first time in a while, Ah'm no behind wi ma maintenance payments, thank f*** fur that.'

'Great!' I said. 'So gie's yir patter.'

At that, Gerry launched into a series of funny stories that had the party rocking with laughter. Half of the people there had never heard patter like it.

'Two unemployed Glesga fellas wur walkin' along the street when they found a pay poke,' he began. 'They decided tae take it tae the polis station but they came past a pub oan the way. "Let's have a wee hawf o' whisky oot o' it before we haun it in." Anyway, wan thing led tae another and another. It wis nearly closin' time and wan o' them complained, lookin' at the empty pay poke, "If the bugger who lost this had worked overtime, we'd have enough fur a carry-oot."'

And there was more: 'A woman calls in tae see her neighbour and spots a statue o' King Billy sittin' oan a horse oan the mantelpiece.

'"Good heavens, Betty, Ah didnae know that ye wur an Orangewoman!" she says, pointin' at the statue.

'"King Billy!" shouts Betty in anger. "Wait till Ah get ma hauns oan that chancer in the Barras who sold me it. He told me it wis Lester Piggot!"'

As the laughter died down, I got into conversation with Gordon, a history undergraduate at Aberdeen University. He was a straight-talking guy with a big mop of curly hair. He said, 'All those idiots in Glasgow who shout about King Billy and the Pope haven't got a clue what they're on about. Today, Rangers fans hate Celtic fans and vice versa but that wasn't always the way it was. Celtic invited Rangers to their first-ever competitive match in 1888. The boys in green won but they all ended up having supper together at St Mary's Hall in Abercromby Street. Now, this thing about 1690: King William of Orange did beat James II at the Battle of the Boyne but at the time King William and the Pope were political allies. Prayers of thanksgiving were said in the Vatican because the battle was seen as a victory for papal intentions.'

This was mind-blowing stuff. So, I asked him, did this mean that all the bigoted banners and chants about King Billy and the Pope were based on a misconception?

'Yes, and all those mindless morons who believe in sectarianism have based their anger and hate on a distortion of history.

'I did hear a funny story about it, though. At the River Boyne on the evening of 12 July 1690, King Billy was wandering around the battlefield. He chanced upon his father-in-law, the vanquished King James, sitting dejectedly on a grassy slope. "I can't believe it," King James says to King Billy. "I don't know how we managed to lose. We outnumbered you. We outflanked you . . ."

'"Don't worry about it," King Billy reassures him. "It's just another battle. In a fortnight's time, who'll remember the Battle of the Boyne?"'

As the party was coming to a close and all the wine and beer had been drunk, Peter the Poet was still in deep sleep, snoring on a bed. Gerry came up with a madcap idea. 'Right, let's get his troosers and underpants aff,' he said. One of the students helped him to do so, leaving Peter half naked. Gerry and his new pal were laughing uncontrollably. Gerry then pulled out a condom, placed it over a pencil and inserted it into Peter's behind, pulling the pencil out and leaving the condom in there. We left the room and Peter, still snoring on the bed. The next morning, he came into work with an extremely worried look on his face. In fact, he was in a very sullen mood and didn't say a word to anyone for a week. I never saw him get so drunk at a party again.

28

ELECTROCUTION LESSONS

D URING THE SUMMER, STAYING IN THE STAFF HOUSE was like living on a university campus. I can barely recall having what I would then have considered a 'normal' conversation with my fellow residents; everything seemed to have an intellectual slant. The living conditions, however, meant that, ironically, we all lived like primitive beings. Every morning, there was a long queue at the house's large kitchen sink, where we bathed before going to work. I had to laugh, thinking that here I was cooped up with some of the best minds in Britain and yet we were all washing ourselves in the same manner as I had as a child in my Gorbals tenement.

Most mornings, I would strike up a conversation with Peter the Poet, who eventually recovered from the condom-up-the-bum incident. He was able to laugh about it after I told him all about Gerry's prank. I thought it would have been far too cruel not to reveal the truth to him.

'Bastard!' he said in his posh voice. 'That fellow should go back to the f***ing gutter where he belongs. Thank goodness you told me! I was convinced that I'd been rogered. My guttural Glasgow friend, you have done me a favour, so I am going to do you a favour: I am going to teach you how to speak properly and get rid of that dreadful accent. When I first met you, do you know what I had images of when I heard you speak?'

'Whit?' I replied.

'Poverty, violence and general harshness. I'll try to help you train your voice so that you will be able to go anywhere and speak with confidence.'

I agreed, rather reluctantly, to these lessons, joking with him,

'Thanks very much, Peter, fur the kind offer o' electrocution lessons.' Later, another Oxford student told me that Peter supplemented his income by giving elocution lessons to foreign students, for which he made a pretty penny. He also taught the art of public speaking and had been very successful. So I felt that I'd got a good deal, being given these tutorials for free.

Over the course of the summer, Peter and I would sit down with a bottle of wine and he would drum his lessons into me. 'The Glaswegian working classes tend to speak with a lazy tongue,' he said, 'which results in slurred words. What's more, many of them seem to find it hard to put their thoughts into words without uttering an expletive. Glaswegians swear in everyday communication and this marks an impoverished vocabulary.

'Let me give you an example,' he said, smiling now. 'A soldier from Glasgow goes to see his commanding officer and tells him he has domestic problems.

'"Well," says the officer, "tell me all about it, man to man, and don't hold back."

'The soldier says, "Ah went f***in' back hame last week, oan unexpected leave. Ah got intae the f***in' hoose and there wis nae sign o' ma wife in the f***in' kitchen. Ah went intae the f***in' livin' room and there wis nae sign o' her there. Ah went up the f***in' stairs intae the f***in' bedroom and there wis ma wife cohabitin' wi another man."

'There is no doubt about it, Glaswegians are great at swearing but poor at speaking the Queen's English. They can use the same expletive as a noun, an adjective or an adverb, sometimes all at once. It may be a kind of art but it's not one that's going to impress a lot of people.'

To an extent, I agreed with what Peter was saying; but did I really want to speak proper? Wouldn't it alienate me from my real pals in Glasgow? I didn't want to end up sounding like Little Lord Fauntleroy. Over the next few weeks, I worked out a solution: I could be bilingual, speaking Gorbalese with my pals and switching to a more refined accent when I felt I needed to.

My first lesson with Peter was a real eye-opener. He told me off for not moving my lips properly to accentuate the pronunciation of words. 'Most Glaswegians hardly move their lips at all when they speak. They're like ventriloquists. Remember, language is a powerful tool; it's not what you say but how you say it that counts. I don't want to turn you into a snob like me, just a fellow who can be understood by anyone from a dustman to a king.' I'd spoken with quite a few midden-men in the past, so that wasn't a problem; the king part might just be a bit harder.

After a few lessons, we were joined by Hazel, a drama student from Edinburgh who felt she needed more confidence in public speaking. She said, 'I'm really fascinated by the use of the Scots language, among all classes, and I'm writing a comedy show about it to take to the Edinburgh Festival.'

She told us that her mother and father were friends of Scottish showbiz royalty, including comedians Jimmy Logan and Rikki Fulton and the actress Molly Urquhart, and these people often called round to her family's house armed with funny anecdotes.

Hazel told a great story about Molly Urquhart. 'She'd left mainstream drama to become a successful comedienne and after her first appearance in a revue at the Theatre Royal, the audience gave her a standing ovation. With applause and cheers still ringing in her ears and laden with bouquets of flowers, she arrived back at the flat she shared with her widowed father. She rang the doorbell and the door was flung open. Before she could utter a word about her accomplishment, the old gentleman shouted at her, "Dae ye know there's no a slice o' breid in this hoose?"'

I told Hazel about the boys and I going round the city picking up patter and cruising for punchlines and she said, 'That's amazing! I do the same, in Edinburgh and Glasgow, but it's Glasgow that usually provides the better material. I think it's something to do with the different cultures. Edinburgh, of course, is more middle class and everything is done behind net curtains. But in Glasgow it's all out in the open. I remember once I was on a bus heading to Queen Street for a train to Edinburgh when I noticed my former schoolteacher, a very refined Morningside lady, sitting near me. She was dressed in tweeds and had a fancy feathered hat on. The bus got caught in a traffic jam and I heard her say to the clippie, "My dear, can't this bus go any faster? I must get back to Edinburgh to prepare my husband's tea."

'The clippie replied, "Missus, if ye had as many feathers oan yir arse as ye have in yir hat, ye could fly hame."'

We laughed and I chipped in: 'Have ye heard the story aboot the Glesga man who saved up over 25 years tae take his wife oan a cruise? Oan the boat, she got talkin' tae an elderly Edinburgh woman who said she was a regular traveller: "My husband works for Cunard, you see."

'Slightly miffed, the Glesga woman replied, "Aye, hen, ma man works f***in' hard as well."'

Hazel giggled and said, 'What's that famous quotation? "The people of Edinburgh are like they are because they were all conceived while their parents were fully clothed."'

After my electrocution lessons, we all headed to the Caledonian Hotel's bar, the Waterlot, for a pint. Even there, it was hard to escape the ongoing education.

Inside, Gordon the history student was propping up the bar. I told him about our chat on the old Edinburgh versus Glasgow chestnut and he said to me, 'Edinburgh considers itself a lady and thinks Glasgow is like a loud tart. It's the same as the way posh Perth looks at her working-class neighbour Dundee.'

The man was like an encyclopedia on legs. He told me, 'Edinburgh's not always had all the good press, though. In the seventeenth century, Daniel Defoe said: "The town of Glasgow, though not so big, nor so rich, yet to all seems a much sweeter and more delightful place than Edinburgh." And Samuel Pepys described it as "a very extraordinary town for beauty and trade, much superior to any in Scotland". Mind you, you don't want to look too far into what Pepys had to say about Scotland. He also said that "a rooted nastiness hangs about the person of every Scot – man or woman".

'You should be proud to come from Glasgow. It's a very popular name. There are loads of them in the world, one in Jamaica and several in America. There's also a New Glasgow in Nova Scotia.'

I was interested to hear about these other Glasgows and, as I walked home, I thought that I wouldn't mind seeing them. But I also thought to myself that Glasgow was more than just a name, more even than just a place – it was a state of mind.

29

~~~~~~

SWEET SORROW

B Y THE END OF THE SUMMER SEASON IN OBAN, I FELT as if I'd already been to college. I thought I'd probably learned more from these brains of Britain than I would have done at university.

I spent a lot of time with Peter and Hazel, and also got to know Hazel's boyfriend Duma, with whom she had built up a relationship over the course of the summer. He was Ethiopian and a very good-looking bloke – tall, extremely dark, with a slim but powerful physique. Before coming to Britain, he had lived in a refugee camp, where he'd learned some English from the British Red Cross workers who manned the camp. He worked in the restaurant as a pot washer, although he often boasted that when he'd first arrived in Britain he'd worked as a gigolo. 'The older women love a young, fit African man like me,' he laughed, 'and they paid well. The older they were, the more money they'd pay!'

I liked him a lot but my perception of him changed one day when I asked him what his ambition was. 'I want to make a young British woman pregnant. Then my child will be British and so will I.' This seemed a fairly dubious attitude to me and I felt wary on Hazel's behalf. Perhaps his overly pragmatic approach to relationships was understandable, though. His life so far had certainly not been easy. As he told me, there had been times when he had had to fight for survival. 'The civil war left me an orphan,' he said, 'and millions of us were starving. Only the strong made it through and every day was a battle to get food and water. I have seen things that you would not believe but I am a survivor. I have no family left and my only comfort is the love of a good woman. But there are many women out there and I want to love as many of them as I can before I grow old.'

Duma and Hazel joined me and some of the other kitchen staff one night at the Waterlot bar and heads turned when they entered. Even as late as 1974, it was still quite unusual to see a white woman with a black man and indeed I had never seen a racially mixed couple in Glasgow or Oban. Duma didn't drink alcohol because he was a Muslim but Hazel was not averse to a glass of red wine. When Duma went to the bar to fetch her drink, a crowd of drunken fishermen decided to pick on him and one shouted, 'Ya big black bastard, why don't ye f*** aff back tae where ye belang instead o' shaggin' white women.' Hazel's face drained of blood as two big bearded guys made their way towards Duma.

What happened next surprised me. I was expecting Duma to be beaten up but it was he who launched an attack. He head-butted one of them and then knocked out the other. Five more fishermen joined the fray, shouting, 'Ya f***in' darkie bastard, we're gonnae kill ye!' But they had underestimated Duma. He was fast and very effective; within a few minutes, he had either knocked them out or kicked and punched them to the ground. He said that he had learned fighting techniques in the refugee camp, where he had had to fight to survive. I had never seen a man go ahead with such ferocity, not even the hardest of cases in Glasgow.

Afterwards, we were in the staff accommodation when he said to me, 'Why are the Scottish so racist? Hazel and I are in love and colour shouldn't matter.' She agreed, nodding her head, but I wasn't sure if Duma was being absolutely truthful when he said he loved her. Later, we were joined by Gerry who said to Duma, 'Ye're the talk o' the toon! Ye knocked oot three fishermen and ye've sent another three tae hospital. Remind me no tae be cheeky tae ye in future, 'cause ye really know how tae scrap.'

A few days later, we were all preparing to leave. Everyone else was asking one another what they were doing next and most were saying things like, 'Oh, I'm going back to Oxford,' or 'I'm starting a law degree at Cambridge.'

When I answered, a quizzical look came over people's faces when I said, 'Ah'm goin' tae Langside College, Glasgow.' I was too ashamed to admit that it was a further-education college and I was going there to do O grades. When I told Peter how I felt, he said, 'Just tell them that Langside is one of Scotland's top colleges and that you're doing a degree. Most of them are from England and they'll never know. Anyway, don't be ashamed that you're only doing O grades – it's a start on your way to success.'

On the last night of the season, we had one final staff party. It was an interesting affair, and pretty wild, too. Peter and Gerry were both in full flow. Referring to me, Peter addressed the party, saying, 'My young friend here is going back to Glasgow to study, and may he do well. Having said that, that dreadful city has given us one of the worst poems ever written, which is about its coat of arms:

> Here's the tree that never grew,
> Here's the bird that never flew,
> Here's the fish that never swam,
> Here's the bell that never rang.

'I could have written something better when I was three!'

Peter took another glug of wine and suddenly he became very emotional. It had dawned on him that we were all going our separate ways and might never see each other again. 'I've had a fantastic summer here in Oban,' he said, 'and made many fine friends. But, like all good things, it must come to an end. Parting is such sweet sorrow! We are born, we learn, we earn and we buy. We eat and we drink, we sleep and we die!'

I could sense another poem coming on. Peter said, with tears streaming down his face, 'In these final moments of our fantastic summer I am reminded of the words of Robert Burns.' Then he recited:

> Pleasures are like poppies spread,
> You seize the flow'r, its bloom is shed;
> Or like the snow falls in the river,
> A moment white – then melts for ever.

As he finished the poem, almost everyone at the party had tears in their eyes. It was the end of an era, the final moment of summer when we had all loved, laughed and learned from each other.

Gerry came over and said to me, 'It's back tae Glesga fur me, too. Ah'm gonnae try tae gie it another go wi ma missus. Besides, Ah need tae be in Glesga tae pick up the patter fur ma act. Ah've got a chance to dae a support slot at the Pavilion and if Ah go doon well there, it should take aff.

'Ah'll tell ye wan mair funny story before Ah go,' he said. 'A teacher says tae her class, "What vegetable can make you cry?"

'A wee boy sticks his haun up.

'"Yes, Johnny?"

'"A turnip, Miss."

'"A turnip? How do you work that out?"

'"Well, if ye get hit in the baws wi a turnip, it brings tears tae yir eyes."'

With that, Gerry headed off, shaking my hand warmly. 'Remember,' he said, 'we're aw in the gutter but some o' us ur lookin' at the stars.'

As Gerry left, I noticed that Hazel was sitting alone in a corner crying hysterically. I asked her what the matter was. 'It's Duma,' she sobbed. 'He's gone and left me, the bastard. He's run off with that Swedish waitress and flown out of the country with the bitch.'

I tried to console her, saying, 'Ach, he's that sort o' guy. It's aw fur the best. Ah don't think he wis yir type, anyway. Duma's a man aboot toon; he isnae the sort o' fella that can stick wi wan woman. That's the way he is and that's the way he'll always be. Anyway, don't worry, ye've still got yir play tae take tae Edinburgh and Ah'm sure it'll be a big hit fur ye.'

But her tears kept flowing and she shouted, 'There'll be no play next year – no way!'

'But Ah thought ye'd written it?' I said.

'I have,' she said.

'Well, whit's the problem?'

'I'm pregnant,' she wailed. 'F***ing pregnant to Duma and I'll never see him again.'

I didn't know what to say. I gave her a kiss on the forehead and found myself uttering a line that I had heard when I was a child at chapel: 'God be wi ye.'

That wasn't the only sad farewell I had to say that night. While I was going back to Glasgow to start at Langside, Charlotte had decided to stay in Oban. Our relationship had come to an end. I left the room thinking, 'Parting really is such sweet sorrow.'

30

STUDENT LIFE

BACK IN GLASGOW AT LANGSIDE COLLEGE, I LOOKED
every inch the student. I'd bought myself a scarf to go with my
jeans and corduroy jacket. I might have looked like a degree student
at Glasgow University but in fact I was a 19-year-old washed-up
chef doing O grades. At first, this thought made me depressed; that
was until I started to attend the lectures and discovered that there
were a lot of students much older than me.

For example, there was Jim, a 45 year old who had worked in
a factory most of his life. He was studying for O grades and his
plan was to go to Glasgow University and read law. There was
Margaret, a 50-something who had worked as a dinner lady but
now wanted to become an English teacher. Charlie, in his late 30s,
was a wild-looking fellow with a beard who had done numerous
jobs before packing it all in to hit the education trail. Alec from
Hyndland was a former shipyard worker and union official in his
early 30s who wanted to go to Aberdeen University and then into
teaching. There was one really old guy who must have been in his
70s. He said he wanted to do O grades to keep his mind alert. Alec
quipped, 'He wis the wan that cut the breid at the Last Supper.'

The other students, much younger, were a mixture of the bright
and the not so bright. Some had simply been lazy at school and
others had been thrown out for misbehaving. Almost everyone I met
had the same aim: to get to university and make something of their
life. During the first few days, I had genuine doubts about whether
I'd be able to keep up. However, when I talked to my fellow students,
I found that they were nowhere near as educated as my comrades in

Oban and none of them were as streetwise as me, and that gave my confidence a bit of a lift.

The following days and weeks were filled with, amongst other things, learning Latin and reading Homer's *Iliad*. The Latin classes were particularly gruelling. We had to learn by rote things like the verb 'to love' (amo, amas, amat . . .) until my head was filled with the language. Indeed, I began to think in Latin and the smallest things would make me laugh, like when I saw the word 'EXIT' on a pub door and automatically thought, 'he goes out'. The advantages of doing Latin, although it was a dead language, were that it improved my spelling and enabled me to understand big words because so many of them were derived from Latin.

History was a subject I began to love. One day, as the lecturer was explaining the causes of the First World War, I noticed a little window cleaner outside the classroom wiping the windows with his shammy. It was freezing cold outside and I thought, 'It's a great life being a student! Look at that poor little bastard out there cleaning windaes for a living and I'm here discussing the Archduke Ferdinand and his assassin Gavrilo Princip of the Black Hand Society. Yes, it's a student's life for me!' History amazed me. What I learned tied in with what I'd discovered on the streets of the Gorbals. People made mistakes and kept on repeating them. History proved that, over the centuries, people simply did not learn from or take heed of the past. The first two world wars were a classic example of that.

Economics was another subject I warmed to. I especially liked the topic of inflation, which the lecturer defined as 'too much money chasing too few goods'. I had known this all along, seeing prices rise in Glasgow shops when items were in short supply. But now I could articulate it in more educated terms.

It struck me that these subjects were really a matter of common sense. The main thing was to 'screw the nut' and get down to studying as hard as possible. I would spend hours in the college library poring over Latin books and reading up on my other subjects. Some days, I left the library with my head buzzing with the information that I'd crammed in. Biology fascinated me, too. When I looked at the structure of a flowering plant and learned how it attracted bees to pollinate it, I thought that there must be a God, because everything in nature is so perfectly planned, down to the very last detail.

The college social life was very good and we'd often go for a pint to a little hostelry just up the road, the Mulberry Hotel, where we'd discuss what we'd learned that day. Alec, the ex-union guy, was usually the centre of attention and he had a knack for attracting very beautiful young women to go along with him for a pint. Once in the bar, he'd regale all and sundry with his stories.

One evening, he said to me, 'Ah know ye're enjoyin' yir Latin but have ye no noticed that Glesga has its ain language within a language? Ah mean, wan common word is "fondia".'

'Fondia?' I said.

'Aye, fondia. Ye hear it aw the time. Like "he's fondia a good bucket" or "she's fondia big vodka" or "they're fondia laugh". Also, the word "ochawan" is very common. Like "ochwan take a runnin' jump tae yirsel" or "ochawan bile yir heid".'

We got to chatting about Glaswegian speech and I said to Alec, 'Another great thing is the way ye get words jam-packed together. Like when ye go abroad ye might hear Glaswegians say "selluvahoathere" or "ahmferrbilin". And when it rains you hear things like "scummindoonbuckits" or "ahmbliddidrookit". And then there's the familiar wan that we aw use: "allawafurrapint".'

'So ye can stick yir Latin where the sun disnae shine,' said Alec, 'the Glesga language is far mair interestin' and a lot funnier. Dae ye know where wan o' the best places tae go is tae hear real Glesga chat?'

'Whit, the Barras?' I asked.

'Nah, that's too obvious.'

'The pubs or Paddy's Market?'

'Nah, it's the law courts. The Sheriff and High courts ur great entertainment value. Ah've spent many a rainy day there passin' the time away, soakin' up aw the atmosphere, talkin' tae the defendants and the lawyers.'

'The thing aboot Glaswegians,' I said, 'is that we speak wi the heid but we hear wi the heart. There's an auld tale that sums it up. An apprentice joiner wis called in tae fix a neighbour's pulley as a favour. Havin' completed the work, he went through tae the livin' room and said to the woman, "That's yir pulley fixed, Mrs Cameron. Noo ye can get yir claes up." She wis a bit taken aback and said, "Well, awright, but Ah was goin' tae gie ye a bottle o' whisky."'

On these nights in the Mulberry, an element of competition usually developed between Alec and fellow mature student Charlie. Alec hated it if Charlie came up with a better story than him but Charlie often did, as he was also a great raconteur. Alec pretended to think him a bore, saying, 'That Charlie fella is aboot as funny as rabies in a dugs' home.' But Charlie always held his own against what some argued was stronger competition.

That night, he said, 'Ah would disagree wi ye slightly, Alec, when ye say the courts ur the best places tae hear the patter. It's mixin' wi folk when they're oot and aboot that provides the best laughs. Ah wis in the Plaza Ballroom wan night when two wee herries wur comin' oot the toilets. Ah heard wan o' them say, "Hey, hen, dae ye know ye've got a Tampax behind yir ear?" The other wan replied, "Oh God, whit have Ah done wi ma fag?"'

Alec responded with another story: 'There wis a young mother pushin' her pram through Kelvingrove Park when she got intae conversation wi an auld woman, who peered intae the pram and said, "That's a bonnie wean ye've got there. And whit a grand heid o' hair! Is the faither red-heided as well?"

'"Ah don't know," the girl replied. "He never took his bunnet aff."'

One night, we were joined by a crowd of students whom Alec knew from Hyndland and Partick. One of them was a philosophy student, an annoying fellow who kept trying to turn the talk round to his specialist subject so that he could control the conversation. 'Why are we here?' he kept saying in an extremely annoying high-pitched voice.

'Jimmy,' Alec replied, 'ye're here because it wis Hogmanay and yir faither wis oan leave fae the army. If ye don't believe me, ask yir maw – she's the wan that told me.'

After getting steamboats in the pub we would all head to the local fish-and-chip shop, where I would order a fish supper and a steak pie wrapped together. I would then place it on a wall and bash it with my fist so that pie, fish and chips all mingled together. It tasted wonderful. As far as I was concerned, this was eating out at its best.

Some nights, a group of us students would catch a bus over to the city centre. We were outside Central Station one night when I spotted a little chancer pinching a half-bottle of whisky from a shop and stuffing it into his trouser pocket. But a few moments later, he fell on the icy pavement and a wet patch began to spread across his trousers. Alec and I went to help him up and he shouted, 'Oh, naw! Ah hope that's blood.'

Later, Alec and I went into the men's lavatory in the station to relieve ourselves of the vast quantity of beer we had consumed. But when we got inside, the urninals were all occupied and, though we waited for several minutes, none of the men made a move to leave. By this time, Alec and I were bursting but still no one moved from the urinals. Alec just lost it. 'F***in' willie watchers! Let me in fur a pish and then ye can go back tae lookin' at each other's todgers.'

At the time, there were no gay bars in Glasgow and the station toilets, especially on Friday night, were full of homosexuals from all over the west of Scotland.

I was mortified when Alec zipped up his fly and shouted to no one in particular, 'Hey, Ah'm homosexual: Ah like ma sex at home. Ah'm also bisexual: if Ah cannae get it fur nothin', Ah'll buy it.'

31

JEKYLL AND HYDE

IN THE COURSE OF MY STUDIES, I READ ROBERT LOUIS Stevenson's *The Strange Case of Dr Jekyll and Mr Hyde* and thought that, oddly enough, I was a bit like the central character. During the daytime at college, I dressed like my fellow students, while at night-time, with my wild Gorbals pals, I reverted to my sharp suits. I'd also developed two completely different Glasgow accents: a slightly middle-class one for college and my original rough, guttural one for my wayward friends. This worked most of the time and I was effectively living two completely different lives. Sometimes, though, my two worlds collided.

One bright sunny afternoon, I was walking through George Square accompanied by two beautiful student girls from the West End, when I noticed a group of young guys heading in our direction. My heart sank, because they were all Gorbals gang members and they recognised me straight away, although they were a bit surprised to see me kitted out in student-style clothes. One of them, Big John, looked me up and down and said, 'Fur f***'s sake, you've changed yir image since Ah last saw ye. Whit happened tae yir Arthur Black tailor-made shirts and yir sharp suits?'

The two girls looked shocked that I knew this man, who was every inch the ex-jailbird. I turned on my roughest Gorbals accent. 'Naw, the flashy suits ur auld-fashioned. The trouble wi you, pal, is ye're stuck in the past. Ye've got tae move wi the times and casual gear like this is the in thing. Helps ye tae meet beautiful birds like these,' I said, pointing to the girls.

Big John laughed, as did the rest of his gang, and replied, 'Aye, MacFarlane, ye always wur a fly man and if ye can attract women like these two then ye must be daein' somethin' right. Ye should see the state o' ma bird, she's got a face like a ragman's trumpet. Maybe Ah'll start wearin' the casual gear.'

The two girls laughed nervously and I replied, 'Aye, ye've got the patter awright; it's jist that the birds nowadays willnae even look at ye if ye're decked oot in gangster gear. Move wi the times, fur f***'s sake! Ah still wear the suits, though, when Ah'm cuttin' aboot wi the boys at night. But it's horses fur courses: casual gear wi the birds in the daytime and gangster gear wi the boys at night. Anyway, where ur ye headed?'

'Oh, up tae the f***in' Sheriff Court. Ah'm in front o' that auld bastard J. Irvine Smith and he jist loves sendin' people doon. Ah think it's his hobby.'

He and the boys then headed off to find out their fate at the court. One of the girls was blushing as her father was a sheriff and Smith was a friend of his who regularly called round to her house in Kelvinside.

'My God, they were so rough!' she said. 'How in heaven's name do you know them? They looked like the sort who would steal the sugar out of their granny's tea.'

It was time to back-pedal and think of a quick cover story. There was no way I could admit that I was a former gang member who used to roam the streets of the Gorbals armed to the teeth. 'Oh,' I said, 'a few months ago I helped some social worker friends to set up a youth club in the Gorbals. That's where I met those guys. They sound rough and ready but they really are the salt of the earth.'

'But when you were talking to them, your accent changed. You were more Gorbals than they were,' the sheriff's daughter said.

'Yeah, well, that's the secret of communication: change accents according to which social class you're addressing. That way, you can converse with pauper or prince,' I replied. The girls laughed, I laughed and we headed off across George Square. I was beginning to enjoy being a Jekyll and Hyde character.

I thought about what Big John had been saying. J. Irvine Smith was a name that most Glasgow criminals feared; he had a reputation for taking no nonsense in court and sending people to jail without hesitation. He had become a legendary figure over the years and his pronouncements often appeared in the *Evening Times* and the *Daily*

Record. As one chap was being led away to begin a lengthy sentence, he let slip, 'F***in' bastard.' Smith had great hearing and picked this up. Asked to elaborate, the nervous felon, realising he had made a grave mistake, claimed it hadn't been a reference to the sheriff. Smith had a different opinion: 'I don't see anyone else in the courtroom who answers that description.' Another time, when a transvestite appeared before him, he deferred sentence and told the defendant to 'go away now and be a good girl'.

Glasgow's criminals were aware that it was utter folly to be cheeky to him. After he'd sentenced one man to three months' imprisonment, the guy declared, 'Three months! Ah could dae that standin' oan ma heid!'

'In that case,' replied the sheriff, 'you can have another three months for contempt of court. Perhaps that will help you find your feet.'

A few days after my encounter with Big John, I changed into my fly-man gear and hit the town with Alex and Chris. Alex was a handsome bloke, thin with jet-black hair, and when he was done up, he looked like a Mediterranean Romeo. He had the patter to match and the girls loved him. Sometimes, though, he managed to attract really rough women.

That night, he got talking to a group of herries from Possilpark in the Tolbooth Bar at Glasgow Cross. 'There wis a wee Gorbals woman rubbin' expensive cream intae her diddies,' he was saying, 'and she told her man it wis guaranteed tae increase the size o' her tits. Her man said, "Why don't ye jist get a dod o' toilet roll paper and rub it in yir cleavage?"

'"Will it work?" the woman asks.

'"Well, it worked oan your arse," her man says.'

The girls laughed and one of them asked him, 'Where dae ye come fae, Alex?'

'Costa del Gorbals!' he replied.

'Is that no helluva rough?'

'Rough?' Alex said. 'It's got so bad that up in the chapel they've had tae put in a new confessional box: eight items or less.'

He noticed one of the girls, a tough-looking lassie, was heavily pregnant.

'Who's the faither?' he asked.

'Ah couldnae tell ye. Hivnae a clue,' she replied.

'Oh, come oan,' Alex said, 'ye must have an idea who the faither is!'

The young lady thought deeply for a moment, took a drag of her cigarette and said, 'Put it this way: if ye eat a tin o' beans, ye don't know which wan made ye fart, dae ye?'

We had quite a good evening, going from pub to pub, and both Alex and Chris were on top form. A beggar approached Chris and asked him for some spare change, to which Chris replied, 'Away ye go and f*** yirsel. Ye'll jist have tae go oot and shoplift like the rest o' us.'

Alex shouted, 'Listen, pal, Ah've got enough money tae last me a lifetime . . . that's if Ah die the morra.'

On our travels through the city-centre pubs, we bumped into a guy who was selling dodgy gear. 'Dae ye want tae buy a Superman T-shirt?' he asked. 'They're aw the rage in America at the moment.'

'How much?' I said, suspecting the stuff had fallen off the back of a lorry.

'In the shops, ye're gonnae pay a fiver but Ah'm no gonnae charge ye that. Thirty bob!'

It was always wise to haggle. 'A pound,' I offered.

'A pound it is!' said Mr Dodgy.

I slipped on my Superman T-shirt and looked at my reflection in the mirror behind the bar. It looked brilliant, if a trifle unusual.

'A pound tae be Superman fur the night. Noo that is a bargain,' said Mr Dodgy.

About an hour later, we were all standing outside the Royal Stuart Hotel at the Clydeside when a police car pulled up alongside us. A policeman, suspecting we were up to no good, rolled down his window and bellowed, 'Hey, f***in' Superman and pals, whit ye daein' hingin' aboot here?'

Perhaps it was the superhero image that gave me the confidence but I walked straight over to the car and said, 'We've jist been oan a pub crawl. Whit the f*** has it got tae dae wi you, ya big ugly bastard. Tell me, is that yir face or is yir arse up fur a breather?' I was instantly lifted for breach of the peace.

In the cells at the central police station, I decided to plead not guilty and take my case to the Sheriff Court for trial. I was sure I could talk my way out of the charge as I had now developed, thanks in part to the Latin, a wide-ranging vocabulary. I thought I could put many Glasgow lawyers to shame. Also, in my mind, my alternative posh accent was very powerful. I was convinced that I could win the Superman trial.

On the day of my court appearance, I sat in the public gallery watching all the cases before mine. There was a young fellow charged with assault and breach of the peace. The court was told that he was an ardent Rangers supporter who had got into a fight with a Celtic fan.

'And how did this altercation begin, leading you to assault the man?' the prosecutor asked.

The defendant, who wasn't exactly the Brain of Britain, replied in a serious tone, 'He called me a dob. And that jist got me aw riled. There wis nae chance he was gettin' away wi that. Ye jist cannae walk aboot callin' somebody a dob – it's jist no right. That's why Ah stuck the heid oan him, the dirty Fenian swine. Naebody calls me a dob and gets away wi it.'

The sheriff, who happened to be J. Irvine Smith, looked at a complete loss. He leaned over the bench and said to the prosecutor, 'I am a bit puzzled here. What exactly is a dob?'

'Yes,' said the prosecutor, 'this is a trifle confusing. You say the man you assaulted called you a dob. What exactly is a dob?'

The defendant replied, 'Well, sir, dob is short fur dirty Orange bastard.'

The sheriff looked aghast and said, 'Well, you learn something new every day. But even if he called you a dob that's no real excuse for breaking the man's nose with your head. I'm going to fine you £25 and the reason that is so little is because you taught me a new word today.'

Alec had been right: the courts were great entertainment value. It was better than paying to go to the pictures. Here we had real-life comedy and drama, with characters that few screenwriters could have dreamed up.

I'd panicked a little when I saw that it was to be Smith who would deal with my case but he seemed to be in a wry sort of mood as he dealt with a variety of absurd cases. One man offered to pay his £10 fine at a rate of £2 a month, to which the sheriff replied, 'I'm here to dispense justice, not run a catalogue.'

Another defendant appeared before him for 'pishing up a close' – in other words, urinating in a public place. The sheriff asked him, 'What exactly do you work at?'

'Ah work at the depot humphin' ginger crates aroon. And sometimes Ah have tae stack aw the ginger.'

The sheriff asked the defending solicitor, 'Humphing ginger? What sort of job is that? I can't understand what he's talking about.'

The solicitor, a verbose man, replied, 'My client is employed by a soft-drinks company that retails aerated waters to the general public for their consumption. He has the menial job of carrying crates of soft drinks from one establishment to the other.'

'Ah, I see,' said the sheriff. 'Why did he not say that in the first place?'

The use of language in the court fascinated me. It was clear that if you were well spoken you had a better chance of getting off. I remembered a story somebody had told me about a man who appeared in court and when asked if he had anything to say, replied, 'F*** all.'

The sheriff said to the prosecutor, 'What did that man just say?'

'F*** all, your honour.'

The sheriff replied, 'I could have sworn his lips moved.'

When my case came up, although I was a bit nervous, I was confident that I would get off. The prosecutor read out the details of the charge: 'It is alleged that the defendant was approached by a police officer in a panda car who thought he and the group of youths with him were acting suspiciously. The defendant then became abusive to the officer, swearing and shouting, and was subsequently arrested for breach of the peace.'

The policeman then took to the dock and swore to tell the truth, the whole truth and nothing but the truth. 'We wur drivin' near the Clydeside at the Royal Stuart Hotel when we noticed a gang o' youths behavin' in a suspicious manner. Wan o' them, the defendant, was wearin' a Superman T-shirt. When Ah asked whit he wis daein' he acted in a violent and aggressive manner, swearing loudly, and was subsequently arrested.'

Then it was my turn: 'Officer, I don't know how you can swear on the Bible that you are telling the truth when in fact your evidence is a pack of lies. I did not act in a violent and aggressive manner. I merely swore at you after you called me "f***in' Superman" when we first encountered each other.'

'Ah cannae recall sayin' that,' he said, but I noticed a certain nervousness in his voice.

'Well, officer, you did say that and I have several witnesses who will verify this. You acted in an aggressive manner towards me. I was merely defending myself. Do you know that you are in danger of committing the very serious crime of perjury if you persist with the assorted mistruths in your manufactured story?'

The big policeman spluttered. I think he must only rarely have encountered a defendant who could stand up for himself. 'Tae tell ye the truth,' he said to the sheriff, 'ma notes fur that night ur a bit faded because ma notebook got damp in the rain and ma memory is a bit hazy aboot this particular case because we arrested aboot ten people that night fur breach o' the peace and he wis jist wan o' them.'

I then addressed the sheriff, still using my poshest accent: 'It is obvious that the officer has an unclear memory of the events surrounding my arrest and I say there is no case against me.'

The sheriff and prosecutor looked impressed by my legal patter. Smith had a wide grin on his face when he said, 'Very well put, young man. It is not every day we have Superman in court. Case not proven, which means, Superman, you can fly away now and continue to save the world. But try to keep away from police cars in future.'

I felt elated – in fact, I felt like Superman – as I left the court.

When I got back to the flat in Shawlands, there was a letter waiting for me. It was my exam results: five As and one B (Latin, of course). I had cleared two great hurdles that day, one legal and one educational. I was on a roll.

32

A STRANGE SUMMER

NOT LONG AFTER I GOT MY RESULTS, ANOTHER letter arrived out of the blue. It was a strange-looking missive, with the address in weird spidery writing. I recognised the handwriting but I was at a loss to recall where I had seen it before. Then it came to me. 'Ah, Fast Eddie from school.' Now, Fast Eddie was, to put it mildly, a wild bastard. He was always in fights when we were kids and he'd done the odd robbery or two. We'd been at the same primary and secondary schools and he was always up to some trick or other. His speciality was nicking women's purses from coats if he saw them hanging up in a workplace, café, hairdresser's or pub.

At school, during playtime one day, he'd sneaked out of the playground and stolen a wee woman's purse from her coat, which was hanging up in a nearby hairdresser's. I thought it was a despicable thing to do but Eddie was a kleptomaniac and that was just the way he was. Somebody had seen Eddie nicking the purse and a squad of police raided the school and lifted him while he was in woodwork class. He got sent to approved school but he loved it there, saying it was like Butlins, that the food was great and he got to play football every day. It was more than five years since I had seen Eddie, so what was he up to now?

I opened the letter up and it was stamped 'Barlinnie Prison, prisoner letter'. This didn't surprise me. Sure, he was a born thief but he wasn't a very successful one, as he was always getting caught. The letter said:

Hello, pal.

Away ma holidays again! This time for 18 months. Somebody gave me your new address in Shawlands so I have enclosed a pass for you to come and see me this week. See if you can make it and we'll have a laugh. A few of your old pals are in here and they are all asking for you.

   Best wishes,

   Eddie

   PS Bars do not a prison make!

Later that week, I caught a bus to 'the Big Hoose', as Barlinnie was known. I went through some giant gates and was led into a waiting room where the prison guards checked to see if I had any contraband on me. Then I was taken into a large room where all the prisoners were waiting. Eddie was sitting there with his jailbird gear on and had a broad smile on his face. 'Ah knew ye'd come,' he said. 'Ye're the sort o' guy who disnae let people doon. It's always great tae see a familiar face. Mind you, there ur quite a few in here already.'

He was right enough. I looked around the visiting room and half the people there I had either gone to school with or I knew from the streets of the Gorbals.

'So, whit ye in fur?' I asked.

Eddie began to laugh and shake his head. 'F***in' mad, it is, pure mental. Ah got drunk wan night and decided tae haud up a corner shop wi a startin' pistol. Me and a couple o' ma pals went intae the shop and we shouted tae the fella behind the counter, "Gie's aw the money fae the till or we're gonnae shoot ye." The wee Asian guy wis terrified. Even his turban wis shakin'. He handed us aw the money, a few hundred quid, but as Ah turned ma back tae make the getaway, Ah wis whacked oan the heid wi a baseball bat. F***in' sore, it wis. The bastard had it hidden behind the counter. Ah tried tae run aff but he kept hittin' me over the heid until Ah wis unconscious.

'When Ah woke up, Ah wis in the Southern General wi a big polis sittin' beside ma bed. The other fellas got away wi a few quid and aw Ah got wis a thumpin' headache that lasted fur two months. The doctors thought Ah might have brain damage so Ah used that tae ma advantage. When the CID turned up and kept askin' me who the other two robbers wur, Ah said the baseball bat had given me amnesia and fur the life o' me Ah couldnae remember a thing aboot the robbery. In fact, Ah said ten years o' ma life had gone missin'. Ah wis expectin' at least five years in jail but the court took into account that Ah might have brain damage and gave me a lighter sentence o' eighteen months. Ah've got twelve months tae go. Funny how life turns oot. Ah never thought that Ah'd get beaten up by a guy in a turban.'

I had known Eddie since he was a small boy and I reckoned that even then he'd had some sort of brain damage, because he certainly wasn't the full shilling.

He leaned over to me and whispered, 'Anyway, Ah want ye tae dae me a favour.'

'Whit's that, Eddie?' I asked.

'Well, ye know that bird Ah wis goin' oot wi fur years?'

'Whit, Big Ina?'

'Aye, well, since Ah've been inside another bloke has been shaggin' her. Ah want you and the boys tae gie him a doin' fur me. Put him in hospital, the dirty nae-good bastard.' Then he shook my hand and pressed a small piece of paper into it. 'That's got the guy's name and address oan it. Make sure he gets sorted, OK?'

I put the piece of paper in my pocket and nodded my head, saying, 'Aye, OK, Eddie, fur auld time's sake.'

'Aye, fur auld time's sake. 'Cause we've been pals since the Pope wis an altar boy. Jist show him he's been messin' wi the wrang people. Ah know Ina's got a face like a well-skelpt arse but Ah love her; she's been good tae me. Ah'm jist tryin' tae protect ma future interests, if ye know whit Ah mean.' He chuckled as he was led away by a burly guard.

Outside, I looked at the piece of paper with the man's name and address on it. If I'd been a ruthless person I would have passed it on to the relevant violent parties. But I crumpled the paper up and threw it into a puddle. That fortunate man doesn't know to this day what a close escape he had. If I met Eddie again I'd just say that the guy had moved away and I hadn't been able to find him. I didn't know what all the fuss was about, anyway. Big Ina was so ugly we used to joke that strangers gave her sweets to stay out of their cars. Chris said she was so unattractive that dogs closed their eyes when they were humping her leg.

The following afternoon, Chris, Alex and I, with several other guys, were passing by an off-licence in Eglinton Toll when we decided to go in for a carry-out. We only had enough money for a few cans of beer, which we intended to consume in front of the telly during a Celtic–Rangers match. We waited a few minutes and, much to our surprise, nobody appeared, even though a bell had gone off when we'd entered. I shouted, 'Service! Is there anybody there?' but it was like addressing a graveyard. At last, a little old lady appeared and said, 'Whit can Ah dae fur ye, boys?'

'Gie's a dozen cans o' Tennent's lager,' I said.

She disappeared into the back room and we waited – and waited and waited. Alex joked, 'Fur f***'s sake! Ah feel like the guy in the story who waited and waited until he forgot whit he wis waitin' fur!'

Finally, the old lady appeared with the lager.

'There ye ur, boys. Anythin' else Ah can get ye?'

Alex was quick off the mark. 'Aye, hen, we'll have another six cans o' lager.' She went off into the back room once again and we all jumped on the counter and helped ourselves to an abundance of whisky, brandy, vodka and other spirits, passing them to two of the boys who were standing outside. A few minutes later, the old lady came back again with the lager. 'Is that aw noo?' she said.

'Aye, missus,' I replied, 'that'll dae us fur the big game.'

We left the off-licence sniggering and proceeded to get extremely drunk on all the buckshee spirits.

A week later, we decided to try the same tactic once again. The bell on the door went and a young guy ran out and said, 'Can Ah help ye?'

'Aye,' I replied, 'could ye gie's a dozen cans o' Tennents?'

'Aye, nae problem,' he said. And as quick as lightning he placed the cans on the counter.

'Thanks, pal, that wis quick,' I said. 'What happened tae the auld woman who used tae serve here?'

'Auld Bessie?'

'The wumman that wis here last week.'

'We had tae get rid o' her,' he said. 'The auld bastard wis drinkin' aw the stock.'

The time had come for me to get out of town and go on my annual jaunt to Oban. But when I got there, the atmosphere in the restaurant was a lot flatter than it had been the year before. The staff had been cut back and they had severely limited the number of students they were employing. Hamish, the kitchen-porter philosopher, was still there and he warned me, 'A new German head chef has taken over and he's a right little bastard. He reminds me of one of the guards from *The Colditz Story*. We call him 'the Commandant' because working with him is like being in a prisoner-of-war camp.'

'Surely the guy cannae be that bad?' I said.

'Worse!' Hamish replied. 'Just you wait and see.'

I didn't bump into the Commandant for a few days as he had gone to Hamburg to attend a family wedding. When he did arrive back in the kitchen, it was as if a black cloud had descended over the place. He was a small bald man with a manic look in his eyes. I introduced myself to him and he said, 'I've heard about you. You're the Glasgow man who walks around telling funny stories. Well, this year, no funny stories. There is no time for stupid jokes, it will be work, work, work! That is the only way to keep me happy. A hard worker is worth ten times more than a fool who tells funny stories.'

I felt like kicking him in the balls right there and then but I didn't want to throw my job away so I kept quiet, as did the rest of the chefs. A few days later, I was in the kitchen and a big box of apples was sitting on the work surface. I took one out, ran it under the tap and bit into it. It tasted delicious but the Commandant had spotted me. He shouted, 'Is this how you repay us? By stealing from the company? You are a thief and I do not like thieves in my kitchen. You should be severely punished for this.'

I had had enough of his chat. 'It's only a f***in' apple. Whit's the big deal? Probably costs aboot tuppence. Ah took a bite oot an apple and noo ye're treatin' me like wan o' the defendants at the Nuremberg trials.'

At that, his face turned bright red. 'Get out of my kitchen,' he shouted. 'Out now, you thief!'

I thought to myself, 'Who the f*** does this wee German bachle think he's talking to? Did we not win the war against guys like this?' Then I thought, 'F*** it!' I turned round and kicked him right in the balls. It was a cracker, spot on. He went flying across the kitchen and as he did so he collided with a pot of tomato soup, which cascaded all over him. 'F*** you and yir f***in' apples,' I shouted. 'Ye can stick yir job and yir apples up yir arse. Away ye go and raffle yirsel, ya f***in' nasty wee Nazi bachle.' Then I threw off my chef's gear and walked out. 'I shall be mastered by no German bastard,' I thought.

However, there were serious drawbacks. I had to give up my staff accommodation, for a start. I rented a room in a flat near the harbour. The flat was home to a mad guy, originally from Glasgow, his alcoholic missus and his two very hyperactive children. It was hard to get a decent night's sleep in the place. Both the landlord and his wife got drunk on cheap wine most nights and spent hours singing songs out of tune. And when they fell asleep, the kids would be running about the place shouting and bawling.

As an emergency measure, I got myself a job at a seaweed-processing factory that was a 20-minute bus ride from town. The pay was almost double what I had got at the restaurant but, of course, I now had to pay for food and rent, so it worked out about the same. The factory produced sodium alginate, which was used in things like toothpaste as a natural preservative.

When I got to the factory, having caught the staff bus at 7 a.m., it reminded me of the Southside Sawmills. A lot of the older guys had been there donkey's years. My job was to stand at a machine and fill a bag full of processed seaweed. Then another bag and another bag . . . and another bag until my eight hours were up. It was mind-numbingly boring. I asked my colleague Donald how long he had been working on this machine filling bags. 'Oh,' he said, 'more than 25 years. But I never find it boring, I always have my mind on other things. That's the secret: keep your thoughts on other matters – maybe women, beer, holidays, anything to occupy your brain. That way, nothing is boring and the time goes fast. Who knows, if you follow my advice you could be here in 25 years like me.' The very thought of it made me feel as if the life was draining out of me. Twenty-five minutes was long enough in this place.

I had only been in the job a week when a strike was called, something to do with overtime payments. I found myself involved in a union meeting with hundreds of other workers, heckling the managers and shouting things like, 'The workers united will never be defeated!' In a way, it was fun and at first I saw it as another experience, another adventure for a Gorbals guy. But the strike dragged on for weeks and eventually all my money ran out. I ended up walking up and down the front, going into hotels and asking if they were looking for a chef.

I spent most of a day doing this and eventually I found a small hotel that needed an extra pair of hands in the kitchen. When she interviewed me, the owner-manager seemed a bit suspicious and asked where I had worked before. I didn't mention the Oban restaurant I'd got the sack from but handed her two glowing references from Glasgow – forged, of course.

'Hmm,' she said, looking at the references, 'these look pretty good. You didn't make them up, did you?'

I gave a false laugh, 'Oh, no, they're completely kosher. I've worked in some of Glasgow's top hotels and restaurants.'

'OK,' she said, 'you can start tomorrow morning.'

She told me my accommodation would be a large luxury caravan at the back of the hotel. The wages were also very good, ten pounds more than I had been receiving before kicking the Commandant in the balls.

My first day at work was a real eye-opener. The kitchen was run by a woman in her late 50s. At 7 a.m. when we were preparing breakfast, she reeked of whisky. She was also a heavy smoker and walked around the kitchen with a fag constantly in her mouth. She really was an accident waiting to happen.

'Now, young man,' she said to me, slurring her speech, 'I am the boss and what I say goes. If I say it's a Tuesday and it's a Sunday, you've to agree with me that it's a Tuesday. My word is final, understand?'

'Aye, Ah understand,' I replied. 'Sure, it's a Tuesday!'

She laughed and walked off, staggering slightly.

One of the waitresses pulled me aside and said, 'You won't last long here. No cooks do. When she gets really drunk she gets abusive and they all end up walking out. I wonder how long you'll last? We're thinking of running a book on it.'

Over the next few days, I bit my lip as the drunk cook launched insults at me. I didn't want to end up back at the seaweed factory again. I could put up with insults – I'd heard enough of them on the streets of Glasgow – but I'd had a bellyful of processing seaweed.

Her derogatory comments were relentless, though, especially

if she'd been drinking heavily. 'Any similarity between you and a human being is purely coincidental,' she would say, or, 'You know, some would say you're not fit to sleep with the pigs. I stick up for the pigs.' One of her most imaginative ones was: 'I thought I saw your name on a loaf of bread over there. But when I looked again it actually said "Thick cut".' A favourite was: 'It's mind over matter: I don't mind and you don't matter.' After a few days, I began to realise that the insults all had a funny element to them and were never as vulgar as some that I'd heard guys using in the Gorbals.

Nonetheless, she did get to me at times. But how could I wreak vengeance? I couldn't exactly kick her in the balls, seeing as she didn't have any. So what was her weak point? The first rule of battle is to find the enemy's Achilles heel and attack it. It suddenly came to me: smoking in the kitchen while preparing food! However, I decided I would do nothing until she had hurled a particularly nasty insult at me.

The next day, she slurred at me, fag in mouth, 'Are you depriving a village somewhere of an idiot?' That was it. She'd gone over the line. But I stayed calm and said nothing. Instead, I went outside to the pavement and picked up half a dozen cigarette ends. I stuffed them in my trouser pocket then went back into the kitchen. We were serving up mince and tatties for a large Rotary Club lunch. I walked over and placed two fag ends in one plate and then stuck three others in another. The dark mince and gravy covered them perfectly.

In the restaurant, some of Oban's top businessmen were sitting waiting for their lunch. A waitress rushed in and took the steaming plates away. I waited for a reaction. Nothing for a few minutes, then it happened like a bomb going off.

'Aaaaarrgh! My God, there's fag ends in my mince!' one man shouted.

'Christ!' cried another. 'Mine too! This is disgusting! Get the manager!'

The owner-manager went out to try to placate her guests, apologising profusely and asking them if they would prefer another dish.

One man shouted, 'Another dish? Get me a bucket, I want to be sick!'

The other bellowed, 'I will never eat in this place again! Cigarette ends in the mince! If that's what you can see in the food, what about the stuff you can't see?'

The owner was furious. She stormed into the kitchen and shouted at the cook, 'You are a bloody disgrace! You're drunk all the time and you walk about smoking endless cigarettes. You're not a cook, you're a health hazard. I could lose my food-hygiene licence over this. Get out of this kitchen now and sober up. I'm not going to sack you but I am suspending you until you get treatment for your alcohol and nicotine addictions.'

At this, the cook began to cry. I didn't feel sorry for her, though. In fact, I thought I'd done her a good turn, setting her on the road to rehabilitation. The next day, a new temporary cook arrived, who was really quite nice. But I didn't particularly care, because I was back off to Glasgow for my second year at college.

33

THE COAT OF ARMS

BACK AT LANGSIDE COLLEGE, I CONTINUED TO advance along my learning curve. I started to read all sorts of literature: the works of Shakespeare, George Orwell's *Nineteen Eighty-Four* and *Keep the Aspidistra Flying*, Tolstoy's *Anna Karenina*, Dostoevsky's *Crime and Punishment*, Jack London's *People of the Abyss* and a plethora of other works, including major Latin texts. That year, 1975–6, I was doing Highers, the Scottish equivalent of A levels, and I was determined that I would end up on a degree course in '76. I didn't have a bloody clue what I was going to study but psychology was still an option I was considering.

After reading all that high-class literature, I thought back to what Peter the Poet had said about the poem describing the elements that make up Glasgow's coat of arms:

> Here's the tree that never grew,
> Here's the bird that never flew,
> Here's the fish that never swam,
> Here's the bell that never rang.

He'd said he could have written something better when he was three and I could see now that he was probably right. But as I thought about the wee poem, I realised that over the years I'd picked up a Glasgow story for each line.

HERE'S THE TREE THAT NEVER GREW

Strolling through Queen's Park, I'd often spot a young Corporation gardener tending to a little tree. It was as if the tree was his baby. He spent a great deal of time watering it and nourishing the soil around it. But I noticed that, even after a couple of months, the small tree hadn't grown any bigger, despite the care and attention it had been given.

One sunny afternoon, I went up to the young gardener and said, 'That wee tree disnae want tae grow up. Dae ye think it'll ever be any bigger or will it be a wee bachle tree aw its life?' The gardener looked at me and said nothing. I continued, 'Ah suppose that wee tree is jist like a baby tae a guy like you. How long have ye been a park gardener?' He looked away and said nothing. 'Ignorant bastard,' I thought. I tried one more time to see if I could get a response out of him. I thought that a joke might do it. 'Hey,' I said, 'how dae ye stop moles diggin' in yir garden?' He made no response. 'Ye take away their shovels!' Still no response, not even a giggle. 'Ignorant bastard,' I thought once again. I was pretty angry by this point so I said, 'F*** you and yir midget tree,' and I walked off. I couldn't believe that he'd completely ignored me.

But a few weeks later, it all fell into place. It was reported in the paper that a Celtic supporter had been arrested at an Old Firm match for shouting abuse at the police. His lawyer pleaded not guilty on his behalf and two big policemen told the court that the young man had shouted, 'F*** the polis!' and had been singing anti-Protestant songs. It seemed they had a clear-cut case against him until his lawyer said, 'My client has been a deaf mute since birth and it would be a miracle for him to speak. He cannot hear or talk and the policemen have a lot of questions to answer after the debacle of charging such a man with breach of the peace. Somebody is telling lies and it certainly isn't my client, because he has never spoken in his life.'

Of course, the police said it was a case of mistaken identity – nothing to do with the fact that they were very good at making up lies against the accused. When I looked closely at the photograph of the deaf man, I realised it was the gardener who had not replied to me. I was embarrassed at how rude I had been but I was relieved that he couldn't have heard me cursing him and the tree that never grew.

HERE'S THE BIRD THAT NEVER FLEW

In Jamaica Street, there was an amusement arcade called Treasure Island. When it first opened, the management decided it would be a great gimmick to have a large parrot in a cage at the entrance that shouted out things like 'pieces of eight' and 'Long John Silver'. I asked the manager how much this exotic creature had cost and he said, 'A couple o' hundred quid. They parrots ur rare. But it gets the punters in and the gamblers like it.'

'But what if it flies away?' I asked.

'Nah,' the manager replied, 'that parrot is goin' naewhere. It's had its wings clipped and it wis bred in captivity. It's never flown in its life and it's no aboot tae start noo. There's mair chance o' me flyin' oot this gaff than that bird.'

The parrot duly appeared in the local papers, which reported that it had been an expensive acquisition for the arcade. This was not missed by the local criminals. One night, I popped into Treasure Island and the cage was still there but the parrot wasn't.

'Whit happened?' I asked the manager. 'It didnae fly away, did it?'

The manager replied, 'Some bastard nicked it last night when we wur busy and wurnae lookin'. They'll probably sell it oan the black market fur a few bob.'

'Ur ye gonnae get another parrot?' I asked.

'Nah,' the manager replied, 'whit's the point? We bought a parrot that couldnae fly but it still left the premises – in the hands o' some dodgy swine. Some people in Glesga will steal anythin', even birds that cannae fly.'

HERE'S THE FISH THAT NEVER SWAM

Big Archie was a guy in his late 50s who had never been married. He lived near Gorbals Cross in the last of the crumbling tenements. Every now and again, I'd see him in either Glasgow Green or Queen's Park with a little fishing net, which he would use to catch tiny fish known as 'baggie minnies' in the park ponds. But Archie had aspirations: he dreamed of becoming a professional fisherman and one day winning the pools so he would be able to buy a boat to get big catches. Of course, it was all a pipe dream and he could come across as a bit of a sad character, hanging around the park ponds.

I bumped into him one day and he invited me back to his house for a cup of tea. We strolled along from Queen's Park, Archie carrying a small jam jar containing two minute tiddlers. He seemed very proud of his pond-life catch. As he was making the tea, he explained his philosophy in life. 'Fishin' is the greatest hobby in the world,' he said, 'and Ah'd love tae dae it properly but ye need the money behind ye. There ur two kinds o' fishermen: those who fish fur sport and the wans that actually catch somethin'! There's a fine line between fishin' and standin' oan the shore lookin' like an idiot.'

I asked him when he started fishing and he said, 'Aboot ten years ago. There's a story behind it. Ma faither wis a right auld swine and we never got oan. He and ma maw lived up the Gallowgate and when Ah moved tae the Gorbals, Ah used tae drop in and see them at least wance a week. Ma faither wis in a good job as a clerk wi wan o' the big whisky firms and when Ah started workin' as a building-site labourer, he looked doon oan me. Fae when Ah started workin' at 15, we barely exchanged a word. He couldnae stand the sight o' me. When Ah went tae visit ma maw, he would leave the hoose and we didnae speak fur years.

'Aboot ten years ago, ma maw passed away and me and ma da began talkin' again. He said that, as a boy, he'd often fished in the great lochs o' Scotland, and, although he wis in his 70s, he wanted tae dae it again. So we ended up goin' salmon and trout fishin' together in the Tay, the Dee, the Ness, the Spey, the Tweed and the Helmsdale.

'Deep in the lochs there wis an abundance o' wild trout, some as big as 18 inches long. When we went fishin', it wis as if the terrible past between us had never existed. It's strange but true; we wur able tae talk aboot things like we never had before. Fishin' together healed aw the auld wounds that had kept us apart. We wurnae that interested in how many fish we caught or how big they wur. It really wis aboot enjoyin' a good friendship fur the first time in our lives.

'Although Ah was in ma late 40s and he was in his late 70s, we wur like two little boys, gettin' together and enjoyin' life. We laughed most o' the time and a wee bit o' good malt whisky in our flasks made things even mair pleasant. Fishin' changed both of our lives. The point wis, it was a chance tae put the past behind us and forgive each other. When Ah wis growin' up, we hated each other but fishin' made us love each other. He died a few years after we took it up and at that time he was ma best pal.'

Tears began to run down his cheeks. He wiped them with a large hankerchief and asked, 'Dae ye know whit the secret o' happiness is?'

'Whit?' I replied, shocked at his sudden display of emotion.

'Go fishin' and enjoy life! Maybe some day we can be pals, wet a line and catch a fish together. Noo that would be somethin'!'

In his living room, there was a large fish mounted on a plaque on the wall. It looked beautiful. I asked him, 'Where did ye catch that beauty?'

He laughed. 'The Barras!'

'The Barras?' I said. 'They don't sell fish like that there. The best yir gonnae dae in the Barras is a fish supper.'

'It's no real,' he said. 'If ye look closely, it's made o' plastic. It's the fish that never swam!'

HERE'S THE BELL THAT NEVER RANG

Rab was a funny fellow. He was always changing his mind. Like me, he was a guy who'd grown up on the streets and tried numerous jobs since leaving school. I met him at Langside. At first, he planned to end up at university but he found it hard to study, and reading and writing were problems for him. He ended up going to a doctor who arranged for him to take some tests and it was discovered that he was dyslexic. In those days, this was considered a huge disadvantage academically and he decided to pack in the studying. However, he came up with an alternative scheme.

'Ah'm gonnae start runnin' a pub,' he told me. 'Ma uncle ran it fur a few years. He hardly made any money oot o' it but Ah'm sure, if Ah gie it a go, it could be the goose that lays the golden egg fur me.'

The pub in question was situated on one of the back streets near the Gallowgate. I called in to see Rab the first week he was in charge. The place was absolutely dead and I joked, 'Hey, Rab, ye don't need a chucker-oot here, ye need a chucker-in.'

'Aye, but Ah've got a plan,' he said. 'Ah'm gonnae start gettin' in aw the heavy drinkers, like those guys who live in the models, and wance they're in, the money'll be pishin' doon.'

It was a strange plan but I hoped it would work for him. Certainly, if he could attract his clientele from the models then he might have a chance of making a tidy profit. At the time, the model lodging houses in Glasgow, such as the Great Eastern Hotel, housed hundreds of homeless men whose downfall had been the demon drink. Most of the beggars in Glasgow lived in such places and they spent all their earnings on booze. It was the same with the other residents; as soon as they got their dole money, it was quickly spent on alcohol.

I called back in to Rab's pub a few weeks later and it was teeming with people. They were rough-and-ready characters who would scare the shite out of ordinary law-abiding folk. They drank cheap red wine and beer, and it looked like many of them hadn't been near a bar of soap for a long time. But this conglomeration of drunken characters was a delight to watch and listen to. They were old-time Glaswegians, up for a bevy and a laugh, and they didn't give a damn.

I was sitting beside one old shabby fellow when suddenly a terrible smell wafted from him throughout the pub. Rab came over and said to him, 'Have you jist shat yirsel?'

'Aye,' said the old fellow.

'Well,' said Rab, 'why don't ye go tae the lavvy and clean yirsel up?'

But the old guy replied, 'Ah've no finished shiteing yet.'

These so-called undesirables defended their heavy drinking with a great sense of humour. One confessed to me, 'Ah went tae see the doctor and he said, "There are two reasons for your poor health: drinking and smoking."

'"Thank f*** fur that," Ah said, "Ah thought ye wur gonnae say it wis ma fault."'

The inebriated regulars often gave Rab a hard time but he had been around the block and knew how to handle their cheek. One shabby bearded fellow staggered over to the bar and shouted, 'Hey, Rab, this beer tastes like pish.'

But Rab didn't lose his cool. He shrugged his shoulders and merely replied, 'Listen, pal, you've only got a pint o' pish; Ah've got three barrels o' it.'

I noticed that some of the drinkers had a certain degree of style when they ordered at the bar. A wee bachle came in one night and shouted to Rab, 'Ah'll have a Southampton, and make it quick.'

Rab looked confused and said, 'Whit's a Southampton?'

The wee drunken bachle replied, 'A large port, ya stupid bastard!'

At closing time, Rab would take a large maritime bell from behind the bar and ring it loudly. As he did so, he'd shout to the shabby degenerates, 'Time up, ya drunken bastards! Get back tae yir models. F*** aff before the polis come.'

At this, they'd all drink up and leave with hardly any trouble. The last thing any of them wanted was to be banned from the place, as they couldn't get served anywhere else.

After everyone had left one night, I watched Rab counting the money from the till. It was a considerable amount. He waved a wad of notes at me, saying, 'Ah told ye! Ah'm aboot the only guy in Glesga that's mad enough tae sell them drink. It's jist a pity Ah had tae ring the bell fur closin' time, otherwise Ah could have coined it in even mair.' We sat down for an after-hours drink. Rab had put all the notes on the table in front of us. 'Ah've got an idea!' he said. This was not a good omen because Rab was a bit of a greedy guy and I had a premonition that his idea could lead to trouble. 'F*** ringin' the bell fur last orders!' he said. 'Ah'm gonnae start openin' night and day.' About a week later I returned and you could hardly move in the place. Word had got round that Rab's place was open all hours.

Sometimes social workers and probation officers called into the pub to see their clients, whom they knew they could always find there if they'd not turned up for an appointment. I remember watching one young social worker, wet behind the ears, sitting with a bunch of the regulars. He seemed fascinated by the experience, as if he was researching material for his PhD. One of the old men was rubbing a little ball between his fingers. 'This looks like plastic but it feels like rubber,' he slurred.

'Let me have a look,' said the young guy, rubbing the ball between his fingers. 'You're right, strange material. Where did it come from?'

'It jist fell oot ma nose,' responded the drunk.

For months, closing time came and went, and the bell never rang for last orders, although the till rang constantly. Rab simply locked the doors, pulled the curtains and let the customers drink themselves into oblivion until the early hours.

Finally, one morning the place was raided by police and everyone was arrested. Rab got a heavy fine, was threatened with jail and lost his publican's licence. He said to me after the court case, 'Ah still made a few bob oot o' it, thanks tae the bell that never rang.'

34

THE GODFATHER

IN MY SECOND AND FINAL YEAR AT LANGSIDE, I CAME across a variety of individuals who looked quite normal and acted in a respectable manner but were in fact half cracked. One such fellow was Eric, a middle-class teenager from out of town who had just been released from a mental institution having served ten months there. When I asked him directly, if rather bluntly, what had led him to be 'carted aff tae the funny farm', he replied cheerfully, '*The Godfather*.'

'Whit, the gangster movie *The Godfather*?' I asked.

'Yeah,' he said. 'Well, my mother and father sent me to boarding school and it cost them a pretty penny. They gave up a lot to ensure that I had a top-class education, which doesn't come cheap.' He asked, 'Did you go to a good school?'

'Aye,' I replied, 'it was so good it was approved.'

He continued, 'Anyway, I was doing fine but then this new master arrived and he was a real sadistic little bastard who delighted in giving me the belt or the cane for no apparent reason other than that I was me. In my dorm at night, I'd cry myself to sleep thinking about the pain he'd inflicted on me and I vowed revenge. After yet another beating from him, I went to see *The Godfather* and it gave me an idea.'

'Whit wis that?' I asked.

'Well, you know that scene where Al Pacino goes into the restaurant and picks up a gun from the toilet cistern then walks back into the dining room and shoots the guy through the head?'

'Aye?' I said.

'Well, I tried to do the same. I knew that the teacher ate alone every Friday night at a certain table at a local Italian restaurant. So on the Thursday night, I went in with a revolver wrapped up in waterproof material and hid it in the cistern.'

'But where did ye get the gun?' I asked.

'Easy. My uncle was the chairman of the local gun club and I stole one from his collection. The next night, the Friday, I walked into the restaurant and saw the little bastard sitting alone at his corner table. The place was so busy he didn't notice me as I strolled to the toilet. I got the revolver out of the cistern and calmly ambled right through the restaurant to his table. I put the gun to his head and he spluttered through a mouthful of spaghetti bolognese. I pulled the trigger but the revolver didn't go off. The next thing I knew, I was jumped upon by three Italian waiters, who wrestled me to the ground before the police arrived. They wanted to charge me with attempted murder but the psychiatrist said I wasn't well, not fit to plead. That's why I spent ten months in an asylum. It could have been worse; I could have got ten years.'

'But wur ye mad?' I asked.

'Well, I was, and I wasn't,' he replied. 'I'm a great film buff and I saw that scene in *The Colditz Story* where the prisoner of war pretends to be mad to the Germans. I did a bit of that, sort of play-acted for a while. And then after a few months in the loony bin, I acted as if I'd returned to my normal self. They soon gave me the all-clear and let me go.'

'Hey, Eric,' I said, 'can ye dae me a favour?'

'What's that?' he said.

'Well, if ye crack up again and ye want tae dae everybody in, will you promise to spare me?'

He laughed, replying, 'No problem! I'll make an exception for you!'

It turned out that Eric's parents had shipped him off to Glasgow to escape the shame. After his Highers, he hoped to study (of all subjects) law at Glasgow University. The guy was always full of surprises.

He and I got elected to the Entertainments Committee, which meant we were responsible for things like hiring bands and arranging disco evenings at a nightclub in the city centre. Eric was on a limited allowance so he was always thinking up money-making scams. A big disco was to be arranged for near Christmas and we sat down to discuss the plan.

'Right,' he said, in the tone of a commanding officer leading his troops into battle, 'we will have 1,000 tickets printed but officially there will be 800. That means me and you keep 100 each and sell them on for a tidy profit.'

I agreed to go along with the scam. I felt sure that nobody would find out about the extra 200 tickets. Besides, like him, I was a poor student and any income was a helpful boost, especially £200 each, which was what we ought to end up with.

Eric was so good at thinking up such schemes that, with his ill-gotten gains, he was able to buy a second-hand Mini, which he used to chauffeur me about Glasgow in. He loved to meet all the characters I knew and they in turn usually said it was a pleasure to meet him.

One night, the Mini broke down in Sauchiehall Street and we looked under the bonnet. 'The piston's gone,' Eric said.

A drunk fellow staggered over and shouted, 'Hey, pal, whit's the matter wi yir motor?'

'Piston broke,' said Eric.

'Well, so am Ah!' said the drunk before staggering off.

Another of Eric's scams was to order 12,000 rag mags (a booklet of jokes produced and sold to raise money for charity), keep 2,000 for himself and then sell them, pocketing the profit. I'd often see him going up and down the streets of Glasgow shouting, 'Get your rag mag here, full of great jokes and it all goes to charity.' The joke was that the charity was Eric.

When I got to know Eric a bit better, he told me his problem was that he had never felt loved by anyone, not even his mother and father. Perhaps that explained his almost manic-depressive behaviour. One minute he'd be up and the next down.

'We'll have tae find ye a nice woman,' I said. 'Somebody that ye can love and she can love you.' I suggested he try harder at the discos we had arranged to get talking to a nice young girl who could transform his life. But it turned out that Eric's chat-up lines were a disaster. He said things like 'I seem to have lost my number. Can I have yours?' and 'If I could rearrange the alphabet, I'd put U and I together.'

The problem was that his lines were too tame and most of the girls thought he was a creep. I suggested that he make them more saucy, stuff like 'I may not be Fred Flintstone but I can make your bed rock,' or 'Shag me if I'm wrong but is your name Helga?' Even this was not successful, though. When he walked up to one gallus young lady and said, 'I know how to please a woman,' she replied, 'Good, that means ye'll f***in' leave me alane, ya ugly bastard.'

These rejections only made him more depressed and he told me that he had gone to the doctor for antidepressants. In the college refectory, he showed me a large bottle of pills and said he had to take two, three times a day. 'They've made me feel a lot happier. They put you on a real high. They're better and a lot cheaper than alcohol. Try a couple, they'll cheer you up.'

I wasn't really into drugs but, seeing him in a happy mood, I thought that I'd at least have two of his happy pills to see what happened. At first, I felt nothing. I left Eric at college and walked into a newspaper shop in Langside, intending to buy a copy of the *Daily Record*. But a few moments later, I found myself outside the shop in a daze wondering what I had gone in for. I was suffering from instant amnesia; perhaps that was the secret of beating depression. As an old guy told me once, 'The secret o' happiness is good health and a bad memory!' It was quite true but I didn't trust drugs that made you forget things. Sure, I was in a game now where we had to remember and memorise things daily.

A few days later, Eric phoned my house in Shawlands and announced, 'I've had enough. I'm going to throw myself off Jamaica Bridge.'

'Nah, nah, nah,' I said, 'don't dae anythin' till Ah get there.'

I jumped in a taxi and when I got to the bridge, Eric was standing there looking intently at the Clyde. I talked him out of drowning himself and we ended up in McSorley's pub, where I bought him a couple of large whiskies.

'I feel as though I have nothing to live for. I can't even get myself a girlfriend,' he said.

'Look,' I told him, 'the summer's comin'. Why don't ye join me and we'll get a job in a hotel fur the season? Fur the past few years, Ah've been in Oban but Ah want tae try somewhere different. Any ideas?'

Eric seemed to cheer up at this. 'Yes! Brighton in Sussex. It's a beautiful place. My parents took me as a kid and I felt really happy there. There was wonderful sunshine all the time. The climate's great and the place is really lively.'

It was agreed then that we would both find a job in a Brighton hotel. We even went to Buchanan Street bus station the next day and booked single tickets down south for after our exams the next week.

We both felt our exams had gone well. The bus was due to leave at ten on the Friday night. We arranged to meet at a local pub beforehand for a few bevies before the 12-hour journey. In the pub, I got talking to a guy who had a suitcase with him. It turned out he was a waiter and was also heading to Brighton.

'Have ye got a job lined up?' he asked.

'Nah, me and ma pal Eric ur jist gonnae try our luck.'

'Don't worry aboot findin' a job. Ah'm good pals wi the manager o' a hotel and Ah'll get the two o' youse a start straight away. The hotel's right on the seafront.'

I waited and there was still no sign of Eric. My new friend the waiter, a weedy-looking man with prematurely grey hair, explained that he was from Parkhead and went to Brighton every summer. 'The beach, sunshine, birds galore, plenty o' nightlife – ye cannae beat it,' he said.

I was excited by this description. But there was still no Eric.

'Listen, pal,' the waiter said to me. 'Ye couldnae lend me a tenner until we get tae Brighton? Ah'll pay ye back as soon as Ah get ye fixed up at the hotel.'

I only had about £15 on me but I handed him the tenner. After all, he was getting me a job and the money would be paid back in the morning.

Then the BBC news came on the pub's telly. The stern-faced announcer said, 'A gunman was arrested on the campus of a Glasgow college today after threatening staff and students.' There was footage of the guy being led away and, sure enough, it was Eric.

After another drink, I climbed aboard the bus with my new friend. I just thought, 'Eric is the past; forget about him. Brighton is the immediate future. Another town, another adventure.' Anyway, it seemed to me that problems were only regional: a problem in Glasgow is not a problem in Brighton.

35

SUMMER OF LOVE

AH, BRIGHTON, THE JEWEL OF THE SOUTH COAST! As the bus pulled in, the place was a complete contrast to the greyness of Glasgow. It was as if the colour button on your television had been turned up. The coach ground to a halt at the bus station, and the waiter and I got off. It was early but the sun was shining and the air warm.

'This is jist like bein' abroad and we're still in Britain,' I said to him, in an excited mood. But he merely grunted as we went to unload our suitcases from the back of the bus. 'Ye know,' I said, 'Ah think ye're right, this place is gonnae be fantastic.' I looked round and he had gone. Disappeared, vanished into thin air! What about my tenner? What about my promised job in the hotel? It was all a fairy tale he had told me to get money out of me. And I was a Gorbals street boy – how could he have conned me like this?

I picked up my suitcase and checked how much money I had in my pocket: just over three pounds. Enough maybe for a few pints and a pie but it was going to be a struggle to survive more than a day. I sat down in a local park but, funnily enough, I didn't feel all that downhearted. The sun was streaming down and I thought that it would be easy enough to sleep rough in a place like this.

I went into a nearby newsagent's and asked for the local paper, as I wanted to look at the job section. 'It'll be out in a couple of hours,' said the man. 'What sort of job are you looking for?'

'A chef in a hotel,' I said, 'wi accommodation thrown in, preferably.'

'Oh, you're a chef, are you? At this time of year there are plenty of jobs for chefs here.'

My heart lifted a bit and I headed to the nearest public toilets for a wash and brush-up. I was shampooing my hair in one of the basins when a large fat man appeared from a little room and shouted at me, 'Hey, you! You can't come in here and wash your hair! It's not that sort of toilet!'

'Whit sort o' toilet is it?' I said, my head covered in soapy bubbles.

'It's a toilet for tourists to use, not for down-and-outs to clean themselves up.'

I was getting increasingly annoyed by this pompous fellow. He had just called me a down-and-out. If I'd been back home in Glasgow, that would have earned him at least a punch in the face. I changed tack: 'Look, pal, this is a f***in' public toilet and Ah'm no daein' anybody any harm. Who the f*** ur you, anyway?'

He looked a bit taken aback at my outburst of aggression but I was reminded of what my mother had told me years before: 'Sometimes ye've got tae show people yir bad side before they see yir good side and respect you.'

He puffed up his chest and announced, 'I am the lavatory supervisor, the boss in here.'

I replied, 'Look, pal, ye're a f***in' shitehouse cleaner, so don't even think o' messin' wi me or Ah'll flush you and yir big mooth doon wan o' these toilets.'

He looked frightened. I began to dry my hair and he said, 'If you don't go now, I'm going to call the police!'

'Call the f***in' polis,' I shouted like a maniac, partly to frighten him more. 'Whit they gonnae arrest me fur? F***in' washin' ma hair? Is there a law against keepin' yirsel clean in this toon? Go and get the polis noo but ye've got wan big problem.'

'What's that?' he said in a tembling voice.

'If they arrest me, they've eventually got tae let me go and when they dae Ah'll be back here lookin' fur ye. Remember, Ah know where ye work; ye're easy to find. So that means Ah've only got to be lucky wance and you've got to be lucky aw the time.'

Suddenly, he ran off to his toilet attendant's room and locked himself in.

Ah! A victory over all the jobsworths in the world! Surely that was one battle worth fighting, even if it only involved a lowly toilet attendant.

I bought the local paper and scanned the situations-vacant section for hotels and restaurants. One advert caught my eye: 'Breakfast chef required for luxurious hotel. Free board and accommodation for the right candidate.'

'Fate!' I thought. I phoned the hotel and arranged to meet the head chef after lunch service. When I arrived at the hotel, the splendour took my breath away. There were chandeliers everywhere and Rolls-Royces and Bentleys outside. I showed the head chef my glowing forged references and he said, 'If you're this good, why have you come to Brighton all the way from Haggisland?'

I replied, 'Well, chef, I heard that this was one of the top hotels in the world and that you were the man to work with. That's why I've travelled all this distance to work under you and learn from your great culinary skills.'

It was all bullshit, of course. I had never heard of the hotel before reading the ad. But I could have sworn he blushed before saying, 'You look and sound like just the person I am seeking for this breakfast chef's position. The only problem is that the staff accommodation is full. You can start tomorrow morning but can you find yourself alternative accommodation for a couple of weeks until we have a spare room for you?'

I put on my best disappointed face. 'No, chef, I can't. I spent all my money to get here from Scotland, so there's nothing left in the pot, not a bean.'

He had a worried look on his face. 'Hold on, I'll sort this out for you,' he said. He picked up the phone, 'Hello, reception? Head chef here. I have a talented young Scotsman here who is coming to work for me as a breakfast chef. Can you find him a room?'

He put the phone down and after a few moments it rang.

'You can? Great! I'll send him along to reception now,' he said.

At reception, they handed me the keys to a luxury suite overlooking the sea. It was the sort of suite only millionaires used during the summer. As I lay back on my big double bed, I thanked God for my luck. I soon fell asleep. I had to be up at 6.30 for my first breakfast service.

In the morning, the sun was already streaming through the windows as I put my work gear on. When I got into the kitchen, I was surprised to see a brigade of ten chefs there, all immaculately dressed in ultra-white clothes and hats. By comparison, my whites looked very much like Glasgow sometimes does: drab and grey. The head breakfast chef, Roger, introduced himself to me and joked, 'F***in' hell, mate, where did you wash your gear, in a puddle? Don't worry about it, though. We have a great laundry here and by tomorrow you'll be decked out in the brightest chef's gear you'll ever wear. This is one of Britain's most exclusive hotels and they don't want to see any of the chefs looking scruffy.'

I struggled not to laugh as I thought of the old joke: 'How exclusive is it?'

'Well, it's so exclusive the guests have to wear a tie in the shower.'

Roger and his team were a highly skilled and organised brigade. Each chef had his own job: one would make the porridge, another the scrambled eggs, another fry the eggs, another cut and grill the bacon, and so on. So as not to make it boring, our tasks changed every morning. My first job was to cut and grill the bacon for the 200-odd guests.

Roger had a ferocious temper and when he saw me slice the bacon in a different way from his method, he quickly laid into me. 'No, not that way, you stupid clod!' he shouted. 'This way!' Over the next few days, he showed me how things should be done. It was his way or the highway. As so often in the past, I had to bite my lip, as I had no intention of giving up my luxury suite and the other trappings that went with the job. Besides, I'd noticed that many of the waitresses were the most beautiful women I had ever seen; some of them were aspiring models and former beauty queens working there for the summer.

As in the other restaurants where I had worked, there were a number of employees who were clearly round the bend. Take, for example, Manuel the Midget. He was a little Spanish fellow who was no bigger than a ten-year-old schoolboy. However, he boasted that he was a great lover. He said to me one day, 'There is an old Spanish saying: "Sex is like air – it doesn't matter until you aren't getting any."' He came into the kitchen most mornings with a scented hankie. He would claim that the hankie, or sometimes hankies, belonged to guests whom he had made love to the night before. He would approach fellow staff members and say, 'Sniff this handkerchief. This is the perfume she wore last night when I seduced her.' It always gave off a powerful smell of perfume, although that didn't really prove anything. I don't know if he was telling the truth about his seductions but the hankies were certainly amusing.

He certainly knew how to laugh at himself and was never short of midget-lover jokes. 'I met a woman last night,' he would say, 'and she told me, "I have never made love with a midget and I've always wondered about the size difference." I told her to take her clothes off and lie back on the bed. Within a few minutes, I had given her seven orgasms. I said, "If you think that was good, wait till I get both legs in there!"'

One of the kitchen porters was a guy called Roy from Babbacombe. He was as mad as a hatter and he specialised in naughty limericks, which he would recite with great gusto, especially if he had been at the bottle of scrumpy he kept hidden under his sink full of pots and trays. Limericks were not exactly a Glaswegian thing, so it was a real experience for me to hear them, especially in Roy's South Devon accent:

> There was a young fellow from Sparta,
> A really magnificent farter.
> On the strength of one bean,
> He'd fart 'God Save the Queen'
> And Beethoven's 'Moonlight Sonata'.

The hotel even had its own staff social club, where we all congregated. The club was run by the staff for the staff on a non-profit-making basis, which meant the beer was quite cheap. It was at the rear of the hotel and had a small bar, lounge and TV room. It was there I first got talking to Willem, a waiter from Holland. We got on well, as he had a good sense of humour and reminded me of some of the guys I'd been to school with in the Gorbals. I did notice one thing, though: he was always talking about his sister and how proud he was of her. He often showed me a photo of her and tears would form in his eyes. The photos showed she was a pretty dark girl in her early 20s.

'Dae ye miss her?' I asked.

'Yes, my friend, very much. There is not a minute in the day when I do not think of her.'

One night, Willem began talking about his sister once more but, this time, when he pulled out the photo of her, he began sobbing uncontrollably. I was a bit taken aback at his sudden change of mood and asked, 'Whit's the matter, Willem? If ye really miss her, why don't ye gie her a phone?'

'I can't,' Willem said, shaking uncontrollably.

'Why no?' I asked.

He sobbed as he replied, 'She was murdered five years ago. Her boyfriend strangled her after they had an argument. You know what I'm going to do?'

'Whit?' I said.

'I'm going to stay in this country until he comes out of prison, then I'm going to kill him.' He pulled out a photo of the guy with his sister and told me he knew where the guy's family stayed. 'I've been planning this for years,' he said. 'As soon as he comes out, I'll kill him. I'm just waiting for the time to come.' I could tell by the crazy look on his face that he was deadly serious. He pulled a sharp knife from his leather jacket and said, 'This will end his life quickly. I will slash his throat like a pig. He will squeal like a pig before he dies.'

What could I say? I heard myself come out with, 'Willem, when ye dae it, make sure Ah can visit ye in jail in Holland. Ah cannae disagree wi ye. Where Ah come fae, auld scores have got tae be settled, nae matter whit the consequences ur.'

A few days later, Willem seemed in a more upbeat mood. He came up to me at the club's bar and said, 'Do you know Kathleen and Lucy from Armagh? They're two of the most beautiful women I have ever met. They're coming down here in a few minutes to join me for a drink.' Willem was always praising women to the skies, no matter what they looked like, so I didn't really expect that much. But when the two girls walked into the club it was as if the sun had come out. They were both extremely beautiful, aged around 21. Kathleen had light blonde hair, a tremendous figure and a face that could have launched a thousand ships. Lucy was in the same league but dark-haired and sultry. They'd both been teenage beauty queens and it certainly showed. I got on with them straight away and all that night we couldn't stop laughing. The Northern Irish sense of humour is very similar to the Glaswegian one. As we got to know each other, a romance developed between Kathleen and me.

The summer of '76 was the hottest for almost 200 years and, after sunbathing every afternoon, we all looked rather bronzed and beautiful. One day, I was walking through the centre of town with Kathleen and Lucy when a crowd of guys stopped and just looked at us. I heard one of them say, 'It isn't fair. Some guys have all the luck!' There was one drawback, however. Kathleen had a rich boyfriend back home. One weekend, he turned up in his sports car in Brighton. I kept a low profile until he'd gone, as someone had told me he had IRA connections and I certainly didn't want to get on the wrong side of him.

At the height of the summer, I was walking along the high street and stopped at a newsagent's where I saw a pile of *Melody Makers* with the headline, 'Ross Reigns Supreme'. A giant photo of my brother Ross was on the front. He had been voted the best singer-songwriter in Britain at the age of 17. A recording contract and parts in *Jesus Christ Superstar* and *Evita* were to follow. Both of us were doing well – thanks to my father's Glasgow confidence lessons.

One day, a letter arrived for me. It was the results of my Highers. I had achieved four As, in economics, history, English and modern studies, and a B in Latin. This meant I was university material. Aberdeen had told me I would be accepted onto their English degree course if I got results that good. I went down to the club to celebrate with the girls and Willem. I told them that I would get in touch with Aberdeen University the next day. But Willem said to me, 'I have a better idea, my friend. Why don't you leave it for a year and join me in Barcelona?'

'Barcelona?' I said. 'Whit's happenin' there?'

'My best friend is opening a restaurant and he wants me to be head waiter. You can join me as a waiter or a chef. We'll have a great time. You can always be a student next year.'

As the beer flowed, the idea grew on me. I had had two winters of studying, so perhaps it was time for a break. The way Willem described Barcelona sold it to me. I agreed at the end of the season that I would go with him to Spain and leave university until the following year.

36

EPIPHANY

WITH THE SUMMER OVER, WE ALL HAD DIFFERENT plans. Kathleen was going back to her rich boyfriend, Lucy was being pursued by a variety of suitors, and Willem and I had our sights set on Barcelona. But we had to wait until Willem's friend had raised the money to open up. Willem headed for London and found himself a small bedsit in Earl's Court. He also got a job at a nightclub that was a jet-set hangout at the time. Armed with the money I had saved up over the summer, I decided to go on a trip to Ireland.

I got the train from Brighton to Cardiff. From there, I would travel on to Fishguard, where I would catch the boat over to Rosslare, County Wexford. I had a few hours to spend in Cardiff and decided to treat myself to a bit of a pub crawl to get to know some of the locals and hear their patter. I had never been in Wales before and I was interested to see what it was like. All I knew about Wales was dragons, choirs, miners and rugby. And, of course, I had been brought up going to parties in Glasgow where someone always sang a Tom Jones song.

When I came out of Cardiff Central Station, I was surprised to see a lot of the street signs in Welsh. It was like being in a foreign country. I stopped a guy in nearby St Mary Street and asked him where the best pubs were; he looked like a bevy merchant with local knowledge. 'Awright, butty, go to the Old Arcade and then the Prince Albert. Full of bloody characters, they are.' I went into the Old Arcade and it reminded me of the Horse Shoe Bar in Glasgow. When the locals heard my accent, they were all extremely friendly, saying they loved the Scots because of the rugby and how well they had been treated when they'd been to Murrayfield for international matches.

I found them to be down-to-earth people with a great sense of humour. The barman poured me a pint of the local ale (Brains SA, which they called 'skull attack') and when I'd paid for it he lifted it up and drank it down in one go. It was a wind-up and everybody in the bar was laughing. 'I'm only taking the mickey, Jock,' he said, and poured me another foaming pint. For more than an hour, I sat with the pub's regulars and we couldn't stop laughing as we exchanged jokes. Everybody seemed to be called Dai and many of them had unusual nicknames: Dai Daps (because he had worn his 'daps', or sandshoes, when he got married), Dai Bungalow (because he had nothing upstairs) and Dai Could Have Been Worse (because no matter what you said to him he always replied, 'Could have been worse').

The patter was certainly different:

Dai: Have you heard about Dai up the road?

Pal: No, what happened?

Dai: Well, his wife has left him for another man!

Pal: Duw [God], never! She's so beautiful, too.

Dai: Well, you know what they say, don't you?

Pal: What's that?

Dai: If you've got a Christmas tree, you've got to keep it decorated!

'Have you been in God's country before, Jock?' one of the many Dais asked me.

'No,' I replied, 'the nearest Ah've come to Wales is when Ah read *Moby Dick*. But when Ah go tae parties in Glesga somebody usually sings Tom Jones' "The Green, Green Grass of Home". It's a great song. That fella's got a brilliant voice.'

Dai Daps nodded his head in agreement. 'Aye, the Jones boy can sing for sure. But we all bloody can, butty. Let me tell you a story. A fellow goes to the doctor and says, "Doctor, when I wake up in the morning, I can't stop singing 'The Green, Green Grass of Home'."

'"Ah," says the doctor, "I know what's wrong with you. You've got Tom Jonesitis."

'"Is it common?" the fellow asks.

'"Well," says the doctor, "it's not unusual."'

I moved on to the Prince Albert and stood in the back room with a crowd of guys from the Rhondda Valley, who also gave me a good welcome. In fact, I almost felt like a celebrity. They had a great sense of community, very much like the atmosphere I had known growing up in the old Gorbals. I got a warm feeling listening to these guys. I felt as if I'd come home.

They told some great anti-English jokes, something else they shared with the Scots. One man at the bar, clad in a red Wales rugby shirt, said to me: 'There were two Irishmen, two Scotsmen, two Welshmen, two Jewish men and two Englishmen. They all got stranded on a desert island. After two weeks, the Irishmen were trying to kill each other, the Scotsmen had started up their own whisky distillery and were pissed all the time, the Welshmen had established a rugby club, the Jewish men set up their own business selling coconuts and bananas, and the Englishmen were still waiting to be introduced to each other.'

I noticed, though, that some of these guys became extremely melancholy when drunk. One man harped on about his divorce. 'Once I had everything,' he said. 'A nice woman and a happy home. But now that she's left me, I've got nothing.' The Welsh seemed to me a sentimental breed but, unlike in Glasgow, there was no aggression in the air at all.

I caught my train down to Fishguard, got on the boat to Rosslare and then took a train to Dublin. The scenery was wonderful and I was amazed at how green the countryside looked. It was a different shade of green from that you found in Scotland, too, bright and dazzling.

What a city Dublin was! In many ways, it reminded me of the Gorbals in the 1960s, when thousands of Irish labourers and their families had descended on Glasgow to find work. At times back then, living in that part of Glasgow was almost like living in Ireland.

I found myself a cheap bed-and-breakfast joint up a close near O'Connell Street. When I rang the doorbell, a large lady with grey hair opened up and said, 'It'll be bed and breakfast ye're lookin' for?'

My first thought was 'I wouldn't like to meet her in a dark lane.'

'Aye that's right, missus,' I said. 'How much is a night?'

'Three pounds up front,' she said. 'For that, ye'll get a nice soft bed and a full Irish breakfast in the mornin'.'

She showed me into a rather shabby, dark room, which was decorated with a number of holy pictures. I felt as if I'd just entered a little chapel. But of course this was Ireland, the land of priests, so I shouldn't really have been surprised.

The landlady told me her name was Mrs Brady and that she'd been 'doin' lodgin'' in Dublin for more than 30 years. 'All my brothers are priests and my two sisters are nuns. I'm the black sheep o' the family – the only one that's earnin' money. I don't know if I'll end up in heaven like my brothers and sisters but I'll have to take that chance. I'll have your three pounds now, if you don't mind, young sir.' I handed her the money and she added, 'The rules of this house are simple: if ye're goin' to the pub, try to come back as quietly as ye can, and no pissin' in the sink. There's a toilet down the corridor. Apart from that, it's all plain sailin'. May God be lookin' after ye.' With that, she turned and walked out of the door.

I lay back on the bed and it was extremely soft and comfortable but I noticed that there was another bed in the room. I just hoped that Mrs Brady hadn't let it out as I would find it uncomfortable sharing a wee room with a complete stranger. I was too scared to ask her about it, however, and, after a 20-minute snooze, I headed out into the streets of Dublin.

It was a Friday night and everywhere I went people seemed to be singing Dublin's version of 'I Belong to Glasgow', 'Molly Malone'. 'In Dublin's fair city, where the girls are all pretty, I first set my eyes on sweet Molly Malone . . .' I ended up in a Victorian pub in a back street near O'Connell Street. The locals seemed friendly enough at first but when they heard my Scottish accent the atmosphere changed slightly.

'From Scotland, eh? What regiment ye with? The Scots Guards?' one burly man asked.

'Naw,' I laughed, 'Ah'm no a sojir. Ah'm a student daein' a wee visit of Ireland.'

The stout Irishman laughed, took a sip of his Guinness and said, 'Ah, to be sure, that's what all you f***in' sojirs say. Ye'll never admit to bein' in the army. Ye're all the same – all f***in' liars!' He said it in a jovial way and I didn't think it was intended to be intimidating.

Then he invited me to sit down with his pals for 'a bit of the old craic'. They were all chatting away and one retired fellow, an ex-bank manager, regaled us with this tale: 'I was busy in the bank when one o' the clerks came into my office and said, "Sir, there's a gentleman outside called Barney who would like to speak to ye. I think he's in showbusiness." I told the clerk to show this Barney fella in and it was then I realised he was a well-known hypnotist. He went all over hypnotisin' people in theatres. I'd read in one newspaper that he'd landed in trouble after hypnotisin' one man to be a duck. When his act finished, the fella was still a duck, going, "Quack, quack, quack!" The police and the ambulance were called but this Barney couldn't break the spell. Anyway, the man quacked like a duck for three days solid until he came round and got back to normal.

'I said to Barney, "What can I do for ye, sir?"

'And he said, "Things are a bit tough at the moment and I wonder if ye could arrange for me to have an overdraft?"

'Well, I fetched out his file and he was deeply in debt, so I said to him, "I'm sorry, but there's nothin' I can do. Ye already owe us several thousand pounds."

'And that's the last I can remember o' the conversation. I fell asleep. When I woke up about 45 minutes later, I was alone in my office.

'I asked the clerk, "When did that Barney fella leave?"

'"Oh," he said, "about 30 minutes ago, with the £2,000 you gave him from the safe."

'I couldn't believe it. I'd been hypnotised into givin' him the money!'

A group of younger fellows, very drunk, joined us. One of them was wearing a Celtic shirt and he joined in the craic with a series of one-liners: 'What's the difference between an Irish weddin' and an Irish funeral? There's one less drunk at a funeral!'

'Go on, Paddy, tell them more,' one of his young pals shouted.

'Did ye hear about the Kerry man who got a camera for his birthday? He just got back his first roll of film: 24 shots o' his right eye.'

They were all in extremely high spirits, and as they drank more, one of the young guys started shouting, 'Up the IRA! F*** King Billy! Our day will come!'

I had often heard this refrain from Celtic supporters in Glasgow and I said to the guy with the Celtic shirt on, 'Ah see ye're a Celtic supporter. Have ye ever been tae Parkheid?'

He looked suspiciously at me and said, 'Are ye Scottish?'

'Aye', I replied, 'fae Glesga.'

He sipped his beer and glanced at his pals before asking, 'Oh, and what regiment might ye be servin' with?'

'As Ah said tae wan o' yir pals earlier, Ah'm no a sojir. Ah'm a student.'

He spat on the floor and said, 'Well, ye look like a sojir, ye talk like a sojir and, as far as I'm concerned, ye're a f***in' sojir!'

'Look, pal,' I said, 'the nearest Ah've come tae the army wis when Ah gave a guy fae the Salvation Army two bob fur a *War Cry* last week.'

But there was no laughter, nothing. I got up to go to the toilet and the barman followed me in. 'Listen, Jock,' he whispered, 'there's an unlocked door opposite this toilet. I've left it open for ye. F*** off through it as soon as you can. Scarper. Those guys are the IRA and they'll end up kidnappin' ye and shootin' ye through the head if ye don't.'

I did as I was told and ran as fast as I could through Dublin's dark streets to my boarding house. Before long I was lying on my bed, out of breath and feeling lucky to have escaped. A few minutes later, I dozed off. It had been a long day. But in the early hours of the morning, a drunk man crashed into the room, singing loudly, 'I've been a wild rover for many a year and I spent all my money on whisky and beer . . .'

So my fears were confirmed: the landlady had let the bed without telling me! The big fellow, who was oblivious to my existence in the darkness, wandered over to the sink and began to piss heavily and noisily into it. He then staggered over to his bed, fell fast asleep and snored loudly all night.

I never slept a wink. F*** the breakfast! I left as early as I could and found myself lying exhausted on the grass at Trinity College. The sun came out and I had a pleasant sleep for a couple of hours. When I woke up, I watched the students going to and from the college. I thought they looked so happy, as if they didn't have a care in the world. 'I want to be one of them,' I murmured to myself. It was a sort of epiphany, another turning point in my life.

37

FIBS

FTER I'D SPENT A FEW DAYS IN DUBLIN, I CAUGHT A train to Belfast. At the railway station, I noticed a middle-aged guy glancing over at me now and again. Did I know him from Glasgow? Had I met him in the pub? I couldn't recall. As the train trundled through the countryside towards Northern Ireland, I dozed off, as I had a bit of a hangover. I woke up after about an hour and was admiring the beautiful scenery when a ray of sunshine shone through the window. Reflected in the glass, I could see myself and a man sitting in the seat behind me. It was the same fellow who had been looking at me in the station. I glanced round but, on seeing this, he peered into his newspaper. 'What's going on?' I thought. 'Am I being followed? Nah! It must be paranoia!' I often got paranoid after drinking too much; it was a classic side effect.

At Belfast's main railway station, I phoned both Kathleen and Lucy. They seemed delighted to hear from me and said they'd drive up and pick me up. When they arrived, we all hugged each other and started talking a mile a minute. Kathleen said I could stay in her house.

When we got into the car to drive back to Armagh, alarm bells began ringing in my head when Kathleen said, 'Look, we're all going out for a drink later. My boyfriend's coming and Lucy's boyfriend's coming. I have a friend called Sadie and the plan is this: you'll have to pretend you're Sadie's boyfriend from Glasgow. Don't mention Brighton and pretend you've never met me or Lucy before. Just act as if you're in love with Sadie.'

'Haud oan a minute!' I said. 'Ah've never met you or Lucy and

Ah'm in love wi Sadie, a woman Ah don't know? Only the Irish could have thought up such a plot! Nae wonder there's so much trouble in this country!'

At Kathleen's house, I had a wash and brush-up before we headed out. Sadie arrived and to put it mildly she was not my type. She was overweight and had the face of a saint – a St Bernard. I felt like doing her a favour by squeezing some of her yellow plukes. 'Hiya, Colin!' she said. 'I hear a good-looking fella's to be my boyfriend for the night. I'm certainly not complaining – Kathleen's loss is my gain!'

I pulled Kathleen aside and said, 'Hey, ye cannae make me pretend Ah'm in love wi that! She's so ugly she'd make onions cry!'

Kathleen said, 'I know she's not very good looking. When we were at school, the boys used to say that when she walked into her kitchen the rats jumped onto the table screaming. But she really is a nice person. She's got a heart of gold. Anyway, you only have to pretend to be her boyfriend for a night and you always told me that you liked new experiences. So think of it as an adventure. More importantly, have fun while you're here!'

I decided to go with the flow. Kathleen, Lucy, Sadie and I caught a taxi to a country pub. We were soon joined by Kathleen's and Lucy's boyfriends. I had been told by the girls to hold Sadie's hand at all times and pretend that we were very much in love. I would deserve an Oscar after this. Lucy's boyfriend was a tall, dark, thin fellow who didn't say much. Kathleen's man was much more outgoing and gregarious, very much like me. He looked surprised when he saw me holding Sadie's hand.

'How long have you known Sadie?' he asked. 'Where the hell did you meet?'

'Oh,' I said, getting into bullshit mode, 'we met when Sadie came over tae Glesga tae visit wan o' her relatives. Since that first meetin', we've been in love.'

I could see a slight smile on his face, as if he was about to erupt into laugher. The three girls all looked a trifle nervous but I carried on. 'We might get married next May. We're thinkin' o' a wonderful white weddin', either here or in Glasgow. When ye're in love as much as we ur, you want tae get married as soon as possible.'

'Let's celebrate,' said Kathleen's boyfriend, and he fetched a bottle of champagne from the bar. He then proposed a toast. We all raised our glasses.

'To the happy couple!' he said.

'To the happy couple!' we replied.

I kissed Sadie gently on the cheek. It was that sort of night.

When the girls went to the toilet, Kathleen's man confessed to me, 'Look, perhaps it is better getting involved with a woman who's not – how can I put it? – exactly beautiful. I worry all the time that because Kathleen's so gorgeous some eejit's going to steal her away from me. She's just spent the summer in England and I don't know if she had a lover there but if she did, and I find out, there'll be big trouble, believe me. I've got a gun, in fact I've got several of them, and I'll shoot the bastard. Or, even better, I'll get one of the boys to shoot him.'

Later, I was lying in bed in the darkness at Kathleen's house when I heard the creaking of floorboards. I looked up and it was Sadie, standing in the shadows.

'Can I join you in bed?' she whispered.

'Yeah, awright, climb aboard,' I said and she did.

Any port in a storm. Anyway, we were, to all intents and purposes, an engaged couple.

The next day, I was at the railway station and, as I bought my single ticket to Glasgow, I noticed a man in a raincoat standing reading a paper. It was the same man I'd seen on the train yesterday! Surely this couldn't be coincidence?

I got on the train and then took the Larne ferry to Stranraer. The crossing was great fun. I had a few drinks at the bar with some Irish fellows who were getting into the beer. When we arrived in Scotland, I got the train to Glasgow. I was clutching my suitcase at a busy Central Station when two men approached me, flashed a card in front of my face and said, 'Security services. Will you please come with us?'

They led me into a little office in the station and asked me what I had in my suitcase. I said nothing and that they were welcome to search it. The man rummaging through my dirty laundry was the one I had seen on the train from Dublin and at the station in Belfast.

'What's your full name, address and date of birth?' he asked me. I told him. 'Do you have any identification on you?' he said. I pulled out my student-union card and put it on the table. He picked it up, looked at it closely and laughed. 'That's a good likeness of you!' he said. I had forgotten all about it but the week before my photograph had fallen off the card and, in a daft moment, I had drawn in the blank space a circle with two little eyes and a mouth.

He continued his interrogation: 'Have you or any of your family or friends ever been a member of the IRA?'

'No,' I replied, realising that I was in a serious situation. Who were these men and what did they want from me?

'MI5,' the man who had been following me said. 'We have been tracking you from Dublin, where you had a meeting with the head of the IRA and his foot soldiers. What did you discuss?'

'Whit, those guys in the pub?' I said. 'Ah didnae know they wur IRA but they kept askin' me if Ah was a sojir. Ah'd never seen them before and Ah still don't know who they ur, except that some o' them wur called Paddy.'

'Come off it! Our sources tell us those men were behind a series of explosions in Britain recently and we believe you might have been involved. Where were you this summer?'

'Brighton,' I said, 'workin' as a chef. Check it oot if ye want.'

'Did you go to London or Ireland during that time?'

'No, Ah stayed the whole time in Brighton.'

'What about the man you met up with in the North, the one who bought you champagne? Are you going to tell me that you didn't know he was a major member of the IRA?'

'Look,' I said, 'Ah'd never met that guy before. He's the boyfriend o' an old girlfriend, that's aw.'

'So what you're saying is that you meeting up with terrorists in Dublin and then with a key IRA player in Armagh was all a coincidence?'

'Aye,' I said, 'Ah didnae know who they wur. They wur jist people Ah came across oan ma travels. It wis pure coincidence.'

'Pure coincidence? Are you sure? I'm not,' he said.

'Aye, Ah'm sure. Ah widnae know an IRA guy if Ah found wan in ma soup.'

They kept me in the office for several hours until they'd checked out my story and then double-checked it. They also searched my bag again, looking more carefully to see if it had any hidden compartments or pockets. I was getting extremely paranoid, thinking they were going to fit me up. What if they slipped in some explosives, a gun or even ammunition? I would be finished and facing a 20-year stretch.

But the MI5 guy came in and said, 'There's nothing we can pin on you at the moment. But remember, we'll be keeping tabs on you from now on.'

'Look, officer,' I said, 'Ah know nothin' aboot the IRA or what they're up to. It's jist that Ah have a big mouth and Ah'll talk tae anyone, gie them ma patter, nae matter where Ah go. The last thing Ah blew up wis a balloon at a birthday party.'

He laughed and said I was free to leave. I left the office slightly dazed, thinking that there was something to be said for a quiet life.

38

THE WAITING GAME

BACK IN GLASGOW, I REGALED THE BOYS WITH MY tale. Some of them found it hard to believe, saying that I was worse than *Jackanory*. But I told them that the story of my dealings with the IRA and MI5 was absolutely true. My best pal Chris never doubted me for a minute. 'Mr Mac,' he said, 'no matter where ye go, somethin' always happens. Ye're jist that sort o' guy. Hey, did ye hear aboot the two IRA guys who got talkin' and wan says tae the other, "How's your boy?" and the fella says, "Dead, he died fur the cause." And he says "How's your boy?" and the other fella says, "Dead as well. He also died for the cause." Then the first fella says, "They blow up fast, don't they?"'

A few nights later, I phoned up Willem in London to see how things were progressing with our jobs in Barcelona. 'It's not looking good at the moment,' he said. 'My friend says the banks want more collateral. He's trying to raise it as soon as he can but it might take a few months.' I promptly signed on the dole and decided to play the waiting game. However, Christmas came and went and still the restaurant was nowhere near opening. I decided to visit Willem to see if I could get things moving.

As I was waiting at Central Station for the London train to arrive, a drunk guy with a suitcase approached me. He looked like a reject from the Tartan Army; he was clad in a tartan bunnet and kilt and reeking of alcohol. He seemed a bit confused.

'Ur ye goin' tae London, pal?' he asked.

'Aye,' I replied.

'So am Ah and Ah wonder if ye could help me. Ah've got tae get tae this street where ma brother lives.'

He handed me a slightly crumpled piece of paper on which was written '10 Cavendish Road'. There was no postcode or district.

'Dae ye know where Cavendish Road is?' he asked me.

'Well, Ah don't really. Dae ye know whit area it's in? London's a big place wi millions o' people and streets, so ye need to tell me whit district ye're lookin' fur.'

'Eh . . .' He was trying hard to recall the area in his drunken state. 'Eh . . . Plukes!'

'Plukes?' I said. 'Ah don't think there is a district in London called Plukes. Ur ye sure?'

'Aye, that's where Ah'm sure ma brother said he wis stayin': 10 Cavendish Road, Plukes.'

I knew he was mistaken. Then I thought about it. 'Plukes' is Scots for 'spots'. But there was nowhere in London called Spots, Boils, Zits or Pimples. Then it came to me. 'When ye say yir brother lives in Plukes, dae ye no mean Hackney?'

A broad smile came over his face. 'That's it, man, Ye're a genius! 10 Cavendish Road, Hackney. Ye should be a private detective. Ye're better than Columbo.'

As the train pulled in, he shook my hand and offered to share a bottle of Bell's whisky with me. But I just thought that if whisky made you think that Hackney was called Plukes, it was better to steer clear of it. I bade him farewell and moved to another carriage for some peace and quiet.

But I had not been there long when a Glaswegian fellow with a fat face sat opposite me and began, much to my irritation, rabbiting on.

'Dae ye read the newspapers?' he asked.

'Aye,' I replied.

'Well, did ye read aroon a year ago aboot a double-decker bus runnin' ower a man's heid in Sauchiehall Street?'

I did recall reading something about it in the *Daily Record*. As far as I could remember, the man had escaped from Gartnavel, a mental institution, and had thrown himself under the bus. 'Aye,' I replied, 'that wis a nasty wan. Ah wonder if the guy survived?'

'He did,' said Fat Face. 'That man wis me! Since the bus ran ower ma heid, people ur sayin' that Ah suffer fae madness but Ah tell them Ah enjoy every minute o' it!'

He was obviously not the full bob. I said I was going to the toilet, moved up a few carriages, found a spare seat and swiftly fell asleep.

When the train arrived in Euston, I headed for the Tube. I eventually got to Willem's place in Earl's Court, a bedsit in a rather large Victorian house. I went up the stairs and knocked on the door but there was no answer. I sat on the steps outside and I was sure I could hear movement inside the flat. I knocked on the door again and shouted, 'Willem, it's me! Open up the door, Ah know ye're in there!' Sure enough, he was in and he opened the door. But his face was awash with tears; he must have been crying about his sister again.

'Hey, man,' I said, 'cheer up, pull yirsel together. Ah've jist travelled aw the way fae Scotland tae see you.'

He shrugged his shoulders, wiped the tears from his face and said, 'I'm sorry, my friend. I've just been lying on my bed. I didn't even have the energy to answer you.'

The photo of his sister and the murderous boyfriend was lying on the bed. I decided to say nothing and change the subject to something lighter. 'Right, man, whit's happenin' wi this restaurant in Spain? Ur we goin' or ur we no?'

Willem started making some coffee and said, 'It's still on. I talked to my friend on the phone last night. He's raised most of the money and is just waiting for planning permission from the authorities. Then we should be clear to go.'

'How long?' I asked.

'Maybe a few weeks, maybe a few months, we don't know yet, until we have – how do you say? – jumped over all the obstacles.'

It was May '77. The days were turning into weeks and the weeks were turning into months. Perhaps I had made a big mistake not going to university. This plan was becoming a big waste of time and Willem's mental health seemed to be deteriorating. In fact, when I glanced at him making the coffee, he had a look on his face that I found disturbing. It occurred to me that it could be the look of a madman.

Suddenly, there was a loud knock on the door. 'Willem, open up the door you little bastard! Where is my rent?'

Willem opened the door and in strode two men, one a fat guy whom Willem called Stavros, his landlord, and the other his handyman sidekick, Chico. When I looked at Stavros, I thought of the Glaswegian line, 'He's got mair chins than a Chinese telephone directory.'

Willem smiled but it was a false smile. 'Ah, Stavros, my friend, would you and Chico like some coffee?'

Stavros replied in a booming voice, 'No, I don't want your f***in' coffee, I want my rent.' Chico, a thin, tall fellow, nodded in agreement, chewing gum as if he was playing the part of an enforcer in some gangster movie.

Willem said, 'My friend, as I told you, I have a new job and they didn't tell me until I started that I have to work one month in hand before I get paid. So three weeks from now, I will give you all the money plus interest for keeping you waiting all this time.'

Stavros wiped his sweaty brow with a white handkerchief. He seemed to cheer up at this offer. 'OK, we'll wait until then. But if you fail to pay up there'll be trouble.'

I felt like launching into a direct attack but I couldn't put Willem's accommodation at risk, so I kept my mouth shut. 'Fat bastard!' I thought, 'I could take him and his cardboard gangster pal any time.' However, some things are better left unsaid, and Stavros and his sidekick left without any Glaswegian-accented expletives issuing from my mouth.

The atmosphere was very gloomy so I said to Willem, 'Get the glasses oot and Ah'll go doon tae the corner shop and get us some wine and beer.' I thought of a line I'd heard many years before in Glasgow: 'Nae matter whether it's win or lose, we'll have a damn good feed o' the booze.' I came back with a substantial carry-out and told Willem to wire in. After a glass or two of wine and a few beers, he began to cheer up a little. 'Don't let the bastards get ye doon! It's onwards and upwards fur us – Barcelona or bust!' I said.

I walked over to the bed, where the photo of Willem's sister and the boyfriend was. I picked it up and looked at the murderer's face. He had a kind face – the kind you'd like to kick in. 'Ah'll tell ye whit, Willem, get me a pair o' scissors and we'll cut that tube oot the photo. Then we'll stick it oan that dartboard and chuck darts at the ugly nae-good bastard.' He agreed so we put the face of the murderer on the board and took great delight in playing a game of darts. This seemed to cheer Willem up no end. He had gone from almost suicidal an hour before to giggling like a schoolboy every time a dart hit the monster's face.

We sat down and talked about our experiences in the hotel in Brighton. When Willem tried, which was seldom at that time, he could be a really funny guy. 'I was on room service when the phone rang,' he told me. 'A French guy was on the line and he said to me, "I would like some pepper, please."

'"Certainly, sir," I said. "Black pepper or white pepper?"

'"Neither," he said, "I want toilet pepper."'

The darts and the funny stories made us feel more optimistic and we decided to go down to Brixton to meet a friend of Willem's for a few beers. However, as we were heading back towards the Tube station, I noticed three black men were following us. Willem stopped to light a cigarette. I looked back and as we stopped so did the three men. They were obviously going to mug us but what was the best course of action? I saw a light coming from a corner shop. Salvation! 'Right, Willem, we've got tae think quick here,' I said. Inside, I said, 'Ah'll have two bottles o' lemonade.' I handed one of them to Willem, saying, 'This is an auld Glesga ploy. If they try tae attack us, jist get stuck in wi yir bottle.' Willem looked nervous but agreed. We walked out and, sure enough, the three muggers were still there. The tallest was in his mid-30s and had a large beer belly. His two cohorts were younger, with intimidating looks on their faces.

Next minute, Fatty approached us. He shouted, 'Right, give me your money or you'll get this.' I looked down at his right hand and he had a Stanley knife – a carpet cutter – in it. He came closer, followed by his pals. 'Time to use a bit of Glaswegian game-as-f*** psychology here,' I thought. 'Hey,' I shouted, 'ur ye a carpet layer? 'Cause ma auld granny's jist bought a new carpet and she wants a big fat useless bastard tae try and lay it.'

Fatty looked taken aback. 'Don't f*** about with me. Give me your money now.'

I shouted back in my loudest, most aggressive voice, 'Nae chance! Come ahead, then!'

He moved towards me and raised the knife but I put my arm up and it caught the thick sleeve of my jacket. Bang! I hit him over the head with the bottle and Willem ran towards the two other guys, who ran off. Fatty was lying on the pavement with his head split open. It was time to get out of town fast, before Fatty's pals returned to the scene to do us in. We ran to Brixton tube station and boarded a train.

'Phew! That wis a close shave. Ah thought ye said Brixton wis safe?' I said to Willem.

'Brixton was safe until a mad Glasgow bastard like you arrived!' he replied with a grin on his face.

39

~~~~~~

ADVENTURE

I STUCK AROUND IN LONDON FOR A WHILE TO SEE IF I
could help get things moving. But I hated the whole killing time
business. This Spanish job was a bit like Billy Bunter's postal order:
there was much talk about it arriving but it never did. As May turned
to June, then July and Willem was still making the same excuses
about the restaurant, I decided to go home.

When I got back to Glasgow, I considered my options. Where
could I go to study if our restaurant plan ended up falling through
altogether? Aberdeen? I'd sort of ruled that out because some of
the guys who I'd gone to college with had gone up there and got
sucked into a very heavy drinking culture. Some had ended up
joining Alcoholics Anonymous. I thought about Dublin. I'd liked
the place but my close shave with the IRA had put me off a bit. I
ruled out Glasgow and Edinburgh universities because they were
too close to home and I wanted an adventure, to go somewhere
completely different. Suddenly, I thought of Cardiff. I'd enjoyed
myself there and I'd been impressed by the honesty and friendliness
of the people. Also, the folk there had seemed much less aggressive
than your typical Glaswegian. I hadn't seen a single fight or even an
argument in Cardiff. I didn't really know what to do so I thought I'd
leave it to fate and let the gods decide where I ended up.

Then, one day, I bought a copy of *The Guardian*, which I had
never done before, and on that particular day it had an education
supplement advertising courses all over Britain. I spotted a rather
large advert that asked, 'Are you interested in psychology and the
mass media? New BA (Hons) degree in Communication Studies
starting in September at the Polytechnic of Wales, Pontypridd, only

12 miles from Cardiff, set in beautiful countryside.' The course sounded exciting and the advert also stated it was 'a good launching pad for those interested in a career in psychology ... or journalism'. Right up my street! The gods were doing overtime for me.

I wrote a short letter stating my qualifications and popped it in the post. Then I went out to meet the boys for a drink in St Enoch Square. When I got to the pub, Alex, Chris and the rest of the boys were in full flow. They all had some job or other and here I was feeling like a nomad with no definite direction in my life. One of the boys, Johnny, was a binman and he said to me, 'Ah think it's the best job in the world. Ah'm up every mornin' and Ah can always see the sky. As long as Ah can look at the sky every mornin', Ah'm happy. Look at aw they depressed bastards workin' in offices – they hardly ever see the sky. But in ma job, Ah jist look up. Magic, it is.'

Johnny said his job had got easier because they'd brought in wheely bins to some areas. 'Ah knocked oan a door last week and a wee man answered it.

'Ah says, "Awright, pal, where's yir bin?"'

'He looks at me and said, "Ah've been oan the toilet."'

'So Ah says, "Naw, mate, where's yir dustbin?"'

'He replies again, "Ah've been oan the toilet, Ah told you."'

'Ah wis nearly pullin ma hair oot wi this guy, so Ah says, "Look, pal, ye're misunderstandin' me. Where's yir wheely bin?"'

'"OK, OK," says the wee guy, 'Ah've really been havin' a wank."'

Johnny offered to get me a job in the council's cleansing department. 'Ye'll love it,' he said. 'Start early, finish early and the money's good. Jist say the word and Ah'll have a natter wi the gaffer. We're short o' people at the moment and Ah could probably get ye a start as a binman next week. Ye'll probably be oan the same wagon as me and Ah'll show you the ropes. And remember, ye get tae see the sky every mornin'!' My plan for '77 had been to be at university; then I'd changed my mind to go to Barcelona; now I was being offered a job as a dustbin man. 'How the mighty have fallen,' I thought.

Alex had been in and out of jobs ever since he left school and he said one of his main problems was getting through interviews. At one point, he'd considered working on the railways as a signalman but the interview had been his undoing. He told us, 'The interviewer asked me, "What would you do if two trains were coming towards each other on the same line."

'Ah said, "Ah'd switch the points in the signal box."

'"But what if the signal switch was broken?" he asked.

'"Then Ah'd use the manual lever."

'But he kept oan. "What if that didn't work?"

'"Well," Ah said, "Ah'd use the emergency phone tae call the next signal box."

'So the guy says tae me, "What if there was no answer?"

'Ah wis gettin' pissed aff by this time, so Ah said, "Ah'd ring ma uncle Jimmy and tell him tae come doon."

'"What good would that do?" he asked me.

'"F*** all," Ah said. "It's jist that he's never seen a train crash before."'

We left the pub laughing and we were walking by the Clyde, where a huge development was being built. Towering over the scene was a giant crane. I had read in the newspapers that it was the tallest crane in Europe. At the top was a little cabin where the crane operator sat. I thought it must have been a hell of a climb for the operator to do every day and I wondered what it would be like sitting in that cabin looking down on the whole of Glasgow. The workers had knocked off for the night and the place was deserted. I said to Chris, 'Hey, fancy climbin' up that crane and seein' what the view is like fae that cabin in the sky?'

The boys looked at me as if I was insane. 'Whit? Climb aw the way up there? Ye'll end up killin' yirsel. Don't even think aboot it,' Johnny said.

But Chris said, 'Aye, come oan, let's have a go.'

Chris and I, having consumed about seven pints of lager each, started to climb the crane. It took us about 45 minutes to reach the cabin. When we got inside, we looked out and there were wonderful views of the whole of Glasgow. The city was lit up like a Christmas tree. There was a little table in the cabin with a pen and paper on it, so I wrote, 'The Gorbals boys have been here. No matter how high it is or how low it is – we get everywhere!'

Then it was time to descend the several hundred feet to the ground. By this time, the effects of the lager had worn off and I felt extremely frightened on the way down. I was convinced one of us was going to fall to his death. But we took it step by step, going down slowly and carefully until we reached the ground. The boys, who were astounded that we'd done it, gave us a rousing cheer.

Chris laughed, saying, 'Can ye imagine the morra when that crane operator climbs up and goes intae his cabin? He'll freak oot when he finds yir note! Ye see, no even the highest crane in Europe can stop us Gorbals guys, 'cause we're aw hawf mad!'

Johnny shook his head and said, 'Ah cannae believe ye jist did that. Ah'll be tellin' ma workmates aw aboot it oan Monday but they'll never believe it.'

Over the next few days, I waited for Willem to phone and give me the latest news on Barcelona but there was nothing. This was odd, as he usually phoned me at least twice a week for a chat. I had to clear things up as soon as possible, as I was being left in limbo and it was nearly August.

I decided to give Willem one last throw of the dice and caught the overnight bus to London. When I got to his bedsit, the door was ajar and all his belongings had gone. He had obviously cleared off in a hurry. I heard footsteps behind me and it was Stavros the landlord and his sidekick. Stavros shouted at me, 'Where has that little bastard gone? He owes me hundreds of pounds in unpaid rent. You're his friend, you must know where he is. Tell me or I'll break your face.' Chico stood behind him nodding menacingly.

'Ah don't know where Willem is. Ah hivnae got a clue,' I said. 'Ah've jist arrived fae Scotland and Ah'm lookin' fur him maself.'

Stavros's face clouded with anger. 'Tell me where he is or you'll be sorry. I'll teach you a lesson you'll never forget, you Scottish bastard.'

I repeated that I didn't know where Willem had gone and he lunged towards me trying to grab my throat. 'F*** this!' I thought and promptly gave him a good old Glasgow kiss, a head-butt right on the nose. He went flying down the stairs. Chico made a move towards me but I swiftly kicked him between the legs and he fell to the ground. I jumped over the two of them and then ran like a fox being pursued by a pack of hounds through the streets of London.

Where the hell had Willem gone? I phoned my mother in Glasgow to see if he'd been in contact but she said, 'No, he hisnae, but a man's been oan the phone fae Wales.'

'Fae the polytechnic?' I asked.

'Aye, that wis it, the Polytechnic o' Wales. He says your qualifications look awright and he wants tae speak tae ye over the phone as it's too far tae travel fae Glasgow jist fur an interview. Ah didnae tell him ye wur in London,' she said.

She gave me the lecturer's name and phone number at the college. I went to a bank and cashed two pounds into ten-pence pieces. Then I phoned him from a telephone box in a nearby Tube station. I rang the college and the operator put me through to the lecturer but the box was eating up money. All the time, I was feeding ten-pence pieces into the box and the phone was going 'do-do-do-do-do-do'.

The lecturer said, 'I'd like to ask you a few questions.'

Do-do-do-do-do-do. I put more money in.

'Fire away!' I said.

'Have you ever studied sociology?'

Do-do-do-do-do-do.

I bluffed it: 'Aye, the problems that married women face in society.'

'What do you think the difference is between the news on TV and the news in print?'

Do-do-do-do-do-do. I inserted more coins but my money was running out.

'Well, TV news tends to be more matter of fact whereas newspapers tend to be more sensationalist.'

'You're accepted. You can start this September.'

'OK!'

And the phone went dead – all my money had gone.

I walked out of the station, stunned that I had just agreed to spend three years doing a degree in Wales. Things were at last moving forward. At least now I had a direction in life.

I caught a train back to Glasgow and as soon as I got to Central Station I was reminded of what a diverse and unique city it really is. There was a man glugging from a bottle of Lanliq wine and singing at the top of his voice:

Does yir maw drink wine?
Does she drink it aw the time?
Does she get a funny feelin'
When her diddies hit the ceilin'?

It was the height of summer and the place was thronged with tourists heading to destinations all over Scotland. I heard one wee Glasgow man give directions to a tourist and then add, 'It's only five minutes' walk . . . if ye run.' A rough-looking woman was standing bang in the centre of the station, a fag hanging from her mouth and curlers in her hair, shouting to her little boy, 'Ah've f***in' told ye before, Tommy, don't eat yir sweeties until ye've had yir chips.'

A stroll across the road to the Horse Shoe Bar revealed that the patter merchants were still very much in force. 'Ah wis so pished last night, Ah wis staggerin' roon the hoose,' said one man to other, 'and then Ah wis sick aw over the cat. Ah looked at the cat, aw covered in ma vomit, and said tae ma missus, "Ah cannae remember eatin' that!" But even though Ah had a terrible hangover the next day, Ah could never gie up ma beer. Ah drink tae make other people interestin'. Ma missus says Ah should gie it up completely and stick tae water but Ah told her Ah couldnae drink water because fish shag in it. Besides, beer has been helpin' ugly people have sex since 3000 BC.'

In the opposite corner, two old characters, both wearing tartan bunnets, were exchanging jokes. It was as if they were involved in some kind of unofficial patter competition. One took a sip from his large glass of whisky and said to the other, 'Did ye hear aboot the fella who walked intae a bar and noticed a penguin wis servin' the drink?

'"Whit you starin' at?" says the penguin.

'"Ah'm jist a bit shocked, says the fella, "Ah never thought the monkey would sell the place."'

His pal tried to keep up: 'A young wumman has triplets and her neighbour Mrs McGinty called roon tae see her. The wumman is over the moon at havin' three bonnie babies and she says to Mrs McGinty, "Ye know whit the doctor told me?"

'"Whit's that?"

'"He said it only happens oan average wance every two hundred thousand times!"

'"Wance every two hundred thousand times?" Mrs McGinty says. "When the hell did ye find time tae dae the hoosework?"'

When I got back home, there was a letter waiting for me behind the door. It was from a high-security prison in Holland.

Willem began by apologising for letting me down over Barcelona. He explained that he had decided to get out of London because he owed so much rent. When he'd got home, though, he'd heard that his sister's murderer had been released early and that his family were having a party to welcome him back. Furious, Willem had turned up at the celebration. Everyone had been singing, drinking and laughing, and Willem had become even more enraged, thinking of his sister whose life was over, who could no longer laugh. He had walked over to the murderer and, before the killer had even noticed he was there, he'd cut his throat. In his letter, Willem described the man's death and the way his screams had got quieter as his mouth had filled with blood. Willem had given himself up to the police. His lawyer said that he might get a reduced sentence because of the unusual circumstances.

A week after I received the letter, I left Glasgow for Wales. I felt I needed a peaceful time and I hoped my studies would keep me out of trouble for a while. Besides, it was another adventure for a Gorbals guy to look forward to. As the train pulled out of Central Station, I stuck my head out of the window and shouted to my pals, 'Cheery-bye ra noo!'